Predictive Business Analytics: Forward-Looking Capabilities to Improve Business Performance by Lawrence Maisel and Gary Cokins

Statistical Thinking: Improving Business Performance, Second Edition by Roger W. Hoerl and Ronald D. Snee

Too Big to Ignore: The Business Case for Big Data by Phil Simon

Trade-Based Money Laundering: The Next Frontier in International Money Laundering Enforcement by John Cassara

The Visual Organization: Data Visualization, Big Data, and the Quest for Better Decisions by Phil Simon

Understanding the Predictive Analytics Lifecycle by Al Cordoba

Unleashing Your Inner Leader: An Executive Coach Tells All by Vickie Bevenour

Using Big Data Analytics: Turning Big Data into Big Money by Jared Dean

Visual Six Sigma, Second Edition by Ian Cox, Marie Gaudard, and Mia Stephens

For more information on any of the above titles, please visit www.wiley.com.

Next Generation Demand Management

People, Process, Analytics, and Technology

Charles W. Chase

WILEY

Published by John Wiley & Sons, Inc., Hoboken, New Jersey.

Published simultaneously in Canada.

For general information on our other products and services or for technical support, please contact our Customer Care Department within the United States at (800) 762-2974, outside the United States at (317) 572-3993 or fax (317) 572-4002.

Wiley publishes in a variety of print and electronic formats and by print-on-demand. Some material included with standard print versions of this book may not be included in e-books or in print-on-demand. If this book refers to media such as a CD or DVD that is not included in the version you purchased, you may download this material at http://booksupport.wiley.com. For more information about Wiley products, visit www.wiley.com.

Library of Congress Cataloging-in-Publication Data is available:

ISBN 9781119186632 (Hardcover)
ISBN 9781119227397 (ePDF)
ISBN 9781119227380 (ePub)

Cover design: Wiley
Cover image: © Ralf Hiemisch/Getty Images, Inc.

Printed in the United States of America

10 9 8 7 6 5 4 3 2 1

To my wife, Cheryl, who has always been an inspiration and supporter of my career and written work.

Contents

Foreword

Cuneyt Eroglu
Assistant Professor
Supply Chain and Information Management Group,
D'Amore-McKim School of Business,
Northeastern University

Demand management is one of those essential business functions that every business professional has to know at least a little about regardless of whether they work in marketing, production, finance, or human resources. Sales forecasting and demand management form the foundation for all planning processes. Demand management is also one of those areas that companies continue to struggle with. No matter how good a company is in demand management, there still appears to be more room for improvement. When it comes to demand management, the journey to excellence seems to be an endless one.

In this book, Charlie Chase takes the reader on a journey to excellence in demand management. As a thought leader in this area, he provides a comprehensive and expertly written treatment of demand management for guiding business professionals. He first explains why demand management can be such a challenge for many companies. He then provides a sound framework on which companies can structure or redesign their demand management practices. He addresses many critical issues that are ignored in other books on this topic. He writes about and addresses, among others things, what kind of skills people in demand management should have, what kind of organization is needed for demand management, how to make sense of predictive and descriptive analytics, and how to take advantage of big data and new technologies.

Unlike many other books on the same topic, Charlie provides a big-picture approach to demand management. Based on many years of experience, he integrates strategic, tactical, as well as operational aspects of demand management. Consequently, this book contains useful insights for everyone from an analyst to a manager to a senior executive. Yet as Charlie writes about the different aspects of demand management, he also provides a unifying vision: The goal of demand management is not to increase forecast accuracy; it is to foster sales growth. This is a truly unique and insightful observation.

As my undergraduate students would say, Charlie "keeps it real." He carefully chooses the most applicable parts of the theory that have direct applications in the real world of demand management. Readers can directly apply what they learn from this book. The concepts are illustrated by relevant real-life examples, which make them so much easier to understand and apply. Charlie is also careful in avoiding unnecessary theoretical details that are not applicable or that readers can learn on their own. The practical approach taken in this book makes it an excellent choice for practicing managers.

Before I finish, I must say something about SAS. I admit that I am biased in favor of SAS as I have been using it over two decades. As a company, SAS has been on the forefront of demand management not only because of its technological capabilities but also because it chose to integrate business insights of thought leaders like Charlie in their software. This makes SAS the ideal platform for the readers to implement the framework that Charlie has built based on his extensive experience in demand management over many years. In summary, this book is a gem for all who are interested in demand management, including the students in my future forecasting classes.

Preface

In today's volatile market, businesses are urgently seeking new ways to protect themselves and keep profit margins strong. External market factors are creating challenges, and manufacturers, perhaps more than most, are suffering from the consequences of that ripple effect. According to analysts' research, one of the highest-ranking challenges faced by CFOs is generating revenue growth and growing profit margin, yet CFOs believe it's not the right time to increase risk. As a result, companies are challenged with striking a fine balance between delivering growth while minimizing risk.

Meanwhile, as companies continue to strive to maintain market share and grow revenue it ultimately lies in the hands of the C-level and senior management teams to generate profitable growth across all levels of the business. Importantly, that includes organizations that manage the supply chain. There is a shift in focus influencing how companies are managing the supply chain, which is not simply about how supply drives demand, but how demand drives supply. It has been proven time after time that better predicting of the impact of demand on the supply chain increases revenues by at least 3 to 7 percent, and a third of companies could increase it by 6 percent or more.

For the entire business to become more demand-driven, it must secure better control over data and the ability to turn it into actionable insights. To gain a competitive edge requires a change in operational processes because companies are so used to forecasting supply rather than demand. Sales and operations planning processes are a focus, but becoming demand-driven requires a broader shift in the business model. It also requires a radical change in the corporate culture, people skills, horizontal processes, predictive analytics, and scalable technology. The entire company needs to become demand centric, and better equipped to influence and anticipate what consumers are going to purchase before they know what they're going to purchase.

CHANGING INFLUENCES

There are a number of internal and external factors that are shifting companies toward demand-driven business models. It's essential that business leaders recognize the impact of these factors on their business, and act on them.

Today, the traditional top-down approach to supply chain is no longer applicable. Companies have gone through a process where margins have been compromised by changing retailer and consumer purchasing patterns. When retailers started to reduce stock levels and consumers had a tendency to stockpile products, manufacturers responded by creating more product categories in a bid to increase profit margins. The result, product proliferation on shelf, expanded buffer inventories and wasted working capital. Yet forecasts are still based on an inventory or replenishment response.

There is a more fluid distribution of goods today because customer purchase behavior has changed the way products are created and sold. The rise of the Omni-channel and new purchasing processes such as Amazon.com make inventory management more unpredictable. The Omni-channel also increases the influence of external factors like social media, tweeter, and mobile devices which make it more challenging for distributors and retailers to plan deliveries and stock orders. Regardless, same day or next day delivery is an expectation that manufacturers and the supply chain process are tasked to support. These factors are making demand more volatile, and as a result manufacturers can no longer operate using inventory buffer stock to protect against demand volatility as it can too easily result in lost profit.

AUTOMATED CONSUMER ENGAGEMENT

The definition of *fast* for consumers today is dramatically different from the *fast* of 5 to 10 years ago. Consumers are demanding more, and expect it quicker than ever before. This is being driven by the Millennials, as they want instant response and same-day delivery. Consumer demand is no longer driven by supply availability, but instead, companies must shift their operational models by listening to demand and responding to consumer pull in order to remain successful. A supply push strategy is no longer viable in today's digit world.

Using sales and marketing tactics and a consumer-centric approach, companies are now pulling demand through the channels of distribution. To do so, sales and marketing tactics have to be more focused on the automated consumer engagement (experience). The influence of unstructured data and social media are having a more prevalent impact than ever before on the entire purchase process, which must be factored into the demand management process. This is the result of the openness and availability of consumer feedback that social media influences and delivers. Feedback via social media is both a gift and a detriment for retailers, distributors, and manufacturers. Although it provides insight into sentiment and provides opportunity for brand exposure, it adds additional complexity to how consumer pull can be influenced. It also means demand can be influenced across multiple channels and, more often than not, with very immediate consequences.

Demand is also changing because customers want to consume products in new ways. Subscription lifestyles and shared economies due to the on-demand world have impacted how companies need to plan, design, and create products for an indecisive generation of consumers. The consumer experience must remain at the forefront of retailer and manufacturer priorities. Flexibility, efficiency, and a consumer-centric approach will be the key to their success.

An increasing percentage of revenue will come from new product lines increasing product life cycles, which are getting shorter. Also, levels of stock-keeping units (SKUs) are escalating. This challenges companies to create faster delivery systems for more products, making the supply chain even more complex. In addition, the rise of online shopping and same-day delivery has resulted in consumers expecting quicker turnaround from retailers and the manufacturers that support them. 3D printing at home is representative of this ever-increasing phenomenon. In the near future, consumers who want a product now may well create it themselves. Companies, particularly manufacturers, will be competing with a very short-lived product life cycle. Business leaders will need to adapt their business models in order to cope with more frequent peaks or troughs in consumer demand. This has to be achieved in a sustainable way and without negative impact on revenue and profit.

NEW WORLD ORDER

Business leaders need to adapt their business models for today's demand-driven supply chain. Big data analytics allows a more accurate demand forecasting and planning process to improve production and shipments. To be successful, companies must redefine their supply chain definition to include the commercial side of the business.

The shift to the next generation demand management will only be achieved through better use of data, the implementation of horizontal processes, and more emphasis on predictive analytics. Subsequently, there needs to more importance on *consumption-based modeling* using a process called *multi-tiered causal analysis* (MTCA), which combines downstream data with upstream data and applies in-depth predictive analytics to:

- Measure the impact of marketing programs on consumer demand at retail
- Link retail demand to shipments from manufacturers to retailers
- Enable manufacturers to perform what-if analyses to shape future demand and help them choose the optimal sales and marketing strategy for producing the highest volume and return on investment (ROI)

Consumption-based modeling is an approach that links a series of quantitative methods to measure the impact of marketing programming and business strategies that influence downstream consumer demand (demand sensing). Then, creating what-if scenarios to shape and predict future demand (demand shaping) using point of sale (POS) and/or syndicated scanner data. Finally, using consumer demand history and the future-shaped consumer demand forecast as a leading indicator in a supply model to enhance supply volumes (shipments and sales orders) using predictive analytics rather than judgment.

Once MTCA measures the KPIs (key performance indicators) that influence consumer demand, the demand analyst can model and perform what-if simulations to predict and shape future demand, developing short- and long-term forecasts. These simulations capture real-world scenarios and show what happens in different situations. The demand analyst can simulate the impact of changes on key variables that can be controlled (e.g., price, advertising, in-store merchandising, and sales promotions), predict demand, and choose the optimal strategy for producing the highest volume and ROI.

Through this process, leaders can predict how market influences or changes will impact their supply chain, which allows them to formalize ways in which the business can accurately learn through the increasing automated consumer engagement process. It will require more antici-patory predictive analytics to ensure that the right amount of products in the right product mix make it to the shelves and into consumers' hands. The sheer size makes demand forecasting and planning on a global scale highly complex. Product categories, sales regions, and an abundance of participating internal organizations combine to weave a tangled corporate web. "To have the right quantity of the right products at the right place and time," companies will rely heavily on the com-bination of transactional data and digital information to anticipate and influence what consumers will purchase. The overarching goal is to be able to "take proactive measures instead of simply reacting" through strong horizontal alignment processes, stronger collaboration with key accounts (customers), and the use of predictive analytics supported by scalable technology.

GAME CHANGER

To make the shift to the next generation demand management, leaders need to bring together different aspects of the organization to make informed decisions based on a holistic view of available data. Previously, the technology available to companies did not facilitate the integration of data, nor facilitate predictive analytics. This is especially true for the sales, marketing & operations planning organizations. They will all be required to source and share data on a continual basis and learn from not only the shared knowledge collected from across the company, but from information collected digitally by sensors, as a result of Internet of Things (IoT). This is why the corporate culture is crucial to the success of this new demand management model. The culture requires an atmosphere of horizontal collaboration, trust of predictive analytics, and scalable technology in order to ensure all the ingredients are in place. Similarly, organizations need to be ready to work quickly with minimal latency to act on the trends and insights produced. Failure to do so risks a reactive culture prevailing.

There needs to be people with the appropriate skills to provide advice to drive the process with the right domain expertise to make more informed fact-based decisions to support business strategies. There is also a broader requirement for those involved to better understand how supply chains are managed under the new demand management model. For example, making sure demand and supply data are not confusing, but, rather, integrated—working in lock-step to deliver value to consumers and customers. Finally, sales and marketing organizations will need a new way to source and organize information in order to feed into the new generation demand management model. The frequency and the way in which the company collects data will require changes, as well.

Like all change management, transitioning to the next generation demand management model while working in a volatile marketplace is a journey that requires time and does not happen overnight. Data and predictive analytics provide the insights and quantify the challenges a company is facing, but it is business leaders who see the bigger picture, realize the urgency and are not afraid to tackle changes, and the frequency of recurring common problems. So to make informed decisions on how to reorganize and resource the business will require leaders, not followers.

The myriad forces impacting the relationship between demand and supply are set to expand their influence. Finding ways to be better prepared means implementing a corporate culture and structure that brings together organizations, and most of all, data from different sources. The analytics and technology capability is now available, so organizational changes and skills must be the focus to transition to the next generation demand management. However, it will also require ongoing change management to not only gain adoption but sustainability that will eventually become the new corporate culture.

Acknowledgments

A number of friends and colleagues over the course of my career have been influential in my success as a thought leader and trusted adviser. Their continued support and encouragement made it possible to write this book.

I also want to thank my SAS editor Stacey Hamilton and publication advisor Lou Metzger for their continued support and help with the editing and distribution of this book. Their encouragement to write the first book ultimately led me to write this third book. Their input and suggestions have enhanced the quality of the book.

Most of all, I want to thank my wife, Cheryl, for keeping the faith all these years and supporting my career. Without her support and encouragement, I would not have been in a position to write this book.

Charles W. Chase
Advisory Industry Consultant and Trusted Adviser
SAS Institute, Inc.

About the Author

As Advisory Industry Consultant and Consumer Packaged Goods (CPG) Team Lead for the Global Retail/CPG Industry Practice at SAS Institute, Charles Chase is a thought leader and trusted adviser for delivering demand-driven solutions to improve SAS customers' supply chain efficiencies. Chase has more than 20 years of experience in the CPG industry and is an expert in demand forecasting and planning, market response modeling, econometrics, and supply chain management.

Prior to working as Advisory Industry Consultant, Chase led the strategic marketing activities in support of the launch of SAS Forecast Server, which won the Trend-Setting Product of the Year Award for 2005 by *KM World* magazine. Chase launched the SAS Demand-Driven Planning and Optimization Solution in 2008, which is being used by more than 100 large corporations globally. He has also been involved in the reengineering, design, and implementation of three forecasting/marketing intelligence process/systems. He has previously worked for the Mennen Company, Johnson & Johnson, Consumer Products, Reckitt & Benckiser, the Polaroid Corporation, Coca Cola, Wyeth-Ayerst Pharmaceuticals, and Heineken USA.

Chase's authority in the area of forecasting/modeling and advanced marketing analytics is further exemplified by his prior posts as president of the International Association of Business Forecasting, associate editor of the *Journal of Business Forecasting*, and chairperson of the Institute of Business Forecasting (IBF) Best Practices Conferences. Chase currently writes a quarterly column in the *Journal of Business Forecasting* titled "Innovations in Business Forecasting." He also served as a member of the Practitioner Advisory Board for *Foresight: The International Journal of Applied Forecasting*.

In 2013, Chase won the Institute of Business Forecasting Lifetime Achievement Award, and the following year he was certified in professional forecasting by the Institute of Business Forecasting. In 2004, he was named Pro to Know by *Supply and Demand Chain Executive* magazine. He is the author of *Demand-Driven Forecasting: A Structured Approach to Forecasting*, which is now in its second edition (Hoboken, NJ: John Wiley & Sons, 2013), and, with Lora Cecere, *Bricks Matter: The Role of Supply Chains in Building Market-Driven Differentiation* (Hoboken, NJ: John Wiley & Sons, 2013). He served as an adjunct instructor in the Masters of Science in Analytics program at North Carolina State University in 2012–2013.

CHAPTER **1**

The Current State

Today's business challenges are numerous due to globalization pressures, supply chain complexity, rising customer demands, and the need to increase revenues across global markets while continuing to cut costs. Adding to these challenges is the current economy in which the last several years supply has outstripped demand. Intense *market volatility and fragmentation* are compelling companies to develop and deploy more integrated, focused, demand-driven processes and technologies to achieve best-in-class performance. As a result, there have been major shifts in demand management.

Unfortunately, there has been more discussion than actual adoption, and where adoption has occurred, there has been little if any sustainability. Demand-driven processes are challenging and more difficult to get right than supply, and they tend to be *politically charged*. Furthermore, implementing a demand-driven process in support of a new-generation demand management process requires investment in people, process, analytics, and technology. Adoption requires an executive *champion* who has the influence to change corporate behavior, encourage new analytics skills (descriptive and predictive), and integrate processes horizontally utilizing new scalable technology. Strategic intent and interdependencies play a key role in maintaining long-term sustainability. Without sustainability, the adoption of new conceptual designs like *demand-driven* tends to fail over the long-term. In most cases manufacturers lack the necessary analytical skills, horizontal processes, and scalable technologies needed to capitalize on *big data* and digitally collected information. After all, it's not just about process anymore.

As shown in Figure 1.1 investment in *people, process, analytics,* and *technology* requires a champion not only to facilitate adoption but also for sustainability purposes. Sustainability can only occur if the strategic intent and business interdependencies are horizontally aligned and supported by scalable technology.

Companies are realizing that moving to the next generation demand management will require a laser focus on four key areas:

1. Investing in their people's skills, which requires change in behavior
2. Reorganization around horizontal processes

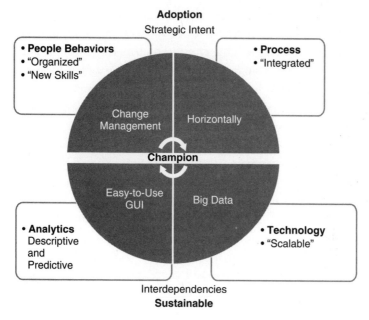

Figure 1.1 People, process, analytics, and technology required for adoption and sustainability.

3. Integrating predictive as well as descriptive analytics into the process

4. Investing in large-scale automatic forecasting technology

These four areas are the key catalysts to move from the current state to the future state, along with good metrics to measure progress. Although adoption requires changes in people behaviors that include new skills and horizontal processes, it will also require more focus on predictive analytics supported by large-scale technology that can adapt and scale to big data. It requires changes in corporate culture led by a champion who has the authority and leadership to not only drive adoption, but also create a new corporate culture that stresses account-ability with a focus on customer excellence. Finally, sustainability can only occur if the strategic "intent and business interdependencies" are horizontally aligned and supported by scalable technology.

In many cases, companies get adoption, but once the champion moves on to a new project, the process participants tend to go back to the old process, stop investing in new skills, bypass the analytics, and create Excel workaround programs to avoid using the technology. This suboptimizes the process and technology, not to mention creates poor results. In other words, the intent becomes self-serving to all people and all things—except for the *right* thing, generating revenue and profit. We have become so immersed in achieving low MAPEs (mean absolute percentage error) that we have lost the original intent of the process.

Before a company invests in people, process, analytics, and technology, they need to define their true intent. We all know through experience that the one number forecast does not work. It might work in theory, but not in practice. Plus, only a handful of companies are forecasting true demand (e.g., POS and/or syndicated scanner data). Most companies are forecasting the supply replenishment signal (sales orders), and/or the supply response (shipments). Finally, most demand planners really don't do forecasting. They manage data and information. This is another reason why more and more companies are looking to hire demand analytics and data scientists who have strong statistical skills. The key word is *intent*. Is your demand management process intended to create accurate forecasts (lower MAPEs) to reduce inventory costs or to provide business decision support to grow revenue and profitability?

WHY DEMAND MANAGEMENT MATTERS MORE THAN EVER

Demand management concepts are now 20 to 25 years old. The first use of the term *demand management* surfaced in the commercial sector in the late 1980s or early 1990s. Previously, the focus was on a more siloed approach to demand forecasting and planning that was manual, using very simple statistical techniques like moving averaging and simple exponential smoothing, and then, Excel, and a whole lot of gut-feeling judgment. Sound familiar? In the mid-1990s, demand planning and supply planning were lumped together, which gave birth to supply chain management concepts of demand planning and integrated supply chain planning.

Most supply chain professionals are quickly realizing that their supply chain planning solutions have not driven down costs, and have not reduced inventories or speed to market. Companies globally across all industry verticals have actually moved backward over the course of the last 10 years when it comes to growth, operating margin, and inventory turns. In some cases, they have improved days payable, but this has pushed costs and working capital responsibility backward in the supply chain, moving the costs to the suppliers. To make matters worse, Excel is still the most widely used demand forecasting and planning technology in the face of significant improvements in data collection, storage, processing, analytics, and scalability.

According to a 2014 *Industry Week* report (see Figure 1.2), moving averaging has now become the preferred statistical model of choice for forecasting demand, digressing from Holt-Winters Three Parameter Exponential Smoothing based on studies conducted by the Institute of Business Forecasting in the late 1990s. Furthermore, with all the advancements in analytics and technology, there has been minimal investment in the analytic skills of demand planners.

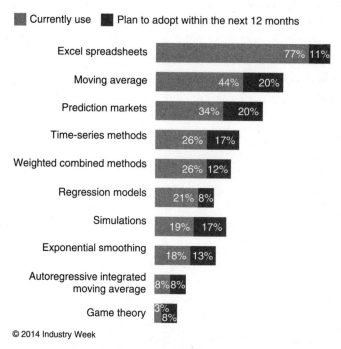

© 2014 Industry Week

Figure 1.2 Current use of forecasting methodologies and tools.

To make matters worse, downstream data—with all the improvements with data collection, minimal latency in delivery, and increased coverage across channels—is still being used in pockets across sales and marketing, rather than the entire supply chain, for demand forecasting and planning.

Companies are quickly learning that in order to move forward, they need to admit their bad practices of the past. They must be willing to risk failure in order to move forward. Leaders must confront a number of mistakes made in the design of their demand management processes over the course of the last decade. The mistakes are many, but all can be corrected with changes to the process, use of downstream data, and most all, the inclusion of analytics. Here are a number of good intentions with poor execution that have caused companies to make key mistakes in demand management.

The One-Number Forecast

Well-intentioned academics and consultants tout the concept of one-number forecasting. Enthusiastic supply chain executives have drunk the Kool-Aid, as they say. But, the reality is, it does not reduce latency and it is too simplistic. In other words, it is conceptually appealing, but not practical in execution.

The sole concept of a one-number demand forecast is that *if everyone is focused on one number, the probability of achieving the number is great.* As a result, the concept adds unintentional, and in many cases, intentional bias, adding error to the demand plan. It is too simplistic; all the participants have different purposes, or intentions.

I ask supply chain managers, "What is the purpose of your forecasting process?" They say, "To create an accurate demand forecast." I respond, "What is the true purpose of their demand forecasting and planning process? Is it to create a financial plan, set sales targets, or create a shipment forecast?" They pause, and say, "All the above." I say, "*All the above* are plans, not an unconstrained consumer demand forecast."

There is only one true forecast—the unconstrained demand forecast, or as close as possible to "unconstrained," given the inherent constraints, whether self-inflicted or customer specific. There is no such thing as a shipment forecast, financial forecast, or sales forecast. They are all plans created from the unconstrained consumer demand forecast. Furthermore, most consensus forecasts are a blend of different plans and financial targets. The people who push the one-number concept really do not understand demand forecasting and planning. An unconstrained consumer demand forecast is used to build a demand plan, financial plan, sales plan, marketing plan, and operations plan. Each plan has a different intent, or purpose, and as such, will be different. There are many separate activities including workflow that require different skills (people), process, analytics, and technology capabilities.

A demand forecast is hierarchical around products, time, geographies, channels, and attributes. It is a complex set of role-based time-phased data. As a result, a one-number thought process is naïve. An effective demand forecast has *many* numbers that are tied together in an effective data model for role-based planning and what-if analysis. Even the eventual demand plan is sometimes not reflective of the original unconstrained demand forecast due to capacity constraints, which results in demand shifting to accommodate supply lead times and materials availability. In fact, most companies who describe demand shaping during interviews with supply chain executives actually describe demand shifting, not true demand shaping. A one-number plan is too constraining for the organization. A demand plan is a series of time-phased plans carefully architected in a data model of products, calendars, channels, and regions. The numbers within the plans have different purposes (intents) to different individuals within the organization.

So, instead of a one-number demand plan, the focus needs to be a common set of plans for marketing, sales, finance, and operations planning (supply plan) with different plan views based on an agreement of market assumptions and one unconstrained consumer demand response. This requires the use of an advanced enterprise demand forecasting and planning solution with the design of the system to create a true demand response and visualize role-based planning views. The legacy systems implemented over the past decade were not designed to accommodate different plan views based on an unconstrained consumer demand response.

Unfortunately, the concept of the one-number forecast often does more damage than it does good, especially when taken literally. What is important is that an entire organization (sales, marketing, finance, and operations planning) is working together to achieve aligned goals based on a set of aligned and integrated plans. This can only be achieved via a well setup and functioning set of cross-functional horizontal planning processes, with plans generated from the S&OP/IBP (sales & operations planning and/or integrated business planning) process driven based on a one-number unconstrained consumer demand forecast. In reality this results in multiple sets of numbers, and ideally, multiple plans are generated and used as inputs into these processes. It is the processes themselves that convert multiple inputs into an aligned set of plans. The notion of a single number to represent the forecast for all departments is a frequent, but incorrect, interpretation of the phrase "a single agreed-to plan."

If you can imagine that marketing, sales, finance, operations planning, and manufacturing all came to a consensus plan discussion with the same numbers, what would they discuss? The idea of all teams meeting to discuss how they arrived at the same number (forecast) is impractical and impossible. Conversely, to arrive at consensus, you want several views with multiple assumptions to discuss. Multiple perspectives of the market and business will enable discussion and debate on how the company can meet and agree to a set of integrated plans. In other words, how much of that unconstrained consumer demand forecast are we willing to fill to meet the most profitable sales revenue goal?

To clarify this process, the demand signal, and corresponding demand response created by sales and marketing, will most likely "not" match the financial plan and senior management's strategic goals. This is where the one-number forecast falls apart. Generally, they hold to the financial plan, particularly when the demand response is below the financial plan. In a demand-driven forecasting and planning process this is where data, analytics, and domain knowledge kicks in. Using data, analytics, and domain knowledge, the sales/marketing teams collaborate using what-if scenario analytics to determine how to close the gap. In other words, what KPIs can be increased/decreased to close the gap between the demand response and the financial plan? Then, the finance team determines what the costs will be to add, say, another sales promotion or marketing event. These gap scenarios are discussed in the S&OP/IBP meeting, where a decision is made to either lower the financial plan or provide sales and marketing with incremental spending to close the gap.

The process just described is the only way a one-number forecast can be achieved. You cannot use gut-feeling judgment, nor wish the financial plan to happen. However, this is pretty much how most demand management processes work (e.g., simple baseline forecast using a moving average with a whole lot of gut feeling judgment).

Collaborative (Consensus) Planning

Collaborative planning is a conceptually sound principle with good intentions, but poor execution. The entire basis for the concept of collaborative planning is based on the belief that each department within the company can add insight (value) to improve the accuracy of the demand plan. In concept, if designed properly, this is correct. In reality, the implementation has been flawed. The challenge is that most companies do not hold the groups within the departments accountable for their bias and error. Each group within the company has a natural bias (purpose or intent), and corresponding error based on incentives. The old adage holds true: "Be careful what you ask for because you may get it." Unless the process has structure regarding error reporting and accountability, the process of collaborative planning will distort the demand plan, adding error despite well-intended efforts to improve the planning process.

Many companies that have redesigned their collaborative planning processes only resulted in improvements in their user interface with the intentions of making data collection and manipulation easier for demand management. I call this, "Automate what I do, but don't change what I do." In each redesign, companies do not question the value and appropriate uses of the demand inputs, nor do they apply structure around the input that drives a 40 to 60 percent forecast over/under bias.

We struggle with why more companies do not apply the principles of *lean forecasting* to the consensus forecasting and planning process through forecast-value added (FVA) analysis. This is best described by Mike Gilliland in his book, *The Business Forecasting Deal: Exposing Myths, Eliminating Bad Practices, Providing Practical Solutions.*[1] In its simplest form, FVA measures the impact of each touch point in the collaborative planning process before and after the statistical baseline forecast is adjusted by one of the participating departments (i.e., sales, marketing, finance, and operations planning). If that particular touch point isn't adding value, then you need to either eliminate it or weight the bias up/down. This requires that all the forecasts be captured each cycle and compared to determine any bias.

Forecast by Exception

Given all the acquisitions and consolidation that have taken place over the past 20 years, SKU proliferation, as well as companies selling their products across geographic regions, markets, channels, and key accounts (customers), has made it difficult to touch every product every cycle. It is not uncommon for a company to have anywhere from 1,000 to 18,000 products (SKUs) that span across multiple channels (e.g., grocery, mass merchandisers, drug, gas and convenience, and others), across multiple regions and countries, not to mention customers and demand points. This could lead to millions of forecasts each cycle. We recently worked with a very large CPG company that had over 4.5 million data series across multiple geographies, channels, and customers. This size data set requires a highly scalable enabling enterprise solution, not Excel, to help manage and forecast all those data series.

It is virtually impossible to touch every product every cycle. Companies forecast at some aggregate level in their product hierarchy with little attention to the lower levels (product mix). Then, disaggregate it down to the SKU/demand point using static historical percentage ratios (SKU splits). Imagine managing that disaggregation for 1,800 SKUs by region, channel, brand, product group, product, SKU, and location using Excel. Well, that is reality. The biggest contributor to forecast error is the lower-level product mix due to the sheer number of products and locations (SKU/ship to location). Thus, a large-scale automatic forecasting system is required that can do all the heavy lifting using analytics, and can filter on an exception basis those products and locations that need the most attention based on a set of business rules, and error statistics (e.g., MAPE, weighted absolute percentage error and others). Excel is simply not scalable, nor does it have the depth and breadth of analytics.

Fitting Demand to Supply versus Fitting Supply to Demand

Traditionally, companies focus on forecasting what manufacturing should make, rather than what the market and channel were demanding. It is a supply-centric approach to demand forecasting and planning that compensates for the lack of a strong demand management process. The process needs to focus on identifying market opportunities and leveraging internal sales and marketing programs to influence consumers (customers) to purchase the company's products and services, also known as sensing demand signals and shaping future demand. This radical change with a focus on customer excellence versus cutting costs changes the process focusing on modeling (using predictive analytics) what is being sold in the channel based on market conditions and consumer preferences to determine the best demand response. This difference might sound insignificant, but it is a major change.

An additional step is required after demand sensing and shaping to translate demand into a more accurate demand response (demand plan). Forecasting channel demand reduces demand latency and gives the organization a more current demand signal. It allows the augmentation of the forecast with demand insights (signals) to improve the quality of the forecast. For most companies, this requires a reimplementation of demand management methodologies, analytical skills, and new enabling technologies.

Lack of Statistical Skills (People)

Recently, while meeting with the supply chain management team of a large appliances manufacturer, we were asked to provide them with a detailed description of the skills required to hire demand planners. This is not uncommon as most demand planners have minimal statistical skills. The demand planner's primary role in the demand management process is focused on taking aggregate level forecasts and disaggregating them into ship to location by SKU forecasts. This requires minimal statistical skills. This is done using Excel spreadsheets, and then manually entered into a legacy ERP system. Those companies who invested in demand analysts with advanced analytical skills combined with new demand forecasting and planning enabling technology based on demand sensing and shaping have significantly improved their demand management processes.

Most traditional demand management organizations are positioned in the operations planning departments too far upstream to understand how to apply analytics to downstream channel data. When meeting with supply chain managers, I ask, "Who is responsible for demand generation?" They always respond, "Sales and marketing." Then I ask, "Why then are the demand planners positioned in the operations planning organization?" When in fact, they should be positioned in the marketing organization where the domain knowledge exists. In other words, demand forecasting and planning requires analytics and domain knowledge.

The demand management organization of the future needs to be positioned in marketing for two key reasons: (1) to provide statistical support, and (2) to gain domain knowledge. As marketing product managers move every two to three years, the demand planners (analysts) will remain as the product domain experts, as well as the analytics experts. As a result, companies begin to sell through versus sell into channels of distribution, as demand analysts begin to analyze and measure the effects of those factors that influence consumers and/or customers to buy their products. Subsequently, inventories will be managed more efficiently in those channels, avoiding discounting, sales promotions, and other vehicles required to push products through the channels of distribution. This will have a positive impact on profit margins, resulting in higher revenues, as well as higher market share.

How Do We Know? Several large consumer packaged goods (CPG) companies in the apparel, food, and beverage segments have recently moved their demand analysts and data scientists into the consumer insights departments, and/or aligned their demand management departments with marketing, significantly improving their demand forecast accuracy—not to mention gaining valuable consumer insights, becoming valued analytic advisers, and transferring accountability and ownership to marketing.

Accountability for the Unconstrained Demand Forecast

Sales and marketing are responsible for demand generation, and ultimately for creating the most accurate demand response. Their primary role is to identify market opportunities, translate those opportunities into demand signals, measure the key performance indicators (KPIs) that influence demand signals, and use them to shape (influence) future demand. The collaboration (consensus) should be between sales and marketing, with finance assessing the programs to determine if they are profitable. If not, then it is finance's role to push back on sales and marketing. This is a truly demand-driven planning process. Operations planning should not provide another input into the consensus forecasting process other than to assess the implications from a supply perspective. If there is a capacity challenge, it should be raised at the S&OP/IBP (sales & operations planning/integrated business planning) meeting to determine a strategy to resolve the constraints (i.e., add another manufacturing shift, OEM the capacity to a third-party manufacturer, or shift demand by moving a marketing program to accommodate the capacity constraint).

Nestle Chocolate Company direct store delivery (DSD) does this best by following a structured demand-driven planning process that is supported by new demand-driven forecasting and planning technology that allows it to measure sales promotions and marketing events by mathematically calculating the lift, and then assessing the lift to determine if it generates profit. If not, the sales promotion is not implemented. This combination of data, analytics, domain knowledge, and financial assessment has significantly improved forecast accuracy as well as sales performance, resulting in higher profit margins and lower finished goods inventory safety stock.

While companies want to move forward, and the desire is reemployment of demand management, in my opinion, they cannot be successful unless they admit to their poor practices of the past! Good intentions but bad execution results in poor results.

For the last three decades, inventory has been the primary method for managing demand volatility. Inventory is expensive, and having the wrong inventory only increases working capital. Nevertheless, companies' efforts have been focused on tightening up their supply chains by becoming more responsive to market signals and trends, and reducing inventory while maintaining high customer service levels. Today, only a handfull of companies, 14 percent according to a 2014 *Industry Week* survey, have begun to adopt demand-driven principles to be more than just reactive to supply chain fluctuations. They are monitoring and responding to early demand signals, and they're figuring out how to reduce demand variability itself. Emerging data collection, storage, processing, analytics, and technology capabilities, coupled with real supply-chain collaboration, are making this possible.

CURRENT CHALLENGES AND OPPORTUNITIES

Globalization and changes in customer expectations continue to increase market volatility, adding complexity that makes it difficult to balance supply and demand across multiple product lines, business units, and geographic regions on a daily and weekly basis. The sheer size of the corporate footprint due to the diversity of many multinational corporations, compounded by the multiple channels they sell through, are driving much of this complexity. At the same time, market pressures are increasing the range of product offerings. This is evident by the growing number of SKUs that most manufacturers have to manage. Add shorter product life cycles, longer lead times, declining customer loyalty, and rising expectations for immediate product availability, and it quickly becomes clear that any improvements in demand visibility and responsiveness would pay huge dividends.

According to recent industry surveys conducted by several analyst firms, there are five key trends occurring that impact the supply chain, and particularly demand management:

1. *Continued demand volatility* and expanding product portfolios challenge supply chain leaders across all industries to elevate demand management performance.

2. *Persistent cost pressures* require supply chain leaders to better align supply with demand for improved performance.

3. *New product launch importance* drives supply chain leaders to seek stronger alignment between new product development and supply chain planning and execution capabilities for increased launch success.

4. *End-to-end partner communication and collaborative execution* by all partners in the supply chain from retailers through raw material providers must constantly collaborate on what events are occurring, the data behind those events, and how they can execute as a unified group to respond to the challenges as they unfold. Trading partners are now acting in a concerted manner based on transparent information to resolve issues as they happen. Solving a problem by pushing costs to another supply chain partner is an antiquated proposition as companies realize that cost shifting is not a sustainable, nor a competitive solution.

5. *Big data is becoming mandatory.* Big data has been the big IT story in recent years. Combining the data of multiple supply chain partners, turning that data into information, and being able to react and execute accordingly requires a lot of information. Big data solutions combined with complex event processing (CEP) solutions are being used more than ever to digest the enormous magnitude of available data and turn it into executable actions. Leveraging these tools with supply chain visibility solutions will quickly become a "must have" rather than a "nice to have" as companies utilizing these tools set the bar for the new normal in supply chain performance.

Companies continue to face an uncertain economy, with volatile demand, expanding product portfolios, and increasing cost pressures. At the same time, they need to aggressively focus on growth and revenue acceleration, increased customer responsiveness, and reduced inventory for improved cash flow. Together, these challenges cause leading organizations to invest in demand-driven transformation to improve demand orchestration, and supply and product capability. Supply chain technology is helping to transform the way companies do business with consumers/customers and each other. If there is one thing these five trends have in common, it is that having constant feedback and control over supply chain functions is key to doing business in today's ever-changing environment. For this reason, these trends are likely to continue for the next several years and beyond.

The primary obstacles responsible for impeding companies from achieving their supply chain goals has not changed much over the past decade. If anything, they have intensified, making it more challenging for those companies that continue to allow their corporate culture (bad habits) to guide their judgment. Most executives continue to focus on three core business priorities: (1) leveraging the supply chain organization to drive business growth, (2) driving business process improvements, and (3) improving customer service. These three primary goals and objectives have not changed very much over the last decade.

It is not surprising that these supply centric strategies still focus primarily on cost reduction to support corporate supply chain initiatives. When asked, "What are the top three obstacles to achieving your organization's supply chain goals and objectives?" the number-one response from supply chain executives is forecast accuracy and demand volatility, followed by the inability to synchronize the supply chain end-to-end, and lack of cross-functional collaboration (planning), consecutively.

Twenty years ago, it made sense to use inventory buffers up and down the business hierarchy when comparatively short supply chains existed, and forecasts based on the previous month adjusted for seasonality were sufficient. Now, with longer supply chains stretching around the world, along with ever-increasing demand variability, companies are realizing that they can no longer use inventory buffers to protect against demand variability. In fact, according to companies we have worked with around the world, demand volatility has not decreased. If anything, demand has gotten more volatile over the past one to two years globally, according to executives in the United States, Latin America, Europe, and China.

Subsequently, among the primary influences causing demand volatility are new product launches, the state of the economy, increased globalization, and SKU (Stock Keeping Units) proliferation on shelf at retailers. As companies have become more global and the size of their product portfolios has increased through acquisitions and industry consolidations there has been an enormous increase in SKU proliferation on shelf. In addition, due to ever-changing consumer demands, new product launches have increased significantly.

As data collection, storage, processing, and analytical power have steadily evolved, systems costs have declined. It is hard to determine if supply and inventory management adoption has kept pace with the growing market complexity. Or, if companies in fact created that complexity by enabling massive global supply chains, and endless product configurations and customer choices to appease the never-ending demands of consumers. Why didn't product life cycle management evolve to maintain continuity across the product portfolio to reduce the increasing complexity of their product offerings?

Across most companies, there is a similar ongoing tension between process, people, analytics, data requirements, and technology needs. The ability to collect, cleanse, and share data across the organization originally required a significant investment and justification within already strained IT budgets, often without an immediate ROI (return on investment). Such investments created the foundation for companies that were the early adopters of advanced data management capabilities. As data collection and analytic tools, applications, and solutions have become more affordable and powerful, they've become easier for companies to justify. For many companies, data management capabilities have advanced so quickly that the challenge now is how to report and make practical use of it all. Furthermore, data storage costs have declined significantly over the past decade. Sales transactional data is being collected at increasingly granular levels across markets, channels, key accounts, brands, and product configurations. Faster in-memory processing is making it possible to run what-if simulations in minutes that previously had to be left to run overnight.

Of course, the output and recommendations of any planning and decision-support system like demand management are only as good as the integrity of the underlying data. The road to achieving the benefits from improved forecast accuracy starts where most business process improvement projects start, with the data. It begins by addressing data quality, and then by breaking down the functional siloes and making the data readily accessible to everyone in the demand management process that feeds into the sales & operations planning (S&OP) and integrated business planning (IBP) processes. According to a 2014 report by *Industry Week*, both data quality and data availability have improved for companies reporting wider adoption of demand-driven forecasting and planning methods. That implies that better and more widely accessible data are a prerequisite, or that poor quality data and a lack of sharing are most likely the barriers to adoption.[2]

However, according to the same 2014 *Industry Week* report, companies have not progressed much in the way of using true demand data to drive their demand-driven forecasting and planning processes. In Figure 1.3, the majority of those companies that participated in the study are still using customer orders and/or customer shipments as their primary data to forecast and plan their demand response. What is even more disturbing is that with all the enhancements in data collection, cleansing, and technology improvements, POS and syndicated scanner data (e.g., Nielsen and Information Resources Inc.—IRI) are the least used data for demand forecasting and planning. According to a book written in 2003 by Oliver Wight, *Demand Management Best Practices: Process, Principles and Collaboration*, POS data is closest to true demand. So, after over two decades companies are still using customer orders and shipments to sense demand signals and shape

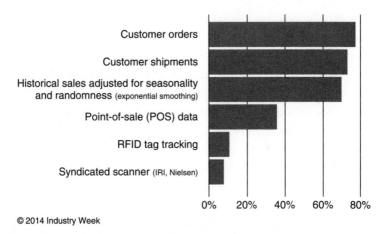

© 2014 Industry Week

Figure 1.3 Demand data used for forecasting and planning.

future demand to create the most accurate demand response, when in fact they are really sensing supply replenishment signals and shaping the future supply plan, or supply response. Consequently, it has been proven that customer shipments are the most volatile data stream due to inventory replenishment policies and other related trade incentives, creating what is referred to as the *bullwhip effect*.

When it comes to preferred technology, it is no surprise that Microsoft Excel remains the most widely used forecasting tool in 2014 (see Figure 1.2), with over 77 percent of the participating companies, according to the 2014 *Industry Week* report. As limited as its capabilities are, spreadsheet applications are ubiquitous on every desktop and laptop computer, as well as most mobile devices. The challenge with spreadsheet analysis, given the SKU-proliferation and data deluge, is that it is simply not powerful or scalable enough to get the job done. Over the last decade, a wide variety of other, non–spreadsheet-based forecasting and planning tools, applications, and enterprise solutions have become available that can scale to the ever-increasing sources of information referred to as *big data*. Consequently, spreadsheets do not have the depth and breadth of analytical methods available for demand-driven forecasting and planning. The good news is that those companies that participated in the study said that they plan to adopt in the next 12 months a number of these more advanced analytical methods, ranging in complexity from simple moving averaging to time series, regression, and other related analytic methods. The really puzzling fact is that simple moving averaging was the number-one analytical method in this study, which indicates that companies have actually regressed, since only a decade ago almost every survey indicated that Holt-Winters Three Parameter Exponential Smoothing was the number-one mathematical method.

The goal for demand planners shouldn't be to use the latest or most complex tools for their own sake, but to identify the analytical method that best fits for a given product line by providing the necessary intelligence on a timely basis. Of course, when it comes to building consensus plans, analytical outputs are only the beginning. Domain knowledge is also necessary to incorporate the correct business inputs that influence demand outside the precursor that fuels the demand forecasting

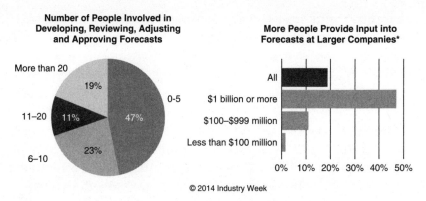

Figure 1.4 Number of people reviewing, adjusting, and approving demand forecasts.

engines with the understanding that such inputs do not take the form of wishful thinking. No matter how sophisticated the underlying statistical algorithms, people often feel that they haven't participated in the forecast process unless they've tinkered with the numbers. Almost half (47 percent) of manufacturers report that five or fewer people are involved in forecast development, review, and approval (Figure 1.4). There tends to be a wider network of perceived responsibility for more people to participate in the demand forecasting and planning process at larger companies, especially those with $1 billion or more in annual revenues.[3]

In addition, translating unconstrained demand forecasts into the appropriate demand response requires not only sensing demand signals, but measuring those KPIs (Key Performance Indicators) that influence the demand signal, and shaping future demand to drive revenue and profit, not just to reduce costs to create the most efficient supply response. Just as collaboration with external value chain partners is necessary to optimize the demand response on the supply side, demand shaping practices using key business drivers, or influence factors such as price, in-store merchandising, sales promotions, and more, require internal collaboration to optimize and coordinate activity on the demand side. More than three out of four manufacturers indicate their demand planning and other planning activities are at least somewhat integrated with fulfillment, manufacturing, procurement, and supply chain functions.[4]

PRIMARY OBSTACLES TO ACHIEVING DEMAND MANAGEMENT PLANNING GOALS

With all the enhancements in demand management over the past decade companies are still faced with challenges impeding the advancement of demand-driven planning. Many organizations are struggling with how to analyze and make practical use of the mass of data being collected and stored. Others are perplexed as to how to synchronize and share external information with internal data across their technology architectures. Nevertheless, they are all looking for enterprise-wide solutions (technology) that provide actionable insights to make better decisions that improve corporate performance through improved intelligence.

Before we can address all the demand management challenges of people, process, analytics, and technology we need to address the many bad practices that must be overcome before companies can truly embrace the benefits of demand-driven planning. The reality is that the obstacles to impeding companies from achieving their goals translate into mistakes and perceptions that hinder the progress of demand management. Those mistakes are still being made today after two decades of data collection, storage, processing, analytics, and technology improvements. In many cases, as we mentioned earlier, the conceptual design is sound, but in practice those designs are flawed due to corporate culture and other related political bias.

In fact, the size of the company or its location doesn't matter. I have sat across the table from several supply chain management teams over the past 10 years at companies that span from less than $1 billion in annual sales to over $109 billion in annual sales. Talk about stirring emotions with the words *demand forecasting*, or *demand-driven planning*, not to mention *being digital-driven*. Although the atmosphere in those rooms could be defined by despair, disillusionment, and most of all skepticism, it was far from hopeless. It seemed like déjà vu when I worked for a large CPG company back the early 1990s—no analytics, no technology other than Excel, and 100 percent gut-feeling judgment injected into the process by multiple departments, including sales, marketing, finance, and operations planning—all in an attempt to create a one-number consensus forecast (technically a supply plan).

The story goes on with no real attention to accountability and little or no attention to the product mix, as the focus was always a top-down forecast (plan). The supply chain leaders didn't just say they wanted to improve their demand management process, but said that they had no choice due to the fact they were sitting on anywhere from $100 million to over $600 million in finished goods inventory, WHIP, and raw materials. Over $75 million to $400 million was in finished goods inventory alone. Talk about being supply centric in their approach to demand management. I guess using buffer inventory to protect against demand volatility doesn't work after all.

Subsequently, demand forecasting and planning is still the key focus area for most companies. For most, it is the biggest challenge that they will face in their supply chain journey. Companies want to improve demand forecasting and planning, but have focused mainly on the process with little or no attention to improving data quality, people, analytics, and technology. As a result, their skepticism has become prevalent among their supply chain leaders, as many have conceded that they can never be successful in improving demand forecast accuracy. As indicated in survey after survey demand forecasting and planning is important to supply chain leaders, but also an area with the largest gap in user satisfaction.

Based on my personal experiences visiting companies, I have found that demand management is the most misunderstood supply chain planning process with little if any knowledge of how to apply analytics to downstream data (POS/syndicated scanner data). Also, well-intentioned consultants have given bad advice, particularly, that a one number forecast process is the key to success. As discussed earlier the one number forecast only encourages well-intended personal bias, and is used to set sales targets, financial plans, and other factors that are not directly related to an accurate demand response. What drives excellence in demand management is the ability to incorporate sophisticated data-driven analytics into the process using large-scale enabling technology solutions to create the most accurate unconstrained consumer demand response. Once that unconstrained demand response is adjusted for sales, marketing, finance, and/or operational constraints, it becomes a sales plan, marketing plan, financial plan, and/or a supply plan.

WHY DO COMPANIES CONTINUE TO DISMISS THE VALUE OF DEMAND MANAGEMENT?

Today, we live in a polarized world that divides family members, friends, and business colleagues. It affects everything we do, from the way we communicate with one another to how we handle business challenges. I have seen long-time business colleagues have passionate discussions defending their supply chain position regarding what adds more value—demand or supply. As a result, we now work in what I refer to as the *polarized supply chain*, where you are either a believer in supply or demand. Sound familiar? We get caught up in what we are comfortable with, or what we believe is the "holy grail" to fixing the inefficiencies in the supply chain. The pendulum seems to swing back and forth from decade to decade, focusing on supply or demand "processes and technologies" with little emphasis on people (skills and changing behaviors), and virtually no attention to predictive analytics.

We are at a pivotal point in the three-decades-old supply chain journey. Are we going to continue to address the symptoms, or finally take action to fix the root cause of our supply chain challenges?

Everyone seems to be high on supply these days as they continue to smoke inventory crack. They justify their addiction on the fact that forecasts will always be wrong. Well, I have news for our supply-driven friends. Why is it that when we underforecast, companies experience significant backorders, and when we overforecast, companies sit on millions of dollars of finished goods inventories? What's more, why are our supply-centric colleagues suddenly abandoning their traditional use of buffer inventory (safety stock) to protect against demand volatility?

By the way, I agree completely that a 1 to 3 percent increase in forecast accuracy may have very little impact if any on safety stock or possibly finished goods inventories, particularly if your forecast accuracy is already above 85 percent on average across the entire product hierarchy. At that point, each additional 1 percent of accuracy (or reduction in error) requires exponential investment in time and resources with minimal effect on buffer inventories. Of course, that is if your forecast accuracy at the lower mix levels (i.e., product/SKU or SKU/demand point) is above 70 percent. We have found that over 90 percent of companies still focus on measuring forecast accuracy at the highest aggregate level of the product hierarchy with little if any attention to the lower level mix accuracy. In fact, the average forecast accuracy across all industries is between 50 and 65 percent on average at the aggregate level, and between 25 and 35 percent or lower at the lower mix levels. How do we know? These numbers have been validated not through analyst surveys but by working directly with over 100 companies during the past 10 years. So, there is a lot of room for improvement regarding demand forecast accuracy—--much more than 1 to 3 percent.

A classic case of poor demand forecasting is when a company ships into a channel, or retailer more products than the retailer can sell, while simultaneously incurring backorders. So, you would think, how could that happen? Well it's all about the product mix. Not only did the manufacturer ship in more products than the retailer sold, they shipped in the wrong mix of products. So, now the retailer is sitting on excess inventory that is not selling. So, what does the manufacturer do? The manufacturer discounts the products in inventory at the retailer by running sales promotions and other related consumer incentives in an attempt to reduce the inventory by pulling it through the channel and retailers' stores. This has a negative impact on profit margins and market share.

In addition, the forecasting methods being deployed, mainly moving averaging and nonseasonal exponential smoothing models, are only accurate one to three periods into the future. As a result, the upper/lower forecast ranges (confidence limits) that are a key input to safety stock calculations tend to be cone shaped (exponentially get larger as you forecast beyond one to three periods). This is why the impact in many cases actually increases safety stock volumes, rather than lowering them. This is not the case when using more advanced statistical methods like ARIMA, ARIMAX, and dynamic regression (predictive analytics) as they are more accurate further into the future, so the upper/lower forecast ranges tend to be tighter (more consistent to the forecast, not cone shaped) as you go further out into the future. These models actually help lower safety stocks not only through more accurate forecasts, but by reducing the upper/lower ranges of the forecast, which is a key input to safety stock calculations. Which demand forecast in Figure 1.5 would you choose to drive your safety stock calculations?

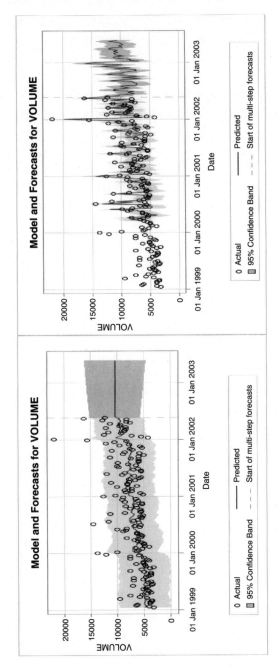

Figure 1.5 Comparing upper/lower forecast ranges for different forecasting methods.

25

The increase in the use of Excel by demand planners over the past decade and the broader use of moving averaging are the result of companies' investment in ERP solutions, which have restricted model selection. They only support simple statistical forecasting methods (mainly exponential smoothing). In fact, the one area of the supply chain that has received the least attention and investment in people, analytics, and technology over the past decade is demand forecasting and planning. If you noticed, I left out process. Process alone cannot improve your forecast accuracy. It requires investment in people skills and behavior, horizontal processes, predictive analytics, and scalable technology putting equal emphasis on all four areas.

Using proof-of-values (POVs use a subset of the customer's data in the software vendor's technology to prove the value—whether it improved forecast accuracy) conducted with multiple companies over the last 10 years, SAS Institute Inc. has shown improvements in forecast accuracy of anywhere between 10 and 30 percent (and in some cases up to 50 percent) on average up/down company's product hierarchies by just deploying "holistic" modeling driven by predictive analytics, not by sales targets, financial plans, and/or judgmental overrides. In fact, it has also been proven using historical demand data (uncleansed—not segmenting demand history into baseline and promoted volumes) combined with predictive analytics that there is no reason to cleanse demand history (shipments/sales orders). Cleansing demand history by segmenting it into baseline and promoted volumes, and for any other reason other than historical realignment or true entry errors, is actually a bad practice. In fact, this type of cleansing makes the forecast less accurate. This cleansing process creates two separate data streams: (1) baseline, which tends to be a moving average, and (2) promoted, which is supposed to reflect promotional spikes and outlier corrections, but is actually a combination of seasonality and promotional volume. Furthermore, the promoted volumes are given to sales and marketing to adjust manually. Finally, the demand planner manually tries to piece these two data sets back together. The result, 1 + 1 now equals 5. In 95 percent of the POVs conducted, there were improvements in demand forecast accuracy in the range of 10 to 25 percent, significantly lowering buffer inventories (safety stock) and finished goods inventory. Furthermore, they found that applying multi-echelon inventory optimization, auto leveling, and other advanced analytics for supply planning along with improved forecast accuracy creates a synergy effect of another 15 to 30 percent reduction in finished goods inventories, thus reducing costs and freeing up working capital.

Another reason why improved forecast accuracy doesn't have a strong impact on inventory safety stock is because no one is actually forecasting demand, but rather supply. Those companies that are moving toward becoming demand-driven and ultimately digital-driven are engaging sales and marketing, and linking downstream data to upstream data using a process called multi-tiered causal analysis (MTCA), or what can be referred to as *consumption-based modeling*. Many have seen as much as a 25 basis point (or 50 percent) improvement in forecast accuracy for shipments on average across their product portfolios. They have also statistically proven that there is a direct correlation between downstream data and upstream data. So, why do we continue to say that improved demand forecast accuracy has no direct impact on supply?

We need to stop relying solely on either demand or supply as a quick fix to our supply chain challenges. Companies need to take a holistic approach to solving the root cause, which focuses on people skills and behavior, horizontal processes, predictive analysts, and scalable technology that is driven by structured and unstructured data addressing both supply and demand. I call it the *holistic supply chain*. Successfully implementing an agile demand-driven supply chain will require a holistic view of demand and supply. *We can no longer make it and hope consumers will buy it.* Companies need to focus across the entire supply chain starting with downstream demand to create a more accurate demand response to fulfilling that demand with the most efficient supply response. It includes a new definition of supply chain management (SCM), which includes the commercial side (sales/marketing) of the business, which is responsible for demand generation. Finally, in order to achieve this new approach to supply and demand, companies need to invest in training people in predictive analytics, implementing horizontal processes with performance metrics, applying and relying on predictive analytics to make better decisions, and implementing scalable technology to allow them to gain the most insights from big data. You cannot get it right by just focusing on demand or supply alone. However, we need to start with demand working with sales and marketing to support demand generation with the intentions of creating the most accurate demand response. Then, work horizontally across the supply chain to meet that demand response with the most efficient supply response.

SUMMARY

As many corporate leaders recognize, investments in people and capabilities are essential for a business to thrive and keep growing. While companies are planning to increase investments in demand management capabilities over the next several years, many are relying on past or ongoing investments to keep moving forward. The top three investment priorities are general demand forecasting and planning, new data management technology, and tools that will help manage new product introductions. When it comes to demand forecast accuracy and maximizing profitability, anything will be better than continuing to use Excel spreadsheets and falling back on simple statistical methods like moving averaging. Excel is simply not scalable, particularly given that SKU proliferation has been on the rise for the past decade. Also, Excel doesn't have the depth and breadth of predicative analytics to support a demand-driven planning process on a large scale.

In order to support an enterprise demand management process, it is critical to have predicative models and a user-friendly, point-and-click user interface. The solution must be highly scalable, allowing the user to sense demand signals and shape future demand up and down the business hierarchy. The rise of demand management capabilities continues to be a broad trend toward improving performance by working smarter without increasing operating costs. Manufacturing leaders readily recognize that the ability to develop more accurate demand forecasts by sensing and shaping consumer demand could have a multimillion-dollar impact on their revenues and cost structures. So, what is impeding them from adopting demand-driven forecasting and planning?

The purpose of this book is to provide a framework and guide for practitioners with a proven structured approach that takes into account *people, process, analytics,* and *technology* to transition to the next generation demand management process. These four areas are the key catalysts to move from the current state to the future state along with strong horizontal performance metrics to measure progress. Although adoption requires changes in people behaviors that include new skills, and an integrated process that includes both descriptive and predictive analytics, scalable technology is required that provides scalability to not only gain adoption but also sustainability. It also requires changes in the corporate culture led by a champion who has the authority and leadership to not only drive adoption but also create a new corporate culture that stresses accountability with a focus on customer excellence in order to maintain sustainability.

The primary goal is to provide readers with a strategic roadmap to transform their current demand management process to the next generation demand management process that is not only adopted but also sustainable, becoming part of the corporate culture.

KEY LEARNINGS

- Number one obstacle to achieving supply chain goals is demand forecast accuracy, followed by:
  - Inability to synchronize end-to-end supply chain
  - Lack of cross-functional collaboration
- Increasing demand volatility is creating a sense of urgency within companies to improve their demand management capabilities.
- Companies can no longer use inventory buffer stock to protect against demand volatility.
- Persistent cost pressures are requiring supply chain leaders to better align supply with demand for improved performance.
- 77 percent of demand planners are still using Excel spreadsheets.
- The most widely used statistical method is moving averaging, followed by exponential smoothing.
- Multiple departments and users (47%) are touching the demand forecast each cycle.
- Too many touch points add political bias, resulting in error.

- Focus is on aggregate level forecasts, rather than the lower product mix.

- The one-number consensus forecast philosophy is ineffective because of the corporate culture and lack of accountability.

- The process is politically charged due to different intentions, purposes, and goals.

- Companies are still struggling to know what to do with big data.

NOTES

1. Michael, Gilliland, *The Business Forecasting Deal: Exposing Myths, Eliminating Bad Practices, Providing Practical Solutions* (Hoboken, NJ: John Wiley & Son, 2010), pp. 1–266.
2. SAS Institute, "Demand-Driven Forecasting and Planning: Take Responsiveness to the Next Level," *Industry Week* (2014), pp. 1–13.
3. Ibid.
4. Ibid.

FURTHER READING

Chase, Charles W. Jr., "Cleanse Your Historical Shipment Data? Why?" *Journal of Business Forecasting* 34, no. 3 (2015), pp. 29–33.

Chase, Charles W. Jr., "Using Downstream Data to Improve Forecast Accuracy." *Journal of Business Forecasting* 34 (2015), pp. 21–29.

Crum, Colleen, and George E. Palmatier, "Demand Management Best Practices: Process, Principles and Collaboration," *Integrated Business Management Series*, co-authored with APICS (2003), pp. 1–206.

CHAPTER **2**

The Journey

Companies are all striving to improve their ability to sense demand signals faster to changes in the marketplace, align their supply faster to fluctuations in demand, and synchronize supply with demand to improved customer service with substantially less inventory, waste, and working capital. Everyone realizes that this is a journey, not a destination. It will take time and vision to actualize. It is also understood that the journey for each company will look slightly different. The biggest obstacle in the path is change itself, and opening up to the possibilities of what might be. The challenge is the uncertain roadmap of how an organization transitions from supply-driven to demand-driven, and finally becoming *digital-driven.*

Manufacturers, retailers, and distributors over the past three decades have created numerous shortcuts and overrides to their enterprise resource planning and supply chain management systems in an effort to make them more efficient. Yet, out-of-stocks persist and inventories continue to climb, negatively affecting the bottom line. Old methods based on spreadsheet forecasting, alerts, expediting, and siloed best practices have forced companies to search for new ways to improve customer satisfaction and lower the cost of doing business.

STARTING THE SUPPLY CHAIN JOURNEY

Still today, many companies focus solely on a supply-centric philosophy, selling into the market channel to obtain operational excellence by matching demand to supply, rather than supply to demand. Because demand was fairly stable with only a few competitors, it made sense to strive for operational excellence that flushed out all the inefficiencies associated with supply—reducing inventories, shortening supplier lead times, and implementing more agile manufacturing capabilities like *lean management.* Also, because demand was fairly stable, simple statistical baseline forecasts focusing only on trend and seasonality provided a fairly accurate forecast. Top-down judgmental overrides could then be used to modify the forecasts to fit demand to supply. Figure 2.1 outlines this very supply-centric approach to supply chain management referred to as being a supply-driven company.

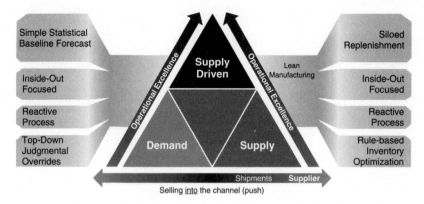

Figure 2.1 The supply chain journey started by becoming supply-driven.

However, as companies became more global, demand volatility increased, and lead times became longer as companies were unable to gain additional efficiency practicing lean management. They found themselves unable to react to economic downturns, which created high carrying costs as inventory escalated due to lower demand for their products. It required weeks of product discounting to sell those inventories through their market channels, reducing profit margins and resulting in lost revenues. Due to the sheer volume of data, supply chains tend to be managed at higher aggregate levels. This means that the forecasted demand and the resulting inventory is viewed in a planning mode at a much higher level versus focusing on the lower level interior product mix. It is not humanly possible to manage any other way. Nor is Excel scalable enough to manage 18,000 SKUs across multiple markets, channels, customers, and ship-to-locations. This type of planning puts a huge emphasis on replenishment activities to overcome out-of-balance demand and inventory positions. In fact, if one looks at most replenishment solutions, they focus almost entirely on three things: (1) monitor potential out of stocks and fill rates, (2) alert to any actions that need to be taken, and, (3) react, react, react! Rapid replenishment is based on the idea that there are and will always be out of balance inventories. The supply chain should be outwardly focused on customer demand, not ever aggregated demand at each step in the supply chain. Indeed, the latency of demand and the aggregation simply amplifies the supply problem that replenishment cannot fix.

INTRODUCING SALES & OPERATIONS PLANNING (S&OP) INTO THE SUPPLY CHAIN JOURNEY

During the second decade of the supply chain journey, sales & operations planning (S&OP) was introduced to help balance demand and supply. S&OP was introduced by Oliver Wight in 1987 and became the go-to process of the 1990s for synchronizing demand and supply. Since then, companies have gained over 25 years of S&OP knowledge and experience. S&OP was designed as a horizontal process to not only synchronize demand and supply but also build efficiency and operations excellence into the supply chain. (See Figure 2.2.) So, why is it becoming so popular again? Haven't we synchronized demand and supply by now?

SALES & OPERATIONS PLANNING CONNECTION

Sales & operations planning (S&OP) has been adopted worldwide by many companies to help them synchronize demand and supply since the late 1980s. Oliver Wight the founders of S&OP continue to find that the quantity, quality, and sustainability of business performance improvements depend on how the process is used. In fact, those companies that have adopted S&OP as the primary process to manage their business tend to get the most significant and wide-ranging results. However, the majority of companies have not seen sustainable

Figure 2.2 Sales & operations planning was introduced to improved synchronization.

results as their businesses have matured along with markets and consumer preferences. As a result, they have not experienced the true benefits of their S&OP efforts.

Outstanding S&OP processes do not appear overnight. S&OP is a journey in itself and requires persistent support and continuous improvements. Obstacles include limited technology enablers, lack of governance, rigid functional silos, lack of shared performance measures, and ingrained company cultures. The overarching purpose of the S&OP process is to set a realistic and profitable overall direction for the company. S&OP brings together all major operational departments (e.g., sales, marketing, operations planning, manufacturing, and finance) to decide how best to manage company resources to profitably satisfy consumer/customer demand and pursue strategic initiatives, which may include new markets, new product introductions, acquisitions, and other related strategic activities. While the objective of S&OP is to create a realistic demand plan that can be executed, today companies view sales and operations planning as a means to execute corporate strategy. A successful S&OP process aligns the company strategically to execute tactically.

Dividing the spectrum of S&OP sophistication into three proficiency profiles helps companies find their level of maturity and chart a path to success. No matter where an organization starts, this journey is well worth the effort. According to research conducted by several organizations, a successful S&OP initiative can:

- Improve revenue by 2 to 5 percent.
- Reduce inventory by 7 to 15 percent.
- Improve new product launch commercialization by 20 percent.

Often, the biggest obstacles to S&OP excellence stem from complexity. For example, it may be too difficult to gather data, there may be too many markets, channels, and SKUs, the process may be too hard to govern, and key data too difficult to analyze and report. Ultimately, the process may become too hard to execute. Leading supply chain teams have discovered that true S&OP success flows from practical thinking, guided by three principles: (1) make it easy to implement, (2) make it easy to execute, and (3) make it easy to sustain.

However, the biggest contributor to S&OP failing is directly related to the focus on supply planning and inventory costs. Most companies forget that the *S* actually stands for sales and marketing. Sales and marketing are not measured as much on costs as they are on market share, revenue, and profitability. In other words, the performance metrics are vertically aligned, rather than horizontally aligned. Not to mention conflicting, creating an antagonistic environment. Furthermore, the S&OP meetings themselves are focused almost exclusively on inventory costs, customer service levels, and production scheduling, all of which are operations planning centric, not customer focused. The only real common metric that sales and marketing share with operations planning is customer service levels.

When discussing S&OP with executives, the biggest challenge they face today is getting the commercial side of the business (sales and marketing) to participate in the process. The main reason for the lackluster commitment by sales and marketing is the fact that there are no real benefits for them. Sales and marketing are focused on downstream demand (POS/syndicated scanner data) not upstream supply (sales orders and shipments).

S&OP is more than getting product managers in a room to agree on a demand plan, which is generally a supply plan based on shipments or sales orders, and it's more than using good modeling and simulation software (both of which are a must). Proper S&OP planning requires sales, marketing, and operations planning working collaboratively toward a realistic and trustworthy demand plan created from an unconstrained consumer demand forecast. S&OP requires both horizontal integration (bringing together demand and supply planning) and vertical integration (bringing together finance and operations functions). So, why is it that the supply chain equation looks like Figure 2.3?

By the nature of the equation, they are only doing OP. Most companies that are supply-driven are doing OP, not S&OP. Also, if the commercial side (sales/marketing) of the business is not attending your S&OP meetings, then chances are you are only doing OP. The *S* stands for sales and marketing, not just sales. So, if you are doing real S&OP, your supply chain equation should be as depicted in Figure 2.4.

• Supply Chain Mangement = S &OP
• S = Sales and Marketing
• OP = Operations Planning
S
OP
Revenue
Finance
Costs

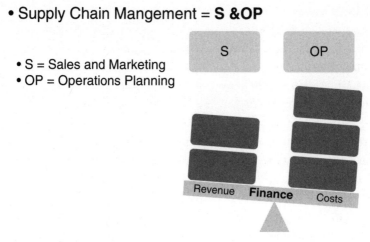

Figure 2.3 Traditional supply chain equation.

• Supply Chain Mangement = S"M"&OP/F
• S = Sales
• M = Marketing
• F = Finance
• OP = Operations Planning
SM
OP
Revenue
Finance
Costs

Figure 2.4 New supply chain equation.

In the past, the *OP* in S&OP created an unbalanced equation where organizations unknowingly biased their supply chains by focusing on the supply side of the business, flushing out inefficiencies in operations (e.g., focusing on reducing inventory costs by improving inventory replenishment capabilities) with little emphasis on understanding how to integrate market opportunities and customer needs. So, if you are

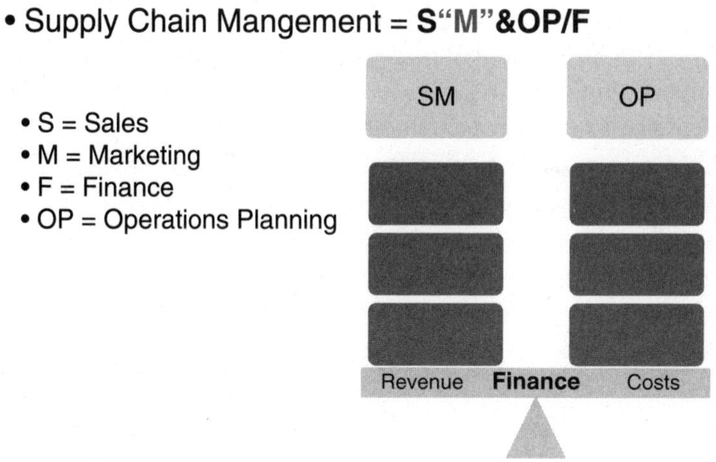

not doing SM&OP/F (sales, marketing & operations planning divided by finance), then chances are you are a supply-driven company.

It has been found that companies that have successfully implemented an SM&OP/F process understand it is a journey over several years. Those companies have combined people, process, analytics, and technology to support and enable the change management activities to evolve their business, market, and products. They also make sales and marketing accountable for sensing demand signals and shaping future consumer demand to create a more accurate demand response. This is a radical change in the process. In addition, finance's role changes with a focus on assessing the implications of sales and marketing activities, such as whether those sales promotions actually make a profit. So, instead of providing another input into the consensus forecasting process, which essentially says, "Hold to the annual plan and roll last month's miss into next month (also, known as *hold-n- roll*)," finance needs to provide financial analysis and assessments of those sales and marketing programs to assure they are actually growing revenue and profit. On the other hand, finance should also be assessing the operations side of the business to assure they provide the most efficient supply response to meet demand. The financial plan is just that, a *plan*, or guide, not the current consumer demand forecast or supply plan.

This new SM&OP/F process outlined in Figure 2.5 defines the roles and responsibilities of this new radical approach to S&OP, as well as the goals of synchronizing the S&OP process to fit supply to demand, not demand to supply.

The missing component in the traditional approach to S&OP is a demand-driven planning process. This requires one single unconstrained consumer demand forecast used for the entire value chain to create sales plans, marketing plans, financial plans, and operational plans over the appropriate time horizon for all value chain members. This concept is known as the demand-driven value network. Becoming demand-driven helps organizations manage the complexities of today's supply chain, offering a viable alternative to traditional S&OP. The key is to create demand-driven value networks (DDVNs), defined as "a business environment holistically designed to maximize value across the set of processes and technologies that senses, shapes and

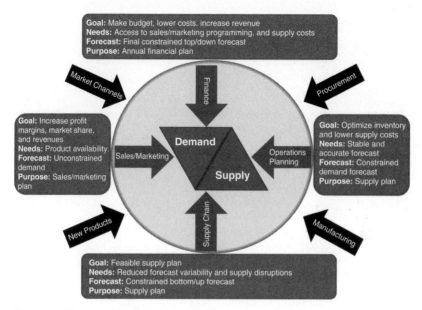

Figure 2.5 The new SM&OP/F process goals, purpose, and needs.

orchestrates demand based on a reduced latency signal across multiple internal supply chain networks along with external trading partners."

In 2003, Colleen Crum and George Palmatier, for consulting firm Oliver Wight, the accepted founders of S&OP, wrote a book titled *Demand Management Best Practices*. In the book, Crum and Palmatier discussed the importance of sales and marketing input in the demand management process.[1] In fact, they said that sales and marketing should own the demand management process, not operations planning where traditional supply-driven companies position demand planners. The book also stressed that without sales and marketing participation in the demand planning process, it is impossible to synchronize supply and demand, as marketing plays a key role in the S&OP process. Finally, true demand is point-of-sale (POS) data, not shipments or sales orders, which are traditionally the data that most companies forecast. Shipments and sales orders are technically replenishment, or supply, not true demand for many companies.

Learning how to better predict the future, rather than letting past forecasting decisions or results constrain future benefits, is well worth

Figure 2.6 Companies are moving to become demand-driven.

the investment in becoming demand-driven. It requires horizontally aligning planning and execution activities based on a single consumer demand forecast in order to drive a profitable balance between marketing investment strategies and operational effectiveness. It's not only about costs, but revenue growth and profitability. A demand-driven planning process takes the actual sales forecast from the retailer POS data and/or sales channel syndicated scanner data to create a consumer demand forecast, which is used to create a customer orders plan (or shipment plan) instead of educated guesses. It then nets these orders against inventory and creates an operational plan (i.e., distribution, logistics, production schedules, and raw material plans) to meet that demand with the most efficient cost-effective supply plan. The process is bidirectional and matches supply to demand in a multi-echelon, multiparty value network while considering capacity and material constrains.

The next step in the supply chain journey requires rethinking demand holistically—the source of demand signals, and the integration of the demand signal into horizontal processes. Figure 2.6 outlines the demand-driven supply chain.

TRANSITIONING TO A DEMAND-DRIVEN SUPPLY CHAIN

Over the past decade, companies have been transitioning to demand-driven supply chain networks focusing on generating a more accurate demand response. It is all about aligning supply to demand with an outside-in focus to obtain customer excellence. Companies are now sensing demand signals and using those signals to shape and translate future demand to improve supply chain processes.

This journey starts with outside-in thinking and focuses on identifying market signals and translating them into the drivers of demand. Demand-driven forecasts focus on accurately predicting what consumers/customers will buy. This is in sharp contrast with the traditional demand management processes that determine what companies will manufacture or ship. The input signals are from the market, channel, brand, product group, product, SKU, and customer. There are many possible inputs, including seasonality, sales promotions, marketing events, pricing, as well as competitive pressures.

The demand-driven planning process relies on data, domain knowledge, and advanced statistical techniques to sense (measure) the key business indicators (KPI's) that influence the demand signal, then using those KPIs to shape future consumer demand and react to changes in the marketplace. The demand-driven planning process provides an unconstrained view or best estimate of market demand based on corporate specific historical sales demand (POS/syndicated scanner data) and translates the demand response into a supply (shipment) plan. The KPIs (demand drivers) used to predict demand (POS/syndicated scanner data) normally include retail price, sales promotions, advertising, merchandising, competitive activities, weather, and other related market factors. Figure 2.7 outlines the key components of the demand-driven planning process.

Demand-driven planning is the set of business processes, people, analytics, and technologies that enable companies to analyze, choose, and execute against the precise mix of customer, product, channel, and geographic segments that achieves their customer-facing business objectives. Demand-driven planning utilizes data from market and channel sources to sense, shape, and translate demand requirements into an actionable demand response that is supported by an efficient supply response. The core focus areas in the demand-driven planning process are:

- *Sensing demand signals:* Sense true consumer demand (POS/ syndicated scanner data) to understand market shifts in demand for their products by measuring the impact of key

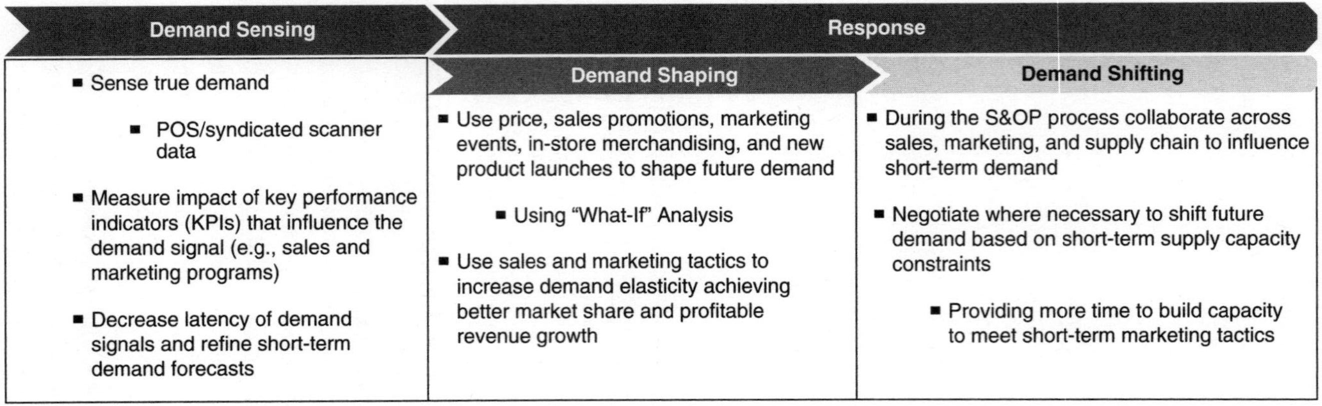

Response

Demand Sensing

- Sense true demand
  - POS/syndicated scanner data
- Measure impact of key performance indicators (KPIs) that influence the demand signal (e.g., sales and marketing programs)
- Decrease latency of demand signals and refine short-term demand forecasts

Demand Shaping

- Use price, sales promotions, marketing events, in-store merchandising, and new product launches to shape future demand
  - Using "What-If" Analysis
- Use sales and marketing tactics to increase demand elasticity achieving better market share and profitable revenue growth

Demand Shifting

- During the S&OP process collaborate across sales, marketing, and supply chain to influence short-term demand
- Negotiate where necessary to shift future demand based on short-term supply capacity constraints
  - Providing more time to build capacity to meet short-term marketing tactics

Figure 2.7 Key components of the demand-driven planning process.

performance indicators (KPIs) that influence consumer demand using predictive analytics.

- *Shaping future demand:* Using what-if scenario analysis to shape future demand by varying the future values of price, sales promotions, marketing events, and other related factors that influence demand.

- *Demand shifting:* During the S&OP process, collaborate across sales, marketing, and operations planning to influence short-term demand by negotiating where necessary to shift future demand based on short-term supply capacity constraints, providing more time for supply to build capacity to meet short-term marketing tactics.

- *Cross-functional collaboration:* Traditionally, companies have adopted techniques of collaboration to increase dialogue between supply chain members in order to create more accurate short- and long-term plans. Those supply members are sales, marketing, finance, and operations planning, but there could be others. This is known as internal cross-functional collaboration. More and more companies are attempting to collaborate with their retail channel partners/customers like Wal-Mart, Publix, Walgreens, and others. This is known as external collaboration.

- *Forecast value added (FVA):* Implement FVA with the intent to reduce touch points in the demand forecasting process, thus increasing forecast accuracy and efficiency (reduced cycle time) by eliminating those touch points that are not adding value. The FVA process measures each touch point in the demand forecasting process before and after someone manually adjusts the forecast. If they are not adding value, then eliminate that touch point, or discount it through weighting, minimizing the bias in the forecast, thus reducing forecast error.

- *Multi-tiered causal analysis (MTCA):* MTCA is a process that links downstream and upstream data (POS/syndicated scanner data to shipments/sales orders data) using a series of quantitative methods to measure the impact of sales and marketing strategies on consumer demand (demand sensing). Then, using the demand model coefficients, MTCA executes various what-if scenarios to shape and predict future demand. Finally, it links demand (POS/syndicated scanner data) to supply (sales orders or shipments) using data, analytics, and domain knowledge. This requires not only data, analytics, and domain knowledge, but also large-scale technology that can handle hundreds of thousands of data series by market, channel, brand, product group, product, SKU, and trading partners. We will discuss MTCA in later chapters.

Several research studies (e.g., Gartner, IDC, *Industry Week, Supply Chain Insights,* and others) conducted over the past decade indicate that anywhere from a 2 to 10 percent improvement in demand forecast accuracy delivers on average between a 5 and 7 percent improvement in revenue and profit growth. Improved forecast accuracy, when combined with software that translates the demand forecast into demand-driven events, will decrease inventory and operating cost, increase service and sales, improve cash flow and return on investment (ROI), and increase pretax profitability. In the last decade, a host of seasoned and practiced supply chain professionals have presented and published articles and research highlighting the returns for companies that use accurate demand forecasts to drive their demand-driven supply chains with a focus on customer excellence. According to those companies, implementing demand-driven supply chain strategies allows companies to:

- Support periods of increasing sales with less finished goods inventories.

- Improve demand forecast accuracy for products that are low-volume while keeping pace with customer demand for those products that have high volume.

- Achieve higher ROI, profits, and overall lower inventory costs and working capital.

This has led companies to move from just inventory management to invest in inventory optimization technologies. What is *inventory optimization*? Having the right amount of inventory, in just the right places, to meet customer service and revenue goals, while minimizing costs and working capital.

The focus should be on correct inventory levels of all products and not just on replenishment. This proactive shift moves the inventory focus to demand-driven synchronized replenishment against the consumer demand forecast with the ability to translate the demand response and meet that response with the most efficient supply response using supply shaping (what-if-scenario analysis) exercises instead of having to rely on outdated days of supply rules.

Constantly changing fulfillment demands have moved inventory optimization (IO) to the forefront as a dynamic process to be evaluated continuously, rather than the traditional once-a-year review and monthly adjustments approach. The demand-driven supply chain is outwardly focused on customer demand, not only aggregated demand at each step in the supply chain. Indeed, the latency of demand and the aggregation simply amplifies the supply problem that replenishment cannot fix. Shifting to an inventory-based system focused on the customer takes away the reactionary replenishment problem and drives efficiency. This shift in practice comes about because of multi-echelon inventory optimization and replenishment. In fact, the shift from replenishment to inventory corrects the operational excellence so that it is outwardly focused on customer excellence. Inventory optimization provides the ERP system with unique, optimized order up-to-level, order level, and safety stocks for each and every product/location combination and links them throughout the multi-echelon supply chain (if needed) to coordinate the inventory. No more rules-of-thumb and stocks can be individually manipulated. This is why you can keep the same service levels with 10–15–20 percent less stock. You are not relying on the inefficiencies of ERP rules-of-thumb. With the right people, process, analytics, and technologies companies have been able to reduce total inventory levels on average by 15 to 30 percent, consequently freeing cash that can be used for more productive purposes.[2]

The journey to become demand-driven requires rethinking demand holistically by understanding the source of demand signals, and the integration of the demand signal into horizontal processes. Demand-driven planning is the use of forecasting technologies along with demand sensing, shaping, and translation techniques to improve supply chain processes. This journey starts with outside-in thinking and focuses on identifying the market signals and translating them into the drivers of consumer demand. Demand-driven plans focus on accurately predicting what consumers/customers will buy, not on what companies think consumers/customers want. This is in sharp contrast with the traditional supply-driven processes that determine what companies will manufacture or ship. The input signals are from the market. There are many possible inputs, including seasonal responses, sales promotions, marketing events, pricing, economic factors, as well as competitive pressures.

Companies have limited ability to reduce supply chain costs using supply-driven levers due to increasingly high demand volatility. Focusing on the demand-driven levers will address the root cause and yield significant benefits to both supply and demand. It has been proven that those companies that have implemented demand-driven supply chain strategies have experienced decreasing inventories simultaneously with increasing sales. With improved demand forecasting and planning, those companies that adopted demand-driven planning manufactured fewer of the products that were low selling and kept pace with consumer/customer demand for what was selling. That led to better gross margin ROI, higher profits, and lower inventory costs, waste, and working capital.

THE DIGITALIZATION OF THE SUPPLY CHAIN

Over the past 10 years consumers have been gaining power and control over the purchasing process. Unprecedented amounts of information and new digital technologies have enabled more control. As a result, there is a major shift underway with the help of technology and advanced analytics that are playing a new and larger role in helping marketers to influence the consumer's purchasing decisions. As consumers increasingly turn to technology to help them make decisions as a result the Internet of Things (IoT), marketers are able to directly engage consumers to influence their purchase decision process.

The next stage in the supply chain journey will be driven by four converging trends:

1. A shift from active engagement to *automated engagement* where technology takes over tasks from information gathering to actual execution.

2. An expanding Internet of Things, which embeds sensors almost anywhere to generate smart data on consumer preferences and trigger actions and offers by marketers.

3. Improved predictive or *anticipatory* analytics technology that can accurately anticipate what consumers want or need before they even know it, based not just on past behavior but on real-time information and availability of alternatives that could alter consumer choices.

4. The availability of faster and more powerful software that crunches petabytes of data, filters it through super-sophisticated models, and helps marketers gain previously unheard of efficiencies to make highly targeted offers.[3]

Technology is helping both marketers and customers take the next evolutionary step in the supply chain journey. Instead of merely empowering customers, technology is making decisions and taking action for them. Customers themselves are initiating this shift. Most are happy to have technology help with presenting and making choices and customizing experiences, as long as they are good choices and desired experiences. In fact, they increasingly demand and expect it. These new trends are leading to the digitalization of the supply chain, or as Figure 2.8 illustrates, the *digital-driven* supply chain.

Analytics technology will be doing more and more of the work for companies by automating activities around research or making actual purchases. It's not merely about *predicting* what consumers want. It's

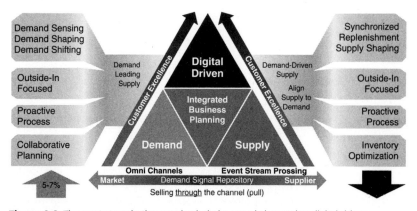

Figure 2.8 The next stage in the supply chain journey is becoming digital driven.

more like *anticipating*, which includes a more sophisticated ability to *adapt* marketing offers and messages to alternatives based on data from hundreds of possible sources. By anticipating something, companies gain a greater chance of influencing the outcome. Consumers' smart phones and other devices can deliver recommendations and offers of where to go, how to get there, and what to buy based on what they are about to do, not just what they've done in the past. Anticipation is about the near-term future, or even a specific time. Prediction is more about things that will happen further in the future. By anticipating something, companies gain a greater chance of influencing consumer purchase outcome.

Demand signal management, (also known as demand signal repositories—DSR) will require more investment in analytics with a strong SM&OP/F (IBP—integrated business planning) process enabled by scalable technology to synchronize demand and supply, visualizing the entire process using what is known as *demand signal analytics*. (Demand signal analytics will be discussed in more detail in Chapter 3.) Companies that are truly digital-driven understand how to translate market opportunities into the factors that influence demand, use those influence factors to shape future demand, and utilize demand synchronization to grow their market share and maximize revenue and profit. They also tend to shape those demand projections through collaborative fulfillment responsiveness, which is focused on visibility and control throughout the supply chain network to coordinate planning activities to actual demand.

Companies will begin to integrate structured and unstructured data into the supply chain management process (e.g., social media, Twitter, RFID, and others). The Internet of Things (also called Internet of Everything or Network of Everything) is the network of physical objects or things embedded with electronics, software, sensors, and connectivity to enable objects to exchange information (data) with the production, operator, and/or other connected devices based on the infrastructure of ITU's (International Telecommunication Union) Global Standards Initiative.

The IoT allows objects to be sensed and controlled remotely across existing network infrastructures, creating opportunities for more direct integration between the physical world and computer-based systems. This will result in improved efficiency, accuracy and economic benefit across complex supply networks. Each thing will be uniquely identifiable through its embedded computing system and will be able to interoperate within the existing Internet infrastructure. Experts estimate that the IoT will consist of almost 50 billion objects by 2020.

As a result of IoT, the capacity for effective commerce will rely on how well companies integrate, including scaling up or down to match new channels and markets while keeping a keen eye on the audience of one. To address these challenges, companies are turning to the omni-channel, which delivers a positive experience across all avenues of interaction, both digital and traditional channels. The omni-channel offers both assisted service and self-service options for retailers, but also for manufacturers as they complement their traditional channels of distribution with an online presence. As companies enter into automated engagement with their brand-loyal consumers, the omni-channel will play a key role. It will also require demand-signal repositories to collect, process, enrich, and harmonize large amounts of data and information from multichannels. Advanced predictive analytics, visualization, and exploration technology will be required to gain insights to make better business decisions in order to anticipate consumer preferences, what they want to buy and when they are prepared to buy.

Finally, *event stream processing* (ESP), which is a set of technologies designed to assist the support and structure of event-driven information systems (EDIS), will include event visualization, event databases, event-driven middleware, and event processing languages, or complex event processing (CEP). In practice, the terms *ESP* and *CEP* are often used interchangeably. ESP deals with the task of processing streams of event data with the goal of identifying the meaningful patterns within those streams, employing techniques such as detection of relationships between multiple events, event correlation, event hierarchies, and other aspects such as causality, membership, and timing. ESP will enable many different applications such as algorithmic trading in financial services, RFID event processing applications, fraud detection, process monitoring, and location-based services in telecommunications. All these new technologies will slowly be integrated into the

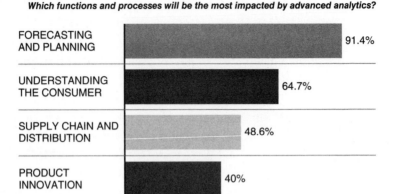

Which functions and processes will be the most impacted by advanced analytics?

Figure 2.9 2015 CGT Report: Forecasting leads analytics benefits.

supply chain network to create an autonomic learning, or self-healing (self-correcting) network system requiring only monitoring and tweaking based on exceptions.

According to a 2015 *Consumer Goods Technology* (CGT) report, consumer packaged goods companies are nearly unanimous (Figure 2.9— 91.4 percent) in predicting the most impact and benefit from advanced analytics and digitalization will come in the area of forecasting and planning, which includes both customer as well as supply chain forecasting and planning.[4] This is an area that has already benefited from analytics to date, so it's reasonable to assume that greater advancements will drive greater impact. Consumer centricity and automated engagement is a dominant theme in consumer products, and the goal of many analytics programs is to get better insights about consumers. So it's not surprising that two-thirds see deeper consumer insights as an absolute business imperative. One underlying assumption for many is likely the ability to factor new data streams into the analysis, such as social media, loyalty data, location, and weather data to achieve not just nuance but reduced guesswork and latency in decisive action.

Finally, product innovation makes a surprisingly low showing at 40 percent. Given the significant working capital bets that are placed on new product development, and the high level of risk, the opportunity to apply analytics to richer sources of data such as social media (Twitter, for example) would seem to be an obvious lever for gaining insights into the appetite for new products, thereby improving confidence.

Very few, if any, companies have risen to the level of being *digital-driven*. Some are making great strides. When companies achieve digital-driven maturity, not only is there better synchronization but also greater agility to match supply to demand. Digital-driven supply chains will allow companies to better balance (synchronize) growth and efficiency, cost and customer service, and demand fluctuations. The bottom-line, digital-driven processes are designed from the consumer back, based on sensing, shaping, and responding to consumer demand, optimizing supply to demand, not demand to supply.

LEVERAGING NEW SCALABLE TECHNOLOGY

Managing demand volatility is no longer just about predicting the future. It is now essential for companies to see and correct imbalances while there's time to deal with them in a cost-effective manner. Companies now need quick and comprehensive simulation that seamlessly links downstream aggregated and detailed consumer plans to upstream supply plans. They also need the ability to combine data from disparate data sources and from all trading partners for instant decision making. Unfortunately, this is not possible with traditional demand forecasting and planning processes, methods, and most of all, technology.

The answer is enterprise technology solutions, not tools, which can manage with an expanded value network, global sourcing for both components and products, as well as customer demands for increasing variety and speed. To this end, organizations today must have strong, effective software solutions for demand forecasting, sales and marketing planning, capacity planning, and operations planning. The technology must also work across all trading partners to create a single demand plan. Demand-driven technology solutions should include a directional link to the financial P&L that focuses on anticipated results. In addition to the demand revenue, a demand-driven solution should include the cost of demand shaping and the respective cost impact based on increased volume and profit. The combination of directional P&L and what-if scenarios helps an organization not only to understand the plan but also to optimize the plan around profitability, not just costs, while weighing it against other criteria such as customer service levels.

BENEFITS

The potential payoffs for more timely and accurate demand forecasts are higher revenues and lower costs. That translates into higher profitability and higher market share. It's as straightforward as basic Business Management 101 class. According to a 2014 *Industry Week* research study, when manufacturers were asked exactly how much of a sales boost they believed they could get from better demand forecasting and planning, the results were insightful. Almost a third (31 percent) anticipated a sales increase between 3 and 5 percent. That's $3 million to $5 million for a company with $100 million in annual sales (and the majority of the respondents reported much higher sales levels). What's even more interesting is that over one-third of companies (35 percent) reported that better forecasting would increase sales by 6 percent or more. And 1 out of 10 manufacturers reported a potential revenue gain of 11 percent or more.[5]

According to those companies that responded, eliminating lost sales due to stockouts and backorders for both existing and new products would account for much of the their sales gain. Subsequently, those same companies anticipated similar multimillion-dollar cost reductions from more accurate demand forecasts. Figure 2.10 outlines

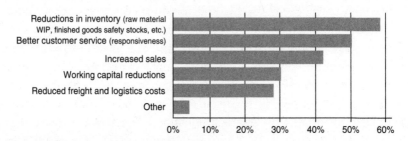

Figure 2.10 Potential benefits of more accurate demand forecasts.

the potential benefits companies will experience from more accurate demand forecasts. The top three in terms of potential impact are:

1. Inventory reductions
2. Better customer service
3. Increased sales

Some of the specific ways more accurate demand forecasting and planning can improve financial performance include:

- Reduced safety stocks, lower carrying costs, and working capital requirements improve overall supply chain efficiencies.
- Reduced inventory ultimately reduces asset requirements through redesigned distribution networks with fewer warehouses.
- Lower freight and logistics costs improve profit margins.
- Enhanced relationships drive superior customer service and responsiveness, which lead to repeat business and growth.

Companies will also see general overhead reductions, higher productivity, reduced overtime, and lower changeover costs as additional benefits from more accurate demand forecasts.

SUMMARY

Investments in people, process, analytics, and technology are essential for a business to thrive and keep growing. Only a third of manufacturers according to the *Industry Week* 2014 research study are planning to increase investments in demand-driven planning capabilities over the next 12 to 24 months, and many are relying on past or ongoing investments to keep moving forward. The top three investment priorities are general forecasting and planning, new data management technology, and tools that will help manage new product introductions. When it comes to forecast accuracy and maximizing profitability, anything will be better than continuing to fall back on spreadsheets. Excel is still the most widely used technology across all industries. However, Excel is not scalable, particularly given that SKU proliferation has been on the rise for the past decade. Also, Excel doesn't have the depth and breadth of predicative analytics to support a demand-driven forecasting and planning process on a large scale. In order to support large-scale demand-driven forecasting and planning, it is critical to have predicative analytics and a user-friendly, point-and-click user interface. This also requires an investment in new analytical skills and talent. The solution must be highly scalable, allowing the user to sense demand signals and shape future demand up and down the business hierarchy for hundreds of thousands of SKUs. Without continuous investment in people, process, analytics, and technology, companies will never gain adoption nor maintain sustainability.

Company leaders are beginning to recognize that the ability to develop more accurate demand plans requires improvements in demand forecast accuracy. The only way to address demand volatility is with more advanced predictive analytics that can sense demand signals by measuring the impact of KPIs and the market dynamics that influence the demand signal, and then use those KPIs to shape future consumer demand to create the most accurate demand response. The result has a multimillion-dollar impact on revenue and profit by reducing costs and maximizing their marketing investment, thus improving overall profit margin and market share.

KEY LEARNINGS

- Companies have been on a supply chain journey for the past 25 years.
- Many companies started the supply chain journey focused solely on a supply-centric philosophy focused on operational excellence.
  - This first stage in the supply chain journey is referred to as being supply-driven.
- The objective of S&OP is to create a realistic plan that can be executed.
  - A successful S&OP process requires getting demand right first.

- You cannot synchronize demand and supply without sales and marketing input.
- S&OP requires sales and marketing input and accountability for developing the unconstrained consumer demand forecast.
- True demand is POS/syndicated scanner data, not sales orders or shipments.
- The new formula for S&OP is SM&OP/Finance:
  - Sales and marketing's role changes, becoming accountable for the unconstrained consumer demand forecast.
  - Finance's role changes to financially assessing and holding accountable sales and marketing for program effectiveness at generating revenue and profitable growth, not providing another input into the consensus demand plan.
- Companies are moving toward obtaining customer excellence by transitioning to a demand-driven supply chain.
  - This requires a focus on six key activities:
    - Demand sensing
    - Demand shaping
    - Demand shifting
    - Forecast value added (FVA)
    - Cross-function collaborative planning
    - Consumption-based modeling using multi-tiered causal analysis (MTCA) process
- Demand-driven planning is the set of business processes, people, analytics, and technologies that enable companies to analyze, choose, and execute against customer-facing business objectives.
- The next stage in the supply chain journey is becoming digital-driven. Four key trends are influencing companies to digitalize their supply chains:
  - A shift from active engagement to *automated engagement* where technology takes over tasks from information gathering to actual execution.

- An expanding Internet of Things, which embeds sensors almost anywhere to generate smart data on consumer preferences and trigger actions and offers by marketers.

- Improved predictive or *anticipatory* analytics technology that can accurately anticipate what consumers want or need before they even know it based not just on past behavior but on real-time information and availability of alternatives that could alter consumer choices.

- The availability of faster and more powerful software that crunches petabytes of data, filters it through super-sophisticated models, and helps marketers gain previously unheard of efficiencies and make highly targeted offers.[6]

- Analytics technology will be doing more and more of the work for companies by automating activities around research or making actual purchases. It's not merely about *predicting* what consumers want. It's more like *anticipating,* which includes a more sophisticated ability to *adapt* marketing offers and messages to alternatives based on data from hundreds of possible sources.

- As companies enter into automated engagement with their brand loyal consumers the omni-channel will play a key role. Advanced predictive analytics, visualization, and exploration technology will be required to gain insights to make better business decisions in order to anticipate consumer preferences, what they want to buy and when they are ready to buy.

- Event stream processing (ESP), which is a set of technologies designed to assist and support the structure of event-driven information systems (EDIS), will include event visualization, event databases, event-driven middleware, and event processing languages, or complex event processing (CEP).

- New technologies will slowly be integrated into the supply chain network to create an autonomic learning, or self-healing (self-correcting) system requiring only monitoring and tweaking based on exceptions.

- Integrated enterprise technology solutions, not tools, are required to support quick and comprehensive simulation that seamlessly links downstream aggregated and detailed consumer plans to upstream supply plans.

- They need the capability to combine data from disparate data sources and from all trading partners for instant decision making.

- The potential payoff for more timely and accurate consumer demand forecasts is higher revenues and lower costs. That translates into several key benefits:

  - Reduced safety stocks, lower carrying costs and working capital requirements.

  - Reduced inventory ultimately reduces asset requirements through redesigned distribution networks with fewer warehouses.

  - Lower freight and logistics costs improve profit margins.

- Enhanced relationships drive superior customer service and responsiveness, which lead to repeat business and growth.

NOTES

1. Colleen Crum and George Palmatier, with Oliver Wright Associates, *Demand Management Best Practices* (Boca Raton, FL: J. Ross Publishers, 2003).
2. Bob Davis, *Demand-Driven Inventory Optimization & Replenishment* (Hoboken, NJ: John Wiley & Son, 2013), pp. 1–217.
3. "Transforming Core Consumer Products Functions with Advanced Analytics, *Consumer Goods Technology* (October 23, 2015), pp 1–10.
4. Ibid.
5. "Demand-Driven Forecasting and Planning: Take Responsiveness to the Next Level," *Industry Week/SAS Demand-Driven Forecasting and Planning Research Study* (2014), pp. 1–13.
6. "Transforming Core Consumer Products Functions with Advanced Analytics," Consumer Goods Technology (October 23, 2015), pp 1–10.

CHAPTER **3**

The Data

WHAT IS BIG DATA?

Big data, what is referred to as the vast quantity of both structured and unstructured information that is now available as a result of the Internet and other sources, can be manipulated in ways never before possible, and is becoming the backbone of corporate performance and economic growth. Big data is the oil of the information economy that needs to be treated as an economic asset. If not, companies are condemned to confirm the old witticism that a skeptic knows the price of everything and the value of nothing. Yet the value of big data is not well understood.

Globally, companies are starting to realize that no matter what industry they are in, one of their most precious assets is their data. If harnessed correctly, the data can unleash new forms of economic value. However, putting a price tag on data is essential. Otherwise, the information will be undervalued, and the potential for further developing and monetizing big data may not be fully realized.

Companies are also finding that big data doesn't necessarily translate into easy success. Furthermore, there is no real means for companies to calculate the true value of their data. To further complicate this situation, according to the *Wall Street Journal's* technology reporter Shira Ovide, roughly 44 percent of information technology professionals surveyed recently said that they had worked on big data initiatives that were eventually scrapped or put on hold. As a result, the value of information captured today is increasingly put to use for reporting purposes (descriptive analytics), rather than the primary purposes for which it was collected (predictive analytics). With big data, information is more potent, and it can be applied to areas unconnected with what it initially represents.[1]

Furthermore, supply chain executives identified data and analytics as two of their top four most important supply chain challenges, according to interviews conducted by Lora Cecere, the editor of the online website *Supply Chain Insights LLC.* Two out of the top four challenges that supply chain executives identified are access to data and actionable analytics (see Figure 3.1).[2] Gaining insights and creating

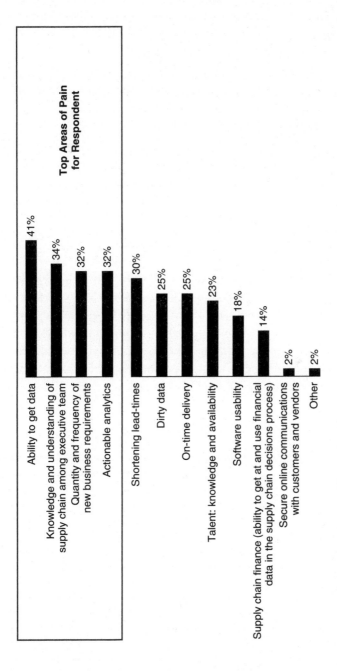

Source: Supply Chain Insights LLC, Logility (Aug-Sept 2012)
Base: Distributors, Manufacturers, Retailers (n = 44)
Question: When it comes to supply chain management, which of the following are the top 3 elements of business pain for you personally? Select no more than 3.
Note: Elements #3 and #4 above are both considered within the "top 3 elements" because they share the same percentage.

Figure 3.1 Top four elements of supply chain management pain for respondent.

actionable analytics from huge quantities of data will require technology and high performance analytics (taking advantage of parallel and grid processing power, and in-store memory). The challenge for companies will be staying ahead of the technology in a cost-effective manner, and developing organizational processes to effectively utilize the huge amounts of data and consume the information into their organizational decision making processes.

During interviews conducted by Lora Cecere and Charles Chase in 2012 (75 in total) with supply chain executives, it was found that their top focus area is improving their demand forecasting and planning process (see Figure 3.2).[3] Other recent surveys found senior executives and managers believe big data to be a forecasting priority for the future. In addition, those same executives plan to make an investment in a new demand forecasting and planning solution. However, many supply chain executives have substantial concerns regarding the costs of the technology, and the requirements essential to make an informed adoption decision for their individual needs while considering costs versus capabilities. They also have concerns regarding change management requirements for adoption of new technology within their organizational processes. To be more specific, supply chain executives will have to overcome the challenges associated with big data. Those challenges are many and require further discussion.

Data versus Actionable Information

Big data enables mining of huge quantities of data. The challenge is converting this massive amount of data into actionable (or usable) information that the organization can absorb, understand, and use effectively to make better-informed decisions. There are two critical elements for success:

1. *Having a good demand forecasting and planning process in place before technology adoption.* This also includes having the combination of statistical skills and domain knowledge. The biggest gap still today in the demand forecasting discipline is the lack of statistical skills, not to mention having the correct consumer marketing acumen. This is accentuated by having demand planners reporting into upstream operations planning, rather

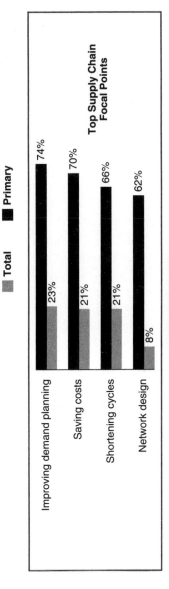

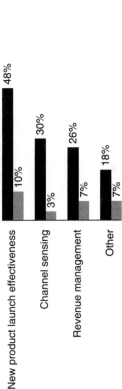

Source: Supply Chain Insights LLC, Voice (April 2012)
Base: Supply Chain Executives—Total Sample (n–61)
Questions:
1. What do you expect to be your primary focus on your supply chain over the next 2 years? Please select one.
2. What other supply chain element, If any, will you be focusing on over the next 2 years? Please select all that apply.

Figure 3.2 Supply chain focal points for next two years.

than downstream in sales and marketing closer to the consumer/customer. Technology layered on top of a poor process only solidifies poor performance. Leading companies understand that they cannot just invest in these technologies without adequate organizational processes in place.

2. *Having an organizational structure that can understand and integrate the information into its decision-making processes will be critical.* This requires creating a learning organization where the learning system is part of the company's future continuous improvement practices. Rules-based ontologies, sentiment analysis, learning algorithms based on industry benchmarking, and real-time learning demand-driven systems for demand planners are all possibilities. Within 10 years, companies will systemically test and learn based on real-time data, while today's response is a fixed and often lackluster response based on historic supply data (sales orders and/or shipments) alone. The demand forecasting and planning process of the future will listen, test, and learn in real time using big data and high performance analytics.

Consumer/Customer Orientation

The primary reason for investing in data, analytics skills, and technology is to improve supply chain efficiencies, not just operational performance. We need to redefine the term *supply chain* to include the commercial (sales/marketing) side of the business. Become more outside-in focused and think market-to-market, rather than supplier forward (inside-out focus). This includes improving demand forecast accuracy, reducing demand variability, and improving supply chain visibility from the customer back to the supplier. Understanding and uncovering market opportunities are the first steps in the next generation demand management process. That requires data, analytics, and technology to perform on a large scale across thousands of SKUs (stock-keeping units), across markets, channels, and key customers. By default, this new focus will improve forecast accuracy, thus improving customer service levels while lowering inventory costs, waste, and working capital. In fact, a large percentage of companies today are placing greater importance on data and analytics to drive growth, rather than merely cutting costs. It's all about making trade-offs based on profit, sustainability, and customer service, rather than just costs. The use of analytics helps identify key elements of the customer's product-service bundle that are most important.

Eliminating Information Silos

Past investments in enterprise technologies, such as CRM, supply chain management, and/or operational supply chain software, have created information silos at many organizations. By learning how to turn big data into information and actionable insights, companies can better integrate information residing in disparate data marts supporting organizational areas, such as sales, marketing, purchasing, operations, and distribution. Effective performance will come from combining these informational silos into one single transparent enterprise data repository.

Sales & Operations Planning

Best-in-class companies are breaking down the silos with big data by sharing information across the organization, improving collaboration, and sharing common performance metrics. Combining and integrating data marts from CRM, supply chain management, and operational supply chain solutions will enable a better understanding of the market-to-market and suppler-to supplier's supplier processes. Incorporating pricing, sales promotions, in-store merchandising, customer inventory, and risk as decision factors within the S&OP (sales & operations planning) and IBP (integrated business planning) processes provides greater understanding and insights.

Technology Can Do It Better and Faster

Automation is the key enabler of any local big data application for one reason only, which is *scalability*. If you combine retailer and manufacturer data across multiple markets, channels, and categories, there is simply too much information for people to review daily, let alone make sense of it to gain actionable insights. It becomes overwhelming to absorb and comprehend all the information quickly. On the other hand, technology helps if it is specifically designed to handle the routine repetitive tasks associated with calculating volumes of data, seeking complex correlations, finding meaningful patterns, and publishing daily reports and outputs for upstream applications and execution systems.

This has a natural extension related to reduced latency and human productivity. Anything technology can do to free people from mundane repetitive work and tasks will increase efficiency. Furthermore, unloading repetitive work to technology frees demand analysts, planners, and supply chain professionals to focus on strategic and tactical initiatives, such as planning sales promotions or changing process design to improve cost efficiency. It is not just theoretical or about descriptive analytics (reporting past results); it's about predictive analytics (predicting what will happen in the future). Those companies that have successfully implemented big data applications to improve forecast accuracy have done so by proactively sensing demand signals and routinely shaping future demand (using what-if scenario analysis), thus recognizing improvements in demand planning performance.

A Structured Process Supported by Technology

Big data applications can only be transformational when used in a systematic and structured way to drive core operational activities across the enterprise. Though many companies store large quantities of retailer data in demand signal repositories, few solutions use this data for more than account-level business intelligence inquiries, such as trade promotion management or retail compliance. While useful for reporting, these systems are far from transformational. On the other hand, big data applications used by skilled analysts in the supply chain can be truly enterprise-wide, encompassing most if not all items and locations performing a structured daily analysis of demand signals to power core activities such as the preparation of short-, medium-, and long-term forecasts; replenishment; inventory management; transportation planning; and supplier visibility. Since daily reporting and review of key performance indicators results are essentially impossible using legacy technology, more robust applications are required. For example, sudden input swings in demand for even a small number of items risk causing disruptive shocks (bullwhip effect).

Another reason why big data applications are designed with layers of safeguards is to ensure that results are always consistent and meaningful. Software developers carefully guard these safeguards as core intellectual property because it is instrumental to make use of big data, and it works. Some of the world's largest consumer packaged goods (CPG) companies with the most respected supply chains already rely on big data applications to create and publish daily forecasts directly to upstream supply planning systems for the majority of their business.

Technology is required to access big data and facilitate actionable information. Using big data to create an agile supply chain that thrives in the face of demand volatility has a significant impact on a company's balance sheet by reducing inventory costs, waste, and working capital while increasing revenue and profitability. Despite market volatility, companies using real-time information with minimal latency to sense demand signals and shape future demand by responding quickly to changes in demand and meet that demand with a more cost-effective supply response have reduced working capital and freed cash. It is not uncommon for companies to see a 15 to 30 percent reduction in inventory costs, which for large manufacturers can represent hundreds of millions of dollars. Furthermore, better visibility to future demand lowers operating costs. Getting products in the right place the first time means fewer instances of transshipments across warehouses, reducing freight expedites, and overall costs. Improved customer service levels translate into fewer lost sales and higher revenues, which can be especially important in more mature, lower-growth markets such as North America and Europe. In my experience, large companies have been able to capture lost sales through the reduction in backorders and save money by cutting inventories by millions of dollars on a monthly basis. Closing the gap between backorders and actual demand is even more important as the economy continues to recover from the Great Recession.

WHY IS DOWNSTREAM DATA IMPORTANT?

Downstream data have been electronically available on a weekly basis since the late 1980s. But most companies have been slow to adopt downstream data for planning and forecasting purposes. Downstream data are data that originate downstream on the demand side of the value chain. Examples include retailer point-of-sale (POS) data, syndicated scanner data from Nielsen, Information Resources Inc., and Intercontinental Marketing Services (IMS).

Prior to electronically available downstream data, manufacturers received this type of data in hard copy format as paper decks (after a 4- to 6-week lag). Once received, the data points were entered into mainframes manually via a dumb terminal (a display monitor that has no processing capabilities; it is simply an output device that accepts data from the CPU). In fact, downstream data have been available to consumer products manufacturers for several decades. Subsequently, the quality, coverage, and latency of downstream data have improved significantly, particularly over the past 20 years, with the introduction of universal product barcodes (UPC) and retail store scanners.

Today, for many companies, data management capabilities have advanced so quickly that the challenge now is how to report and make practical use of it all. Data storage costs have fallen significantly over the past decade. Sales transaction data are being captured at increasingly granular levels across markets, channels, brands, and product configurations. Faster in-memory processing is making it possible to run simulations in minutes that previously had to be left to run overnight.

Companies receive daily and weekly retailer POS data down to the SKU/UPC level through electronic data interchange transfers (electronic communication method that provides standards for exchanging data via any electronic means). These frequent data points can be supplemented with syndicated scanner data across multiple channels (retail grocery, mass merchandiser, drug, wholesale club, liquor, and others) with minimal latency (1- to 2-week lag) by demographic market area, channel, key account (retail chain), brand, product group, product, and SKU/UPC. Consequently, downstream data are the closest source of consumer demand above any other data, including customer orders, sales orders, and shipments. Unfortunately, most companies primarily use downstream data in pockets to improve sales reporting, uncover consumer insights, measure their market mix performance, conduct price sensitivity analysis, and gauge sell-through rates. However, no manufacturers including consumer packaged goods (CPG) companies have designed and implemented an end-to-end value supply chain network to fully utilize downstream data.

According to a recent 2014 *Industry Week* Demand-Driven Forecasting and Planning study, the least two data sources being used for demand forecasting and planning are POS and syndicated scanner data (see Figure 3.3).[4]

It is apparent that companies' supply chains have been slow to adopt downstream data, although POS data from retailers have been available for decades. Initially, it was a matter of data availability, storage, and processing. Today, it is primarily a question of change management due to corporate culture, particularly from a demand forecasting and planning perspective.

So what are the barriers? In large part, the slow adoption rate is because the organization has not approached the use of these new forms of downstream data from a holistic standpoint. Instead of mapping new processes outside-in, the organization has tried to force-fit

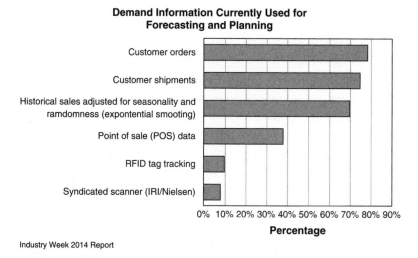

Industry Week 2014 Report

Figure 3.3 Demand information currently used for forecasting and planning.

the data into existing processes using Excel with no real analytics, and a lot of manual manipulation. Despite the fact that channel data are now available for anywhere from 50 to 70 percent of the North American retail channels, and the use of the data has decreased data latency in the supply chain by 80 to 100 percent. However, given all these improvements, many companies still feel downstream data can't be used for demand forecasting and planning.

Meanwhile, confronted with demand challenges, companies have been looking for new ways to predict future demand in the face of a progressively volatile marketplace. The traditional demand planning technology under these changing conditions has been ineffective at predicting future demand. The main reason for the unsuccessful performance of traditional technology is directly related to the fact that most companies are not forecasting demand. They are forecasting supply, which is proven to be much more volatile because it produces what is referred to as the bullwhip effect.

Customer orders, sales invoices, and shipments are not true demand. They are the reflection of retailer and manufacturer replenishment policies (supply). To make matters even more difficult, traditional demand forecasting processes and enabling technology were not designed to accommodate POS and syndicated scanner data, let alone the more sophisticated analytic methods required to sense demand signals and shape future demand to create a more accurate demand response.

To reduce volatility and gain insights into current demand trends, companies are turning to POS and syndicated scanner data, but are finding that using them for demand forecasting and planning is complex. Perhaps it is because they are not familiar with downstream data, as most demand planners report into operations planning too far removed upstream, rather than downstream in sales and marketing. Another reason is that most companies do not collect downstream data on an ongoing basis over multiple years. They normally collect it on a rolling 104-week basis. This trend is no longer a barrier, as companies are creating demand signal repositories (DSRs) to capture downstream data by week for more than 104 weeks to allow them to compare downstream consumer demand to upstream shipments and/or sales orders.

Others will tell you that what retailers sold last week, or even yesterday, is not necessarily a good predictor for what they will order next week or tomorrow. This is another myth, as companies have been keeping inventories low with more frequent replenishment because retailers are not allowing manufacturers to load their warehouses at the end of every quarter with their products. As a result, there is a direct correlation with weekly POS/syndicated scanner data at the product level, and in many cases at the SKU/UPC levels (see Figure 3.4). As you can see, in both cases there is a strong correlation between weekly retailer POS and shipment data, as well as weekly syndicated scanner and shipment data. Most manufacturers now capture their shipment data weekly by channel and key account down to the warehouse distribution point.

Another barrier has been scalability. Many companies feel that adding downstream channel data to demand forecasting involves a magnitude of effort and complexity that is well beyond what most companies can handle to source, cleanse, and evaluate the range of data. However, new processing technology (e.g., parallel processing, grid processing, and in memory processing) leveraging advanced analytics in a business hierarchy, along with exception filtering, has enabled several visionary companies to overcome these difficulties. The promise of downstream data can be realized with the right technology on a large scale.

The only real barriers are the corporate culture, internal analytical skills, and the desire to take that first step. In fact, the best way to get the commercial side of your business (sales/marketing) to participate in your S&OP process is to integrate downstream data into the demand forecasting and planning process. Without it, there is no real reason for sales and marketing to participate. Downstream data are the sales and marketing organizations' *holy grail* to consumer demand.

DEMAND MANAGEMENT DATA CHALLENGES

Most demand forecasting and planning initiatives are abandoned or considered failures due in part to data quality challenges. The right data input to the demand forecasting and planning process has several important dimensions that need to be considered for success

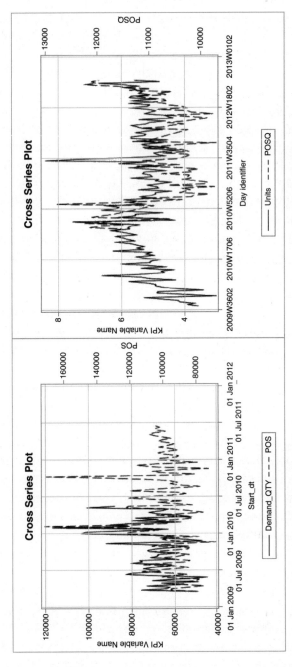

Figure 3.4 Consumer demand (POS/syndicated scanner data) versus supply (shipments).

of any process. Harnessing the right data for demand forecasting and planning always appears to be straightforward and relatively simple. However, bad data, or use of the wrong data, often is the real reason behind a demand forecasting and planning process failure.

What Historical Demand Data Should Companies Use?

Almost all demand forecasting and planning systems use some form of statistical forecasting methods that require historical demand data. In most cases, companies choose to use product shipment data or sales orders data to predict the future, as both are readily available and best understood by demand planners who are responsible for the demand planning process. According to the 2014 *Industry Week* research report, close to 70 to 80 percent of companies still use either shipment or customer order data for demand forecasting and planning.

Unfortunately, product shipment data as well as sales orders contain several undesirable components like incomplete or partial order fills, delivery delays, and load effects due to promotions, which represents supply chain inefficiencies, supply policies that do not always reflect true demand, and sales/marketing strategies designed to increase consumer demand (e.g., sales promotions). Furthermore, shipment data represents how operations planning responded to customer demand, not consumer demand itself. Demand forecasting and planning systems must build plans off a forecast and use shipment data as a measure of effectiveness in meeting those plans. Product order data less any customer returns is the next best data representing customer product demand, but not necessarily the best demand data input for the statistical forecasting process. The closest data to consumer demand is POS and/or syndicated scanner data. Although many companies collect and store POS and syndicated scanner data, less than 40 percent of companies use POS data for demand forecasting, and less than 10 percent use syndicated scanner data according to the 2014 *Industry Week* research report. Everyone agrees that POS and syndicated scanner data are the closest data to true consumer demand, yet both these data streams are among the most underutilized for demand forecasting and planning. Furthermore, roughly 70 percent of companies are using historical sales adjusted for trend and seasonality, and cleansed of promotions and outliers separating the historical baseline volume from the promoted volume.[5]

Manually Cleansing (Adjusting) Demand History Is a Bad Practice

It is a mystery to me why anyone would manually cleanse the actual demand history given all the advancements in data collection, storage, processing, and predicative analytics. In my experience, whenever a company separated historical baseline volume from promoted volume, and then *added* them back together using judgment (also known as layering), 1 + 1 tended to equal 5, instead of 2. The process of cleansing historical data is a manually intensive and unproductive process, in my opinion.

The actual history is what happened unless it was entered into your data warehouse incorrectly. In fact, in all my years doing demand forecasting the only time historical demand data was changed (corrected) was if the data was entered into the data warehouse incorrectly, or if the historical data needed to be restated due to distribution warehouse consolidation. Many companies continue to manually cleanse their historical demand data as a prerequisite for forecasting and planning of their products. It is a manually intensive process that takes up in many cases 80 percent of a demand planner's time. I would only cleanse the data if it were entered incorrectly into the data warehouse, or if the organization was being realigned. There is only a handful of reasons to realign historical demand data (sales orders/shipments):

- Warehouse consolidation and realignment
- Geographic consolidation or realignment
- Acquisitions and realignment of products

The true reason for cleansing historical demand is that traditional demand forecasting and planning solutions are unable to predict sales promotions or correct the data automatically for shortages or outliers. To address this shortcoming, companies embedded a cleansing process of adjusting the demand history for shortages, outliers, and sales promotional (incremental) spikes by separating them into baseline and promoted volumes. The cleansing process has become an accepted activity when a company is using a statistical forecasting solution to model and predict future demand. In theory, manually adjusting (cleansing) demand history by removing promotional spikes and outliers improves the forecast results. Furthermore, it is believed that cleansing the actual history will produce a true historical baseline. On the contrary, it actually makes the forecast less accurate. This is primarily a result of the statistical methods being deployed in the technology—mainly exponential smoothing methods—that are not capable of measuring and predicting sales promotions or automatically correcting for shortages and outliers.

The definition of *baseline history* of a product is its normal historical demand without promotion, external incentives, or any other abnormal situation that may be caused by outliers. An *outlier* is a too-high or too-low sales figure in a product's history that may occur under special, or abnormal conditions. Promotional volume is the incremental volume a company sold due to sales promotions and trade merchandising. Based on these definitions, how would anyone know by how much to raise or lower the data to create the baseline volume? Furthermore, are they actually removing the correct amount of the sales promotion, or are they removing seasonality as well?

In many cases, sales promotions are executed around annual seasonal holidays. This is another reason why traditional demand forecasting and planning systems tend to autoselect nonseasonal models because the seasonality has been removed along with the sales promotion volume during the cleansing process. In fact, they would have been able to use more sophisticated exponential smoothing methods like Holt-Winters, which is one of the best methods for measuring seasonality and predicting the future of highly seasonal products.

CPG COMPANY CASE STUDY

Recently, while conducting a proof-of-concept (POC) with a large CPG company we found the results of the company's normal demand forecasting process of separating baseline and promoted volumes using their normal cleansing process was less accurate than using all the data holistically (not cleansing the data). The results were astounding, showing a 5 to 10 percent improvement in forecast accuracy by modeling the total uncleansed demand history. What we noticed is that the autoselect was choosing only nonseasonal exponential smoothing methods (or moving averaging) for the cleansed baseline, rather than the seasonal exponential smoothing models. With the raw historical shipments data, the autoselect started selecting Holt-Winters (additive or multiplicative) exponential smoothing models over 80 percent of the time. The result on average was a 5 to 10 percent improvement in forecast accuracy.

The original objectives of the POC were to investigate the potential benefits of advanced statistical forecast modeling to become demand-driven. There were three core objectives and activities:

1. Attempt to optimize existing ERP demand forecasting and planning models to improve the accuracy of current shipment baseline forecasts at item/warehouse level.

2. Use advanced forecasting technology and demonstrate the benefits of advanced statistical modeling.

3. Show the value of using syndicated scanner data (using the multi-tiered causal analysis process—MTCA) to become demand-driven.

The results in Figure 3.5 are the results of the POC using uncleansed data, or what is referred to as holistic model. In the first step we loaded uncleansed data into an automated large-scale hierarchical solution (hierarchical forecasting is discussed in Chapter 4, Appendix A), but only turned on moving averaging and exponential smoothing models. Without any data cleansing, the forecast accuracy improved by 10 to 15 percent. Also, there was no human judgment used to adjust the final forecast. We found that 80 percent of the products were selected using seasonal exponential smoothing (Holts-Winters exponential smoothing—additive and/or multiplicative), rather than moving averaging and/or nonseasonal exponential smoothing.

In step two, we introduced ARIMA models (seasonal and nonseasonal) with event variables (intervention variables, or what is referred to as dummy variables—binary variables) to capture the lifts of the

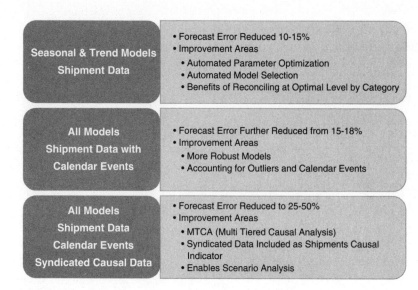

Figure 3.5 Proof-of-value results using uncleansed data: holistic modeling.

sales promotions, and also to correct for outliers. The results were an improvement of another 15 to 18 percent, bringing their forecast accuracy to 83 percent on average across all the products targeted for the POC with no data cleansing or judgmental overrides. Their target for the project was 85 percent for year one. Finally, we incorporated downstream data into the process using consumption based modeling using the MTCA process (discussed in more detail in Chapter 6), which is a two-step process of nesting two models together up/down a business hierarchy. First, modeling and forecasting POS data (in this case, Nielsen syndicated scanner data), and then using the history and shaped future forecast of the downstream data as a leading indicator in a shipment model to predict supply. In this case, we improved the accuracy of the forecast another 25 to 50 percent. The end result was a forecast in the low to mid-90 percent accuracy on average across the products selected for the POC.

So, are cleansing the data and separating it into baseline and promoted volume really worth the effort? Also, how much accuracy or bias do judgmental overrides really add versus letting the analytics do most of the work, or heavy lifting?

DOES DEMAND HISTORY REALLY NEED TO BE CLEANSED?

Many companies feel data cleansing and transformation are required to facilitate the demand forecasting process. This manual process is both time consuming and impractical, requiring various rules that use estimates and experimental tests to assess the results of the cleansed data. The cleansing process is usually completed for all historical data during the premodeling process. The rules developed must be applied in real time as historical data is generated over time. Beyond cleansing, a transformation process is often applied to normalize the input data for units of measure or changes in product sourcing locations in the future. Additionally, for new products that are merely product line extensions, a transformation process is used to fabricate historical data that will provide the necessary inputs for the statistical forecasting engine. There are now two new processes supported by data, analytics, and technology that allow more precision in predicting new product launches. These new processes can now be implemented using new technology capabilities called *product chaining, lifecycle management*, and *structured judgment*, requiring little manual input or rule based transformations.

Data cleansing supposedly removes inaccuracies or noise from the input to the forecasting system. In fact, this so-called normalization tends to create a smoothed baseline that replicates a moving average (see Figure 3.6). Operations planning prefers a moving average forecast for easier planning and scheduling for manufacturing and replenishment purposes. Events such as sales promotions or anomalies are described as unforecastable, and normally turned over to the commercial team to be handled separately using judgment. By removing and separating these events during the forecasting process it is believed to ensure accurate prediction of the impact of future occurrences. These events are also used to assess the lift of a sales promotion that occurred in the past helping to plan for future promotions. Although more sophisticated forecasting systems can detect outliers and correct for their impact on the future forecast, companies still manually remove (cleanse) them from the historical data based on rules and past experience. In my experience, any manual adjustments to the

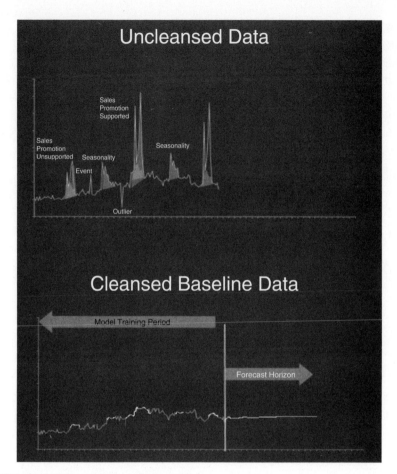

Figure 3.6 Before and after data cleansing.

historical data or to the future forecast tend to make the forecast less accurate due to personal bias whether intended or unintended.

Exponential smoothing methods can only measure trend, seasonality, and level (moving average). As a result, the related sales promotional data needs to be stripped away (cleansed) from the demand history, as well as the demand history adjusted for shortages and outliers. After cleansing the demand history the baseline volume tends to replicate a predictable smoothed trend with little if any seasonality, which is essentially simulating a moving average ideal for nonseasonal exponential smoothing methods. Smoothed trend and seasonal baseline historical data can be easily forecast with a high degree of accuracy using exponential smoothing methods. The sales promotion volume lifts are then layered back using judgment. It's much more difficult to forecast the sales promotional lifts that occur on a regular basis, but may not always happen in the same time frames (i.e., in the same weeks or months into the future) as they did in the past. Also, the durations for such sales promotions may change, or can be different (i.e., 4 weeks, 6 weeks, and overlapping).

Exponential smoothing methods are traditionally deployed in over 90 percent of demand forecasting and planning solutions, making it difficult to measure and predict sales promotions or adjust for shortages and outliers. Once the demand history is cleansed, the demand planner forecasts the baseline history (also known as the baseline forecast). Upon completion of the baseline forecast, the demand planner manually layers in the future sales promotion volumes created by the commercial teams (sales/marketing) using judgment, as well as other events to the baseline forecast to create the final demand forecast.

Today, new demand forecasting and planning solutions can holistically model trend, seasonality, sales promotions, price, and other related factors that influence demand using predicative analytics. In addition, these same models can automatically correct for shortages and outliers without cleansing the actual demand history. Methods such as ARIMA, ARIMAX, and dynamic regression models can be deployed up and down a company's business hierarchy to holistically model trend, seasonality, sales promotion lifts, price, in-store merchandizing, economic factors, and more. Intervention variables (dummy variables) can be used to automatically adjust the demand history for shortages and outliers. There is no longer the need to cleanse the demand history for shortages, outliers, and sales promotional spikes. In fact, these same predictive methods can measure the impact of sales promotions—calculate the lift volumes and predict the future lifts in different time intervals based on marketing event calendars. In addition, the commercial teams (sales and marketing) can spend more time running what-if scenarios with precision, rather than judgmentally layering back the sales promotional volumes to the

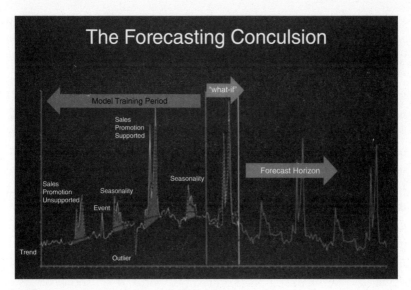

Figure 3.7 Holistic model using an ARIMAX model.

baseline volume. Figure 3.7 illustrates how a holistic model captures the trend and seasonality along with sales promotions while correcting for shortages and outliers without cleansing the data.

HOW MUCH DATA SHOULD BE USED?

An accurate statistically generated forecast has several elements including trend, seasonality, holidays, sales promotions, marketing events, and other related causal factors. There must be sufficient demand history in order to statistically model the patterns associated with these elements to produce an accurate forecast for future periods. In most cases this means a minimum of three years of historical data, and ideally three or more would be best to capture seasonality. Most demand forecasting and planning systems use monthly summaries of product demand separated either by the manufacturing source or the distribution point. In other words, the data must also reflect the business hierarchy with the same periodicity (historical time interval) including geography, market, channel, brand, product group, product, SKU, UPC, and customer/demand point. Although, less data can be utilized one to two years, the results may not completely reflect the true nature of demand, particularly, in regard to seasonality, holidays, and promotional effects.

In 2016, demand planners are still spending over 80 percent of their time cleansing, managing, and disseminated data and information across the organization, rather than using the data and information to improve forecast accuracy. They are merely managers of data and information. As big data continues to grow in volume, velocity, and variability, and with more pressure to drive revenue growth, demand planners will be asked to not only improve forecast accuracy, but also find new insights that are actionable to proactively drive revenue and profit. As such, companies need to invest in data quality, new technology, predictive analytics, and skills. Demand planners will need to transition from managers of data and information to demand analysts with a focus on predictive analytics driving revenue growth and profitability. Recent research indicates that improved forecast accuracy can add as much as 10 percent to revenue and profitability. *Manually cleansing historical demand? Let's make that history.*

DEMAND-SIGNAL REPOSITORIES

There are many challenges to implementing the next generation demand management process. Many of the data sources are new for most companies to manage, so ownership, expertise, and governance are important. Not to mention change management requirements to gain adoption, and governance to make it sustainable. Many executives say that their organizations are still in the basic stages of data integration due to data quality and internal lack of skills about how to maximize analytic benefits. In today's business environment, there are significant financial implications to ineffectively managing all this big data. These challenges can take the form of higher costs and lower revenue due to conditions such as nonoptimized inventory, ineffective demand planning, strained product launches, and higher out-of-stocks.

Companies across myriad industries understand the importance of transforming to the next generation demand management.

The challenge is to gather, cleanse, and access the vast amount of downstream demand data. Downstream data can be difficult to master and govern without a cohesive approach across the organization. As such, companies are investing in demand signal repositories as an integrated information hub that provides the foundation for breakaway analytics and optimization across the enterprise. Utilizing big data to its fullest potential involves integrating information sources such as retailer point-of-sale (POS), syndicated scanner sources (Nielsen, Information Resources (IRI), and others), loyalty programs, consumer panels, and social media as well as ERP transactional systems, and other internal systems, which are all available to drive powerful analytics. Downstream consumption data are now more widespread, with many retailers sharing POS data with consumer products companies on a daily basis. As a result, they are expecting enhanced knowledge from their suppliers. The demand-signal repository is a central data mart that houses all this information.

The successful implementation of a demand signal repository, supercharged by demand-signal analytics, depends on managing POS and syndicated scanner data effectively, and complementing it with specific internal data, such as the company's product hierarchy. This exercise makes the POS and syndicated scanner data a more robust source of information to analyze with more dimensions that can be sliced and diced to gain more actionable insights. This type of data comes from internal corporate systems, local repositories, as well as spreadsheets. Furthermore, it is usually manually maintained, and thus is not subject to good data governance disciplines.

What Are Demand Signal Repositories?

A demand signal repository (DSR) is a data warehouse designed to integrate consumer demand data and leverage that data by consumer goods manufacturers, automotive manufacturers, electronics manufacturers, pharmaceuticals, and others to service retailers and end user customers efficiently. The focus has been on synchronizing POS and syndicated scanner and internal (shipment/replenishment) data, which allows companies to provide business users with a more complete view of their retail performance. The repository itself is a database that stores the information in a format that allows for easy retrieval of information so that users can quickly query the database to identify what's selling, where, when, and how. Identifying marketing opportunities, demand performance, and out-of-stock (OOS), along with control tower tracking and monitoring, are the key requirements for demand forecasting and planning. Leveraging DSR data for demand forecasting and planning using predictive analytics is where the real benefits of such applications can help to identify and measure past, current, and future impacts on demand. With the right architecture, demand signal repositories (DSRs) will continue to grow with the business needs. They will be leveraged across multiple business groups including demand management, channel marketing, supply chain management, inventory management, and promotion and event management.

A demand signal repository is a centralized data repository that stores and harmonizes attributes, and organizes large volumes of demand data such as point-of-sale (POS) data, wholesaler data (electronic data interchange—EDI), inventory movement, promotional data, and customer loyalty data for use by decision support technologies (channel marketing analysis, shopper insight analysis, demand forecasting and planning, inventory replenishment, and more). Demand signal visualization (DSV) provides companies with faster decisions and scenario modeling for outcomes and accurate decisions. Furthermore, demand signal analytics (DSA) combines DSV with predictive analytics, allowing companies a real-time, root-cause visualization and exploration system. DSR/DSV/DSA is at the heart of being demand-driven. The fact is this: To reap the maximum benefit from a true demand-driven planning process takes commitment and a well-conceived plan, which requires a best-in-class demand signal repository (DSR) at the core.

Benefits of Demand Signal Analytics

The augmentation of DSR data into the demand planning process improves visibility and control. POS and syndicated scanner data can be a tremendous asset when used properly. By integrating POS and syndicated scanner data with company-specific attributes, manufacturers can leverage that data by collaborating more effectively across the organization and with their retailer (customer) networks. POS data can then drive commercial and operational improvements, such as:

- Improving demand forecast accuracy, and enhancing demand sensing and shaping activities
- Sensing product category changes more effectively
- Improving evaluation of new product information via integration of sentiment analysis
- Increasing trade promotion effectiveness
- Reducing out-of-stocks
- Lowering inventory and safety stock levels

What Are Users Looking to Gain?

Users are looking for easy-to-use visualization tools with predictive analytics capabilities to uncover market opportunities with the ability to more efficiently synchronize demand and supply to take advantage of the information stored in their DSRs. If they can't, then they have a point solution that is proprietary, and not a true DSR. An open architecture should have an intuitive point-and-click user interface with strong visualization capabilities that lets users easily get reports to help them understand their sales, manage category and brand information, and more. Users should be able to easily drag, drop, and drill into information. They should be able to pull data from multiple data sources, share reports securely, and create alerts. In addition, users that have specific job requirements, such as price elasticity or analyzing promotional ROI that aren't handled in their DSR, require an exploratory capability that uses predicative analytics that leverages POS/syndicated scanner and shipment and supply replenishment data.

Alerts combined with predictive exploratory capabilities, using visualization, will allow users to pinpoint areas of the business that require immediate attention. The goal of a DSR is to provide faster access to more information, improve retailer relationships, maximize ROI, streamline internal efficiencies, improve performance at all stages of the supply chain, and support multiple departments and teams. However, most DSRs fall short of their promise by providing control towers (dashboards) and descriptive reporting to monitor and track their business year after year with virtually no predictive analytics to uncover insights into the data that are actionable.

Why Is It Important?

If you want to be more proactive than simply basing replenishment on shipment data, you need access to downstream data, analysis, and insights to make decisions that put you ahead of the demand curve. There is more to it than just forecasting trends and seasonality. Demand sensing is about identifying and measuring market signals, and then using those signals to shape future demand.

Effectively using customer data requires making an investment in a demand signal repository (DSR) to harmonize and cleanse POS/syndicated scanner data so that it is usable for data analytics. Demand signal analytics using consumption data (POS/syndicated scanner), as well as inventory, shipment, and replenishment data, are today's examples of using *structured data*. While the term *downstream data* is most often connected to consumption and inventory data, unstructured data, like loyalty data, social sentiment, consumer perception attitudinal data, are starting to be used for targeting consumers, shaping demand, and improving new product launch effectiveness.

WHAT IS DEMAND SIGNAL ANALYTICS?

Demand signal analytics uses the combination of visual analytics and predictive analytics to access the data in DSRs to uncover actionable insights with minimal latency. You can think of DSA as comprising three layers. The foundational layer is a demand signal repository (DSR), an integrated database of essential (big) data that companies need to provide insight into sales, marketing, inventory, price, demand performance, and operations. It cleanses, normalizes, and integrates this raw demand data from any source (point-of-sale, wholesalers, social media, weather, EDI, inventory, syndicated scanner data, promotional/marketing information, panel data, customer loyalty data, survey data, and more). It works with any data type or source format from multiple retailers, distributors, and their respective disparate systems to make that data available for retrieval, query, reporting, alerts, and analysis. The second layer uses visual analytics to transform the DSR data into demand signal visualization (DSV) to allow for exploration, analysis, and insight that suggest areas of focus, improvement, and action. Although typical marketing research only provides answers to predefined questions, DSV provides insight into questions companies didn't initially know to ask. The third layer brings the DSR and DSV to culmination by combining DSR and DSV, creating *demand signal analytics* (DSA). The addition of predictive analytics (forecasting and optimization) complements the descriptive analytics of DSV, and quantifies the direction, size, scope, and variability of supply chain replenishment. Figure 3.8 illustrates a typical interactive visualization combined with predictive analytics allowing the demand planner to review both demand and replenishment by combining POS and replenishment data.

DEMAND SIGNAL ANALYTICS KEY BENEFITS

- Optimize data management no matter the source: Always have access to the data you need, from legacy systems to ERP applications to data stored in Hadoop or SAP Hanna Demand Signal Management (DSiM) using in memory processing, from virtually any hardware platform or operating system. New sources can be easily added and security is centrally managed at the user, department, or enterprise level. You'll get improved productivity using a standard interface for building and documenting work. The result is consistent, timely data that lead to improved accuracy and confidence.

- Unlock insights with visual data exploration: Give yourself a competitive advantage and make better, more impactful decisions using all of your strategic data investments. The visual analytics component empowers business users to conduct

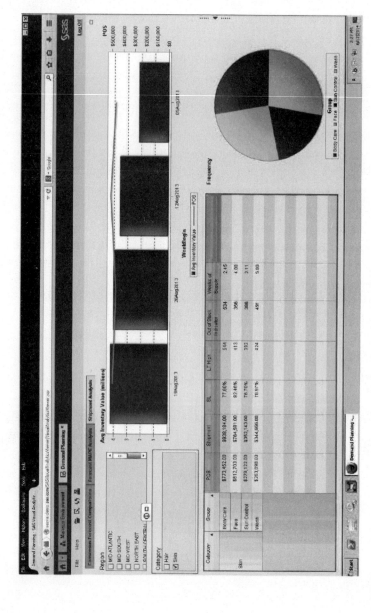

Figure 3.8 Demand signal analytics combining descriptive and predictive analytics.

thorough exploration on all available data quickly without requiring them to know subsetting or sampling techniques. By using all of the data available, users are able to clearly view all options to make more accurate decisions faster.

SUMMARY

As supply chain executives stand at the edge of this new era of big data and look forward, what they see is a new world of opportunities. Big data applications will shape our lives in ways that are hard to comprehend; but one thing is certain, the processes, people, analytics, and technology requirements of big data will undoubtedly transform not only the way we do business, but also the new generation of demand management. So the real challenge is not that companies are acquiring large amounts of data, because they are clearly already in the era of big data. It's what they do with their big data that matters. The hopeful vision for big data is that organizations will be able to harness relevant information and use it to make better-informed decisions.

Analytics and technologies today not only support the collection and storage of large amounts of data, they also provide the ability to understand and take advantage of its full value, which helps organizations run more efficiently and profitably. For instance, with big data and big data analytics, it is possible to:

- Sense demand signals and shape future demand for millions of SKUs as well as determine optimal prices that maximize profit and reduce inventories while maintaining higher customer service levels.
- Mine consumer demand data for insights that drive new sales and marketing strategies for customer retention, campaign optimization, and next best offers.
- Generate retail coupons at the point of sale (POS), based on the consumers' current and past purchases, to ensure a higher redemption rate.
- Send tailored recommendations to mobile devices at just the right time while consumers are in the right location to take advantage of offers.

- Analyze data from social media to detect new market trends and changes in demand.
- Determine root causes of failures, issues, and defects by investigating user sessions, network logs, and machine sensors.

A number of recent technology advancements are enabling companies to make the most of big data and big data analytics, such as cheap, abundant storage and server processing capacity, faster processors, and affordable large-memory capabilities, such as Hadoop. New storage and processing technologies are designed specifically for large data volumes, including structured and unstructured data. Parallel processing, clustering, MPP (massive parallel processing), virtualization, large grid environments, high connectivity, and high throughputs are making it possible to process big data faster. Cloud computing and other flexible resource allocation arrangements are becoming more desirable and cost effective. Big data technologies not only support the ability to collect large amounts of data, they also provide the ability to understand it and take advantage of its value. The goal of all companies with access to large data collections should be to harness the most relevant data and use it for optimized decision making.

The race among companies is to deploy the capabilities required to convert increasingly large, complex, disparate sets of downstream data into retail customer, shopper, and consumer insights that can enable improved decision making and execution across the organization. The transformation from DSR to DSV and ultimately DSA will require leadership, a strategic vision, a roadmap of priorities, and the ability to execute against the organization's strategy. Achieving best-in-class status across every measure could merely mean adding unnecessary cost and complexity. What's important is to invest in people, process, analytics, and technology improvements that are valued by customers. Leaders make conscious trade-offs, with an understanding that it may be appropriate to have benchmarks that are at par with industry averages while, at the same time, having other measures that reflect best-in-class outcomes. Now that many companies have created DSRs, to move to the next level will require the migration to DSV, and then, ultimately, to DSA. Until those companies implement DSV/ DSA, they will not have the capabilities to take full advantage of all the big data collected, cleansed, and loaded into their DSRs. In order to take full advantage of their DSRs, companies will need to add a second layer of DSV, combined with a third layer of DSA. With DSA, companies can get a near real-time picture of retail store level sales and inventory replenishment trends while identifying potential challenges as well as market opportunities. The entire organization can take advantage of the predictive intelligence of DSA by easily visualizing (using DSV) big data libraries of facts and measures at the lowest granularity across account hierarchies, category/item hierarchies, and geographical hierarchies. In addition, DSA can deliver targeted alerts to enable exception-based processes and workflow.

It is very important to understand that not all data will be relevant or useful. It is a widely acknowledged challenge. Most businesses have made slow progress in extracting value from big data by migrating to DSRs. Others attempt to apply traditional data management practices to big data, only to learn that the old rules no longer apply. Investing in DSRs with DSV and DSA capabilities with a set of prepackaged reports, dashboards, and easy-to-use exploration capabilities designed to support demand management, brand management, category management, and product performance along with scorecarding capabilities can accelerate time to value.

KEY LEARNINGS

■ Companies are starting to realize that no matter what industry they are in, one of their most precious assets is their data.

■ The value of information captured today is increasingly put to use for reporting purposes (descriptive analytics), rather than the primary purposes for which it was collected (predictive analytics).

■ The challenge is converting massive amounts of data into actionable (or usable) information that the organization can absorb, understand, and use effectively to make better-informed decisions.

- ▦ Automation is the key enabler of any local big data application for one reason only, which is scalability.

- ▦ Data availability, storage, and processing are no longer a challenge for companies as advancements in technology have solved them.

- ▦ Point-of-sale and syndicated scanner data are still the least utilized data for demand management even though they are the closest to true demand.

- ▦ Cleansing of historical demand is still a standard practice for companies due to antiquated statistical methods deployed—moving averaging and exponential smoothing—as well as lack of predictive analytics skills.
  - ▦ As a result, demand planners are merely managers of data and information.

- ▦ As big data continues to grow in volume, velocity, and variability, and with more pressure to drive revenue growth demand, planners will be asked to not only improve forecast accuracy, but also find new insights that are actionable to proactively drive profit.

- ▦ Demand planners will need to transition from managers of data and information to demand analysts with a focus on predictive analytics driving revenue growth and profitability.

- ▦ If companies want to be more proactive than simply basing replenishment on shipment data, they need access to downstream data, analysis, and insights to make decisions, which requires the demand signal repository (DSR) combined with demand signal visualization (DSV) and demand signal analytics (DSA).

NOTES

1. Shira, Ovide. "Big Data, Big Blunders: Five Mistakes Companies Make—and How They Can Avoid Them," *Wall Street Journal*, March 11, 2013, p. R4.
2. Lora, Cecere. *Supply Chain Insights, LLC.*, August 2012.
3. Lora, Cecere and Charles W. Chase Jr., *Bricks Matter: The Role of Supply Chains in Building Market-Driven Differentiation* (New York: John Wiley & Sons. 2013), p. 109.

4. Demand-Driven Forecasting and Planning Research Study, *Industry Week/SAS* (2014), p. 9.
5. Ibid.

FURTHER READING

Chase, Charles W. Jr., "Using Big Data to Enhance Demand-Driven Forecasting and Planning," *Journal of Business Forecasting* 32, no. 2 (Summer 2013), pp. 27–32.
Chase, Charles W. Jr., "Innovations in Business Forecasting," *Journal of Business Forecasting* 33, no. 4 (Winter 2014–2015), pp. 28–33.

CHAPTER **4**

The Process

C ontinued demand volatility combined with market dynamics is compelling companies to develop and deploy more integrated analytic-driven demand management processes, which require predictive analytics, market intelligence, and more sophisticated technologies to achieve their revenue growth goals and objectives. These changes in the dynamics of the marketplace are driving the process focus of predicting and orchestrating the best demand response, and not simply forecasting supply based on static analysis and gut-feeling judgment. What's more, shrinking product life cycles, combined with a demanding marketplace, are sharply increasing the costs of choosing supply to correct for the wrong demand response. As a result, companies realize that market and channel dominance mandates a highly integrated and dynamic demand response. The strategic objective is to influence consumers in the market based on the strength of prevailing brands to purchase their products, thus pulling their products through the channels of distribution, rather than pushing products into the channel.

Demand management done well encompasses more than just forecasting. It incorporates sensing, shaping, and translation of a demand signal that planners can continuously fine-tune (or shape) based on key performance indicators (KPIs). This requires the combination of data, analytics, domain knowledge, and technology. Unfortunately, demand planning in most companies is based on an expert's gut-feeling judgmental override to a simple baseline statistical forecast built on altered sales history (adjusted for outliers and promotional lift). It's a politically charged naive planning process that assumes what will happen next week will be more or less the same as what happened last week, with some incremental adjustments based on assumptions related to business goals and objectives rather than current market conditions.

There is growing competitive pressure to better understand the dynamics of the market. Then model (sense) and use those factors to influence (shape) future demand to grow revenue and profitability. These same companies have found that no amount of rapid responsive or manufacturing flexibility can rescue them from devastatingly lackluster customer demand. Furthermore, if their demand forecasts consistently fall in the 50 to 60 percent accuracy range, they will continue to experience poor customer service and high expediting and inventory carrying costs. Those companies that respond to this challenge do so by investing in data and advanced analytics to supplement their demand-driven planning process.

It is not uncommon for companies to adopt a supply strategy when experiencing SKU–level forecast errors running on average of 50 to 150 percent, and considering demand management a waste of time and effort. They eventually invest heavily in lean manufacturing and supply chain planning driven by inventory optimization solutions aimed at dealing with the challenge entirely from a supply-driven perspective, addressing the symptom rather than the root cause. Although this does improve manufacturing efficiencies, companies quickly realize that it does nothing to improve customer service or reduce excess finished goods inventories. After several unsuccessful years, most companies begin to augment their supply-centric initiatives with one specifically targeted at improving forecast accuracy and enabling a rapid demand response that is based on prioritizing different market segments. Within six to nine months of doing so, forecast error is generally reduced from an average of 100 to 50 percent, at which time the companies begin to become more confident that a target of 20 percent can be reached within the following year. Segmenting and prioritizing the market has also been a critical factor to success, allowing companies to achieve their targets in terms of inventory reductions and improved customer service. It is now believed that if a company begins with a forecast more reflective of the marketplace, it may not need quite as high a level of sophistication on the supply side. Based on empirical observations, it is clear that superior demand planning and orchestration with the increased frequency (weekly versus monthly forecast cycles) dictated by market dynamics is a prerequisite to an effective demand management strategy.

CENTERS OF FORECASTING EXCELLENCE

Due to globalization and expanded product portfolios, many companies are considering creating *centers of forecasting excellence* within their corporate headquarters, particularly at larger global companies. Furthermore, they are staffing those centers of excellence with demand analysts, not demand planners. So, what is the difference? Demand analysts are responsible for creating the statistical baseline forecasts for all the regions/divisions. Then, pass those statistical baseline forecasts to the regional/divisional demand planners to refine (make adjustments) to the statistical baseline forecasts. Those adjustments are based on local sales and marketing activities, such as pricing actions, sales promotions, and others.

The skill sets of these newly created demand analyst positions are different from the demand planners. The demand analysts have advanced statistical skills and strong business acumen. They also have strong collaboration skills as they work closely with the regional demand planners. The regional demand planners do not necessarily have a strong statistical skill set, but work closely with the local commercial business teams to refine the statistical baseline forecasts reflecting regional sales/marketing activities (i.e., pricing actions. sales promotions, marketing events, and others). Another question that always follows is the ratio of demand analysts to demand planners. Based on my experience, it is recommended that there be one demand analyst for every three or four demand planners. This seems to be the optimal mix between demand analysts and demand planners. Once all the statistical models are generated demand analysts only need to tweak the statistical baseline forecasts on an exception basis requiring fewer resources. The demand analysts also provide ad hoc analysis in support of the global commercial teams to assess business strategic initiatives and tactics.

If you are implementing a demand-driven forecasting and planning process, those statistical baseline forecasts will include key performance indicators (KPI's) such as price and sales promotions, which the demand planners can utilize to make adjustments through what-if analysis, not gut-feeling judgment. Also, POS/syndicated scanner data (true demand) can be integrated into the demand planning process encouraging the commercial teams to engage with the demand planners. The goal is to have demand analysts building holistic all-inclusive statistical baseline forecasts that include KPIs, such as sales promotions, price, advertising, in-store merchandising and more. Then, demand planners work with the commercial teams (sales/marketing) running what-if simulations to adjust the forecasts based on data, analytics, and domain knowledge rather than gut feelings. The what-if analysis is done at the local divisional/country level for tactical planning, but can also be conducted at the corporate (global) level for strategic planning. This is done using large-scale hierarchical forecasting enabled by new technology.

The goal is to reduce judgment bias by using data, analytics, domain knowledge, and scalable technology, thus minimizing bias judgmental overrides that add error. This requires investment in people (skills/behavior changes), process (horizontal, not vertical) that includes the commercial side of the business, using analytics (not just descriptive, but also predictive analytics), and finally, supported by scalable enterprise technology. Most traditional demand planning processes focus only on the process and technology, and then rely on gut feeling judgment to enhance the accuracy of the demand forecast. That traditional process has failed. Furthermore, Excel spreadsheets are not scalable enough to handle thousands of SKUs across multiple market areas on a global basis. It requires an integrated scalable enterprise solution.

DEMAND MANAGEMENT CHAMPION

Companies are quickly realizing that an internal *champion* is needed to drive the change management required to gain adoption, because this new process design and added demand analyst role is a radical change for most companies. Also, even if you get adoption, you need it to be *sustainable*. Many companies gain adoption, but cannot sustain it to make it part of the corporate culture. In order to make it sustainable, companies need to incorporate predictive analytics into the process that are supported by a large-scale enterprise technology solution with an easy-to-use user interface (UI). Also, an internal ongoing champion involvement will be required to assure this new approach to demand planning becomes part of the corporate culture over time.

These interdependencies are also influenced by the strategic intent of a company's demand planning process. In other words, is the intent to create a more accurate demand response, a financial plan, marketing plan, supply plan, or a sales plan (target setting)? These different intentions are conflicting, and are not really forecasts, but rather, plans that are derivatives of the unconstrained demand forecast.

DEMAND-DRIVEN PLANNING

Demand-driven planning is the set of business processes, analytics, and technologies that enable companies to analyze, choose, and execute against the precise mix of customer, product, channel, and geographic segments that achieves their customer-facing business objectives. Based on recent observations and research, demand-driven planning on average is driven 60 percent by process, 30 percent by analytics, and 10 percent by enabling technology, depending on the industry, market, and channel dynamics that influence how companies orchestrate a demand response. Although enabling technology represents only 10 percent, the other 90 percent cannot be achieved without the enabling technology due to scalability and analytical requirements, not to mention data integration requirements that span across the global corporate enterprise. The need for an improved demand planning process focuses not only on process, analytics, and technology but also the importance of integrated collaboration across the global enterprise.

Demand-driven planning utilizes data from market and channel sources to sense, shape, and translate demand requirements into an actionable demand response that is supported by an efficient supply plan, or supply response. A true demand-driven forecast is an unconstrained view or best estimate of market demand, primarily based on corporate specific historical sales demand, preferably POS, sales orders, and shipment information. Demand shaping uses factors, such as price, new product launches, trade and sales promotions, advertising, and marketing programs, in addition to other related sales and marketing information, to influence what and how much consumers will buy.

WHAT IS DEMAND SENSING AND SHAPING?

Demand sensing and *shaping* are common terms that have been used loosely over the past several years with different definitions, depending on the industry and purpose. The most common definitions are associated with the consumer packaged goods (CPG) industry.

Demand sensing, especially in recent years, has come to embody using granular downstream sales data (mainly sales orders, preferably POS/syndicated scanner data) to refine short-term demand forecasts and inventory positioning in support of a one- to six-week supply plan. It is slowly being expanded to cover medium-term operational and inventory replenishment plans that require a 1- to 18-month demand forecast. Eventually, it will also include long-term strategic forecasting and planning (two years into the future and beyond). The term *demand shaping* often describes measuring the relationships of consumer (or customer) demand with respect to sales promotions and marketing events and/or price discounts, then using those consumer demand influence factors to shape future demand using what-if scenario analysis. These new, much broader definitions for demand sensing and shaping have been at the forefront of many conversations with senior executives across all industries globally.

What Is Demand Sensing?

Demand sensing is the translation of downstream data with minimal latency to understand what is being sold, who is buying the product (attributes), and how the product is impacting demand. Overall, three key elements define demand sensing:

1. *Use of downstream data (for demand pattern recognition).* This requires the ability to collect and analyze POS and/or syndicated scanner data (Information Resources Inc. [IRI], Nielsen, Intercontinental Marketing Services [IMS]) across market channels, geography, brands, product groups, products, and so on to understand who is buying what product and in what quantities. This includes the KPIs (key performance indicators) that influence the demand signal, for example, average base price, average retail price, displays, features, feature/displays, temporary price reductions (TPRs), weighted distribution, sales promotions, marketing events, and others.

2. *Measuring the impact of demand-shaping programs.* This refers to the ability to analytically measure and determine the impact

of demand-shaping activities, such as price, promotions, sales tactics, and marketing events, as well as changes in product mix, new product introductions, and other related factors that impact demand lift. It also includes measuring and assessing the financial implications of demand-shaping activities related to profit margins and overall revenue growth—measuring those KPIs that significantly impact the demand signal, and then running what-if analysis applying those KPIs to shape future demand. This includes assessing the impact of those scenarios based not only on incremental lifts but also on revenue and profit generation.

3. *Reduced latency/minimal latency.* This refers to the ability to model and forecast demand changes on a more frequent basis. Traditionally, demand forecasting is done on a monthly or longer basis. Demand sensing requires that demand be modeled on a shorter horizon—weekly or daily depending on the frequency of new information—and that the changes in demand be reflected on a weekly basis (or whatever the frequency of new information).

These three demand elements are used to translate demand requirements into a profitable demand response that can be consumed for planning purposes. Although many companies have developed demand processes to capture volume information and replenishment (sales orders) and shipments (supply) within their supply chain networks, it is the responsibility of sales and marketing to capture demand insights with regard to what sales promotions and marketing activities have influenced consumers to purchase their products. The information translated into a demand response by sales and marketing is used to adjust prior predictions of future unconstrained demand. Traditional sources have yielded structured data, but unstructured sources, such as weather patterns and chatter on the social Web, are increasingly important sources of insight, as well.

Today's supply chains still respond to demand, but do not sense demand. They focus on customer orders and shipments, which is a replenishment signal, and supply signal. Additionally, supply chain latency is accepted and not questioned. Companies have not conquered the bullwhip effect (the ripple effect throughout the supply chain that causes inefficiencies that could have been avoided). Also, the translation of demand from the retail shelf to a manufacturer's replenishment to retailer warehouses remains unchanged. The result is that companies have built long supply chains that translate, not sense, demand.

Sensing Demand Signals

Companies across some industries, particularly in the CPG industry vertical, are taking demand sensing to the next level by leveraging POS and downstream data such as syndicated scanner data to better understand consumer demand. Companies are using this information to make better business and operational decisions. They use a structured approach to transform terabytes of aggregated store-level data into actionable information across their businesses.

These same companies use downstream data to improve their short-term statistical demand forecasts.

They normally define short term as one to six weeks into the future. Their process and enabling technology provides weekly forecasts by item and location level, using downstream data to improve short-term execution (replenishment and deployment), supporting an end-to-end supply chain network. The short-term statistical demand forecast does not replace the operational demand forecasting and planning system (operational plan). Rather, it supplements the operation plan with more real time insights into consumer demand. A benefit of using a short-term statistical forecast allows these companies to expand their sales and operation planning (S&OP) horizon from short-term tactical execution to longer-term operational, and strategic execution and planning. Their downstream data process provides weekly forecast revisions. The analytical models determine the best predictive signal—that is, shipment, order, and customer data—to determine the best tactical demand forecast.

The improvement in short-term tactical demand forecast accuracy using demand sensing is significant, and companies in the CPG industry are able to further improve forecast accuracy when utilizing downstream data as part of their short-term statistical forecast. With that, they have been able to reduce their finished goods inventory on average by as much as 15 to 30 percent while becoming even more agile through sensing demand, and reacting faster to changes in unpredictable demand.

Demand Shaping Is a Critical Success Factor

Downstream data can determine what products consumers want and when, which gives companies a competitive advantage. Previously, companies used to make what they thought they would sell, and now they make what they can sell. Demand shaping enables companies to influence the future volume and profits by orchestrating a series of marketing, sales, and product tactics, and strategies in the marketplace. Several key levers can be used in the development of demand-shaping strategies. These are:

- New product launch (including the management of categories)
- Price management (optimization)
- Marketing and advertising
- Sales incentives, promotions, trade policies/deals
- Product life cycle management strategies

True demand shaping is the process of using what-if analysis to influence unconstrained demand in the future, and matching that demand with an efficient supply response. Based on various industry research studies conducted over the past several years, demand shaping, just like demand sensing, includes three key elements:

1. *Ability to increase volume and profit.* This can be achieved by using predictive analytics to proactively influence future unconstrained demand using what-if analysis. Using predictive analytics companies can measure the impact of changing price, sales promotions, marketing events, advertising, and product mix against demand lift and profitability to make optimal business decisions that impact future demand.

2. *Supply plan/supply supportability analysis.* This refers to how much can be made based on existing capacity, and where, when, and how fast it can be delivered.

3. *Demand shifting (steering)*. This refers to the ability to promote another product as a substitute if the product originally demanded was not available and/or move a sales and marketing tactic from one period to another to accommodate supply constraints. It is especially useful if demand patterns or supply capacity change suddenly to steer customers from product A to product B, or shift demand to a later time period.

Over the past several years, many companies have begun to invest in demand-sensing and -shaping processes along with enabling technology. However, in almost every case, they are doing demand shifting rather than true demand shaping. If anything, they have implemented short-term demand sensing (one to six weeks into the future). Even in those cases, they are sensing sales orders, which is a replenishment (supply) signal. No one is truly sensing and shaping true demand, POS (point-of-sales) or syndicated scanner data (Nielsen/IRI/IMS), or linking unconstrained demand to sales orders and shipments using a process known as *multi-tiered causal analysis* (MTCA). We discuss MTCA in more detail in Chapter 6.

True Demand Shaping

Demand shaping happens when companies use sales and marketing tactics like price, promotion, new product launches, sales incentives, and/or marketing programs to influence future consumer demand, to generate not only incremental unit volume but also profit. All too many times, companies believe that they are shaping demand but find that they are really just shifting demand (moving demand from one period to another). Moving demand from one period to another and selling at a lower margin without improving market share and revenue growth creates waste in the supply chain. The first step in the demand-driven forecasting and planning process is sensing market conditions based on demand signals and then shaping future demand using predictive analytics such as price optimization, trade promotion analysis, new product launch plan alignment, and social/digital/mobile data convergence (see Figure 4.1). Demand sensing reduces the latency of the demand signal by 70 to 80 percent, allowing

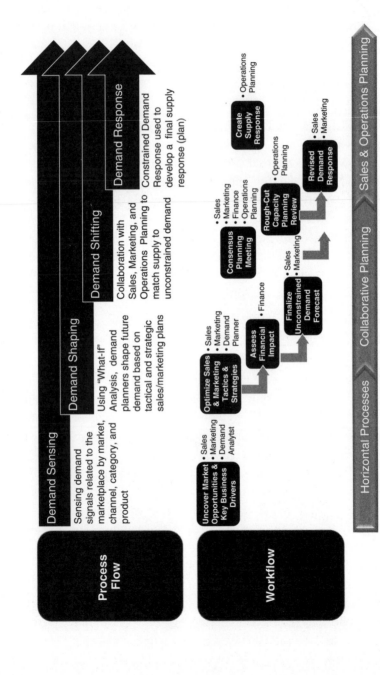

Figure 4.1 Demand-driven forecasting and planning process.

the company to better understand and see true channel demand. Demand shaping combines the tactics of pricing policies, sales promotions, sales and marketing incentives, and new product launches to increase demand.

Traditional demand forecasting and planning systems were not designed to sense demand patterns other than trend/cycle, seasonality, and level (unexplained). For that reason, it is impossible for traditional ERP/demand management systems to conduct demand-sensing and shaping activities associated with price, sales promotions, channel marketing programs, and other related factors. As the global marketplace has become increasingly volatile, fragmented, and dynamic, and as supply chain lead times have become overextended, companies are quickly coming to the realization that their demand management systems are no longer adequate to predict future demand. There are two primary factors that have contributed to this situation:

1. *Limited statistical methods* available in traditional demand management systems:

    a. Can only sense and predict stable demand that is highly seasonal with distinct trend patterns.

    b. Primarily use only one category of statistical models, called time series methods, with a focus on exponential smoothing models, such as simple exponential smoothing, Holt's two-parameter exponential smoothing, and the Holt-Winters three-parameter exponential smoothing.

2. *Process requires domain knowledge* versus judgment to:

    a. Define data availability, granularity, and sourcing.

    b. Assess the dynamics of the market and channel segments to identify factors that influence demand.

    c. Run what-if analyses to shape future demand based on sales and marketing tactics/strategies.

Research continues to show that there is a strong correlation between demand visibility and supply chain performance. As demand visibility yields higher accuracy in assessing demand, efficiencies continue to accumulate throughout the supply chain. Yet in most companies, there is still a wide gap between the commercial side of the business, with its understanding of the market and plans for demand sensing and shaping (e.g., sales/marketing tactics and strategies, new product commercialization, life cycle management, and social media), and the supply chain organization, with its ability to support those efforts.

Demand sensing as a core capability isn't new; retailer POS data, syndicated scanner data, customer insights, and focus groups have guided marketing and sales promotional programming for over two decades. The challenge is how to translate these demand insights into actions that can drive an efficient supply response. The ability to sense, shape, and translate demand into an accurate demand forecast and a corresponding supply response requires more transparency and collaboration between the organization's commercial and operational functions.

The key to demand shaping is cross-functional collaboration between sales and marketing and among the other members of the supply chain (e.g., finance) by coordinating and agreeing on demand-shaping programs (see Figure 4.2). The core purpose of such programs is to drive unit volume and profitability among the company's brands and products.

At first, these activities typically are monitored and managed independently by each functional department, such as sales, strategic marketing, and product management, with little cross-functional integration. For example, a price change occurring simultaneously with a product sales promotion could erode the profitability of the product or create an unexpected out-of-stock situation on the retailers' shelves. Cross-functional collaboration among sales, marketing, and finance requires companies to shift to a cross-departmental market orientation that balances the trade-offs of each tactic and focuses on revenue generation and profit (see Figure 4.3), not just reducing inventory costs.

To better understand the dynamics of demand sensing and shaping, we need to break down the demand management process into a capability framework made up of five key components:

1. *Large-scale hierarchical statistical engine.* A set of more sophisticated statistical models is a key requirement to enable demand sensing and shaping, as well as scalability to forecast hundreds

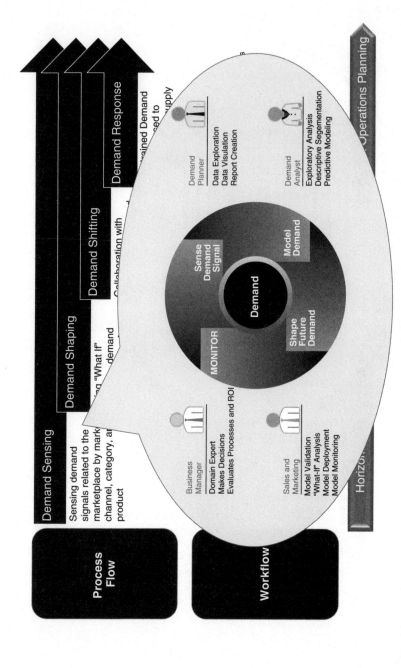

Figure 4.2 Demand sensing and shaping workflow.

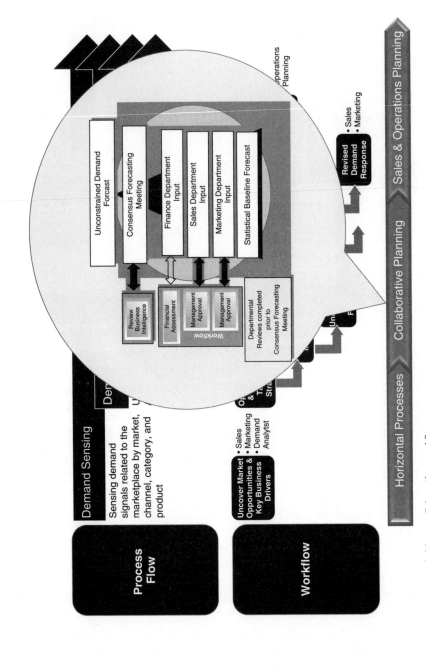

Figure 4.3 Demand-driven collaborative workflow.

of thousands of products up/down the business hierarchy. Such models measure the effects of different sales and marketing events and enable a better understanding of the incremental volume that is associated with them. The ability to measure past events over time and clearly identify which ones are profitable helps companies avoid unexpected planning events that produce negative returns and exploit those identifiable events that are more profitable in driving incremental demand and profit.

Companies can proactively influence the amount and timing of consumer demand by varying the future marketing mix elements that influence demand for a product through the use of what-if analysis. For example, varying future price, sales promotions, levels of merchandising, and advertising can influence consumers to purchase more of a company's products. More advanced methods, such as ARIMA, ARIMAX, and dynamic regression models as well as utilizing downstream POS/syndicated scanner data can help sales and marketing planners better understand consumer demand and uncover insights such as price elasticity. Combining these more advanced statistical techniques with decision-support tools, such as what-if analysis, enables sales and marketing planners (support by a demand analyst) to determine the right trade-offs within the marketing mix by market, channel, brand, and product that drive incremental unit volume and profit. Demand analysts and planners are moving toward the use of downstream data to help capture consumer insights to build on current trends and seasonality, utilizing marketing programs based on the combination of historical data and domain knowledge, not gut-feeling judgment.

2. *Visualization analytics (VA).* VA capabilities combine the power of descriptive analytics associated with monitoring, tracking, and reporting with the power of predictive analytics to uncover actionable insights with user-friendly interfaces. VA control towers/dashboards, along with predictive analytics, allow sales and marketing personnel to collect, integrate, and apply data from the statistical engine and the field to support business tactics and strategies, such as planning pricing changes,

sales promotions, and measuring results against strategic and tactical business plans. Demand shaping can be used to reduce demand volatility, thereby reducing the need for supply network agility. For example, corporate leaders in various industries (e.g., food services, spare parts planning, and electronics) are looking to use Web channels to sense demand signals and shape future demand using distributor networks.

3. *Post reconciliation of performance.* It is important to measure demand-sensing and shaping programs after each completed demand forecasting cycle to determine the success or failure of the programs implemented to drive demand.

    Historically, it took weeks to review and assess the success or failure of a sales promotion after its completion. With new enabling technology, along with downstream data collection and synchronization processes, as well as market sensing and shaping capabilities, today it is much easier and faster to monitor, track, and report on the effects of demand-shaping programs. This allows companies to manage the demand-shaping process around real-time demand signals. Adjustments can be made to demand-shaping programs within a daily or weekly period to better manage the outcome.

4. *Executive alignment to support change management.* Establish clear decision criteria, empower senior managers and their staff, and develop an appropriate incentive program that includes rewards for accurate demand forecasts. Decentralize tactical knowledge-based decision making while balancing corporate strategic unit volume and profit objectives. Stress the importance of building a demand forecast based on sales and marketing programs that are profitable, not just volume generators. There will be a paradigm shift, moving from a view of unit volume in isolation of profitability (not considering profit, but only incremental volume for trial purposes) to a more focused view of how unit volume increases can affect profitability.

5. *Continuous business process improvements.* Short- and long-range business strategy and planning, operational tactical planning, and post-event analysis must be coordinated in the organization. Sophisticated analytics shared across the various departments within a company through well-designed decision support networks will provide more consistency and alignment of internal processes and work flow to drive profitability.

Demand shaping focuses on creating an unconstrained demand forecast that reflects the sales and marketing activities that shape demand rather than using supply to manage demand. Demand shaping is a process that requires predictive analytics supported by enabling technology. The system should be flexible and easy to use, with quick response time and closed-loop feedback to measure and report the value of those adjustments made to an initial statistical forecast. Without access to the intuitive system, the sales organization has legitimate reason to resist participating in the forecasting process.

A NEW PARADIGM SHIFT

Educating sales, creating a well-structured demand forecasting process, clearly defined organizational roles and responsibilities, and access to information are all important to help incentivize the sales team to participate. Among these, there are two axioms that should also be understood: (1) what gets measured gets done; and (2) incentives drive behavior.

Sales team performance metrics often fall into a revenue generation category. Typical measurements are based against a sales quota (gross or net value), and may also be measured based on a margin or profitability target. As a result, the focus becomes how much revenue can be generated by the sales organization and how profitable is that revenue for the company. At its basic level, the quota is a forecast. Since compensation is determined by the results compared to a quota, or forecast, there is a tendency to understate the forecast in order to improve the chances of exceeding the target.

Another common measure for the sales team may be based on customer service. This is normally an order fill rate, such as delivered in-full, on-time (DIFOT), or some other similar measure, such as perfect order fill rates. When customer service measures are used to determine compensation, the tendency is to overforecast demand in an attempt to make sure adequate inventory is available to maximize order fill rates.

Tying sales team performance to forecast accuracy can balance demand and service with the least amount of inventory possible. In order to more closely align sales team performance with forecast accuracy, it is important to establish the correlation between forecast accuracy and the amount of inventory required to support desired customer service levels. Drawing that correlation between forecast accuracy and the costs of inventory can be somewhat of a challenge, but there are experts and processes capable of pinpointing the relationship.

Inventory optimization provides visibility to the multiple drivers of inventory investment, including forecast accuracy and supply lead-time variability to name a few. If an inventory planning function exists within the supply chain team, they can help drive an understanding of current forecast accuracy, as well as the trade-off between customer service levels and inventory investment. With this understanding, performance measures can be developed that provide a much better incentive for meaningful sales team involvement in the forecasting process.

Finally, the forecast isn't a number pulled off the top of someone's head, although in many cases that's not too far from the truth. The demand forecast is the sum of many parts working together toward a common goal. The sales team can add significant value to the forecasting process. However, the process must harness the intelligence the sales organization provides to align consumer demand at strategic and tactical levels with the company's marketing capabilities, resulting in improved revenue and profitability. At the strategic level, the emphasis is on aligning long-term marketing investment strategies with long-term consumer demand patterns while maximizing marketing investment effectiveness. At the tactical level, the focus is on understanding customer demand patterns, and proactively influencing demand to meet available supply, using the marketing mix to sense and shape price, sales promotions, marketing events, and other related factors to influence demand generation and profitability.

LARGE-SCALE AUTOMATIC HIERARCHICAL FORECASTING

Most companies review their forecasts in a product hierarchy that mirrors the way they manage their supply chain or product portfolio. In the past, product hierarchies in most companies were simple, reflecting the business at the national, brand, product group, product line, and SKU levels. These product hierarchies ranged from hundreds to a few thousand SKUs, spanning a small number of countries or sales regions and a handful of distribution points, making them fairly easy to manage.

During the past two decades, however, many industries have gone through major consolidations. Larger companies found it easier to swallow up smaller companies to increase their economies of scale from a sales, marketing, and operations perspective rather than growing their business organically. They realized additional benefits as they flushed out inefficiencies in their supply chains while increasing their revenue and global reach. Unfortunately, with all this expansion came complexities in the way they needed to view their businesses.

As companies consolidate through acquisition and expand globally, their product portfolios have grown exponentially from hundreds of SKUs to excess of hundreds of thousands of SKUs across multiple intersections (e.g., geography, region, market, division, channel, brand, product group, product, SKU, customer, demand point, and others). This situation has required companies to generate a large number of forecasts (millions in some cases) based on time-stamped data stored in their transactional or time series databases. Social media, point-of-sale (POS) data, syndicated scanner data, shipments, sales orders, pricing and promotion data, inventory data and others are examples of data that are stored in transactional databases. A skilled analyst can forecast a single time series by applying good judgment based on his or her knowledge and experience, by using various time series analysis techniques, and by utilizing good software based on proven statistical theory. Generating large numbers of forecasts and/or frequently generating forecasts requires some degree of automation. Common problems that a business faces are:

- No skilled analyst is available (little or no statistical skills).

- Many forecasts must be generated.

- Frequent forecast updates are required (weekly and/or monthly).

- Time-stamped data must be converted to time series data (weekly and/or monthly intervals).

- Difficult to run various statistical forecasting models for each time series.

TRANSACTIONAL DATA

Transactional data are time stamped data collected over time at no particular frequency. Some examples of transactional data are:

- Internet data

- Point of sales (POS) data

- Syndicated scanner data

- Shipment data

- Sales order data

- Inventory data

- Key account data

Companies often want to analyze transactional data for trends and seasonal variation for demand forecasting and planning. To analyze transactional data for trends and seasonality, statistics must be computed for each time period and season of concern. The frequency and the season may vary with the business problem. For example, various statistics can be computed on each time period and season. For example,

- Web visits by hour and by hour of day

- Sales per week by month and year

- Inventory depletions per week and by week of month

- Sales promotion volume per week by month and year
- Price per product by week and year

TIME SERIES DATA

Time series data are time-stamped data collected over time at a particular frequency. Some examples of time series data are:

- POS data per week or month
- Inventory depletions per week or month
- Shipments per week or month
- Sales orders per week or month

The frequency associated with the time series varies with the challenge at hand. The frequency or time interval may be daily, weekly, monthly, quarterly, yearly, or many other variants of the basic time intervals. The choice of frequency is an important modeling decision. This decision is especially true for automatic forecasting. For example, if you want to forecast the next four weeks, it is best to use weekly data rather than daily data. The forecast horizon in the former case is 4, in the latter case is 28.

Associated with each time series is a seasonal cycle or seasonality. For example, the length of seasonality for a monthly time series is usually assumed to be 12 because there are 12 months in a year. Likewise, the seasonality of a daily time series is usually assumed to be 7. The usual seasonality assumption may not always hold. For example, if a particular business's seasonal cycle is 14 days long, the seasonality is 14, not 7. Time series that consist of mostly zero values (or a single value) are called interrupted or intermittent (sparse) time series. These time series are mainly constant valued except for relatively few occasions. Intermittent time series must be forecast differently from non-intermittent time series.

FORECASTING MODELS

There are numerous types of forecasting models that a skilled analyst can use. For automatic forecasting of large numbers of time series, only the most robust models should be used. The goal is not to use the very best model for forecasting each time series. The goal is to provide a list of candidate models that will forecast the large majority of the time series well. Overall, when an analyst has a large number of time series to forecast, the analyst should use automatic forecasting for the low-valued forecasts. Then, the analyst can spend a larger portion of his/her time dealing with high-valued forecasts or low-valued forecasts that are problematic.

The candidate models need to be more robust including all categories of statistical forecasting methods (e.g., time series—moving averaging, exponential smoothing, ARIMA; intermittent demand methods; causal methods—ARIMAX, regression, multiple linear regression, dynamic regression; and weighted combined methods). These models have proven their effectiveness over time. They not only consider the local level, trend, and seasonal components of the time series, but also causal factors like price, sales promotions, marketing events, in-store merchandising, and others. The term *local* is used to describe the fact that these components evolve with time. For example, the local trend component may not be a straight line but a trend line that changes with time. In each of these models, there is an error or random component that models the uncertainty.

The components associated with these models are not only useful for demand forecasting but also for describing how the time series evolves over time. The forecasting model decomposes the series into its various components. For example, the local trend component describes the trend (up or down) at each point in time and the final trend component describes the expected future trend. These forecasting models can also indicate departures from previous behavior or can be used to segment time series.

The parameter estimates (weights) describe how fast the component is changing with time. Weights near zero indicate a relatively constant component, and weights near one indicate a relatively variable component. For example, a seasonal weight near zero represents a stable seasonal component, and a seasonal weight near one represents an unstable seasonal component. Weights should be optimized based on the data for best results using statistics, not human judgment.

Today, with global reach across multiple countries, markets, channels, brands, and products, the degree of granularity has escalated tenfold or more (see Figure 4.4). Company product portfolios have increased exponentially in size due to consolidation through acquisition and global expansion. Subsequently, the proliferation of the SKU base for many companies has expanded into the thousands and in some cases hundreds of thousands. It is not unusual to see companies with more than 10,000 SKUs that span across 100 or more countries (see Figure 4.5).

Further escalation occurs as marketing departments segment their consumer base by ethnicity, channels of distribution, and purchase behavior. The resulting increased granularity has further complicated company product hierarchies. All this proliferation in business complexity has made it difficult not only to manage the data but also to process the data in a timely manner. As such, companies need more robust technology that can not only forecast up/down their complex

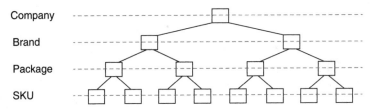

Figure 4.4 Most companies review their forecasts in a product hierarchy.

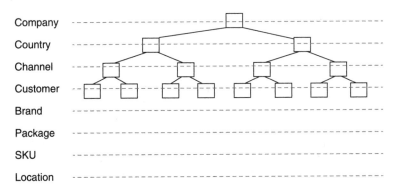

Figure 4.5 Globalization has made product hierarchies more complex.

business hierarchies but also apply more advanced statistical methods to capture and measure the effects of all the marketing activities used to generate demand. This new technology capability provides not only top-down and bottom-up overrides and reconciliation but also middle-out at any middle level in the business hierarchy. In fact, it has been found that on average middle-out overrides and reconciliation tend to be more accurate.

SKILL REQUIREMENTS

Business leaders need to deploy large-scale automatic forecasting systems to aid in their decision-making processes. Deploying such solutions will require different skills to effectively utilize this new technology. Demand analysts (statisticians, econometricians, mathematicians, data scientists and others) speak in terms of statistical techniques (model building, parameter estimations, predictions, statistical testing, etc.). Demand planners who are responsible for facilitating collaboration across the organization with sales, marketing, finance, and operations planning to create a final consensus demand plan speak in terms of *demand management* regarding *forecast accuracy*, *inventory costs*, *rough cut capacity planning*, and other supply chain terms. Finally, business users (marketers, brand managers, category managers, and others) speak in terms of *business domain* (pricing, sales promotions, marketing events, market channels, decision making and more).

Demand analysts who need a rich set of statistical techniques are more skilled or concerned with the information stored in the statistical model repository (model specification, model selection lists, etc.), and may be less skilled or concerned with data management, but require business domain knowledge. If a business does not have statistical analysts, it must rely solely on automation or must contract these skills to outside statistical consultants.

Demand planners need a rich set of extraction, translation, loading, and data quality techniques. They are more concerned with the information stored in the time series data, event repository, and the overall process flow and may be less skilled or concerned with statistical analysis and business domain issues. Business users need a rich set of domain-specific reporting and easy to use point-and-click interfaces. They are more concerned with the information stored in the forecast results repository and may be less skilled or concerned with statistical analysis and data management issues.

A large-scale automatic forecasting system allows the separation of these various skills and permits the necessary intercommunication between skill sets while at the same time applying sound demand forecasting principles to be used by the business.

SUMMARY

Corporate supply chain networks have been evolving from their traditional supply-driven architectures to becoming demand-driven due to global expansion and demand volatility. This has made their supply chain networks increasingly complex, requiring more effort and resources to orchestrate demand. As a result, companies can no longer use buffer stock (inventory) to protect against demand volatility and long lead times. Transitioning from a supply-driven process to a demand-driven requires investment in people, process, analytics, and technology. Process and technology alone is not enough. At the mature stage of the demand-driven transformation process, companies must focus on balancing profitable growth and marketing investment efficiency with inventory costs and customer service while reducing working capital. When demand-driven maturity is achieved, there is not only better balance but also greater agility across the supply chain.

The implementation challenges associated with the transition to demand-driven networks require *change management*, which can be enormous from a people, process, analytics, and technology standpoint. Companies that attempt to navigate a demand-driven transformation process must tackle corporate cultural changes head-on. The most important changes are:

- *Incentives: The role of the commercial teams.* As long as sales are incentivized only for volume sold into the channel and marketing only for market share, companies will never become demand-driven. To make the transition to demand-driven, companies must focus on profitable sales growth through the channel.

■ *Traditional view of supply chain excellence.* For demand-driven initiatives to succeed, they must extend from the customer's customer to the supplier's supplier. Most company supply chain models encompassed only deliver and make. Customer and supplier initiatives usually are managed in separate initiatives largely driven by cost.

■ *Leadership.* The concepts of demand latency, demand sensing, demand shaping, demand translation, and demand orchestration are not widely understood. As a result, they are not included in the definition of corporate strategy.

■ *Focus: Inside out, not outside in.* Process focus is from the inside of the organization out, as opposed from the outside (demand-driven) back. In demand-driven processes, the design of the processes is from the market back, based on sensing and shaping demand.

■ *Vertical rewards versus horizontal processes.* In supply-based organizations, the supply chain is incentivized based on cost reduction, procurement is incentivize based on the lowest purchased cost, distribution/logistics is rewarded for on-time shipments with the lowest costs, sales is rewarded for sell-in of volume into the channel, and marketing is rewarded for market share. These incentives cannot be aligned to maximize true value.

■ *Focus on transactions, not relationships.* Today, the connecting processes of the enterprise—selling and purchasing—are focused on transactional efficiency. As a result, the greater value that can happen through relationships—acceleration of time to market through innovation, breakthrough thinking in sustainability, and sharing of demand data—never materializes.

The demand-driven value network implementations are not a traditional approach of adding ERP + Advanced planning and scheduling/ Customer relationship management + Supplier relationship management, and shake until well blended, as Lora Cecere (Founder and CEO of Supply Chain Insights) mentioned recently in her Supply Chain Shaman blog. In fact, some of the most demand-driven companies have legacy systems that have not supported the process, but actually have hindered it. In order for the transition to be adopted and sustainable, focus on:

- *Process.* The implementation requires a focus on the processes: revenue management, new product launch, downstream channel data management, and use of demand insights.

- *Network design.* The design of the network is an essential element to actualizing this strategy. Demand-driven companies have made deep investments in supply chain modeling software—optimization and simulation—and actively model scenarios for the network reflecting changes in both demand and supply.

- *Demand sensing and shaping.* These companies also have a control tower to actively sense network changes and adapt the network for changes in market demand, constraints, and opportunities. This overarching group crosses source, make, deliver, and sell to work hand-in-hand with customer service to maximize the use of resources while minimizing costs and maximizing profitability.

So, does this mean that we give up on demand-driven concepts? The answer is emphatically *no*. It is the right concept, but it will take more time and investment in people, process, analytics, and technology.

KEY LEARNINGS

- Due to globalization and expanded product portfolios, many companies are considering creating *centers of forecasting excellence* within their corporate headquarters.

- Companies are now hiring demand analysts who are responsible for creating holistic statistical baseline forecasts for all the regions/divisions.

- They pass those all-inclusive statistical baseline forecasts to the regional/divisional demand planners to refine (make adjustments to) the statistical baseline forecasts using what-if scenario analysis, not gut feeling judgment.

- Companies are now investing in downstream data (POS/syndicated scanner) to integrate into the demand planning process.
  - The goal is to have demand analysts build statistical baseline forecasts (demand sensing) that include KPIs, such as sales promotions, price, advertising, in-store merchandising, and more.

  - Then, pass those statistical baseline forecasts to demand planners to run what-if scenarios with sales/marketing to shape future demand.

- An internal champion is needed to drive the change management required to gain adoption, because this new demand-driven process design and added demand analyst role is a radical change for most companies.

- Demand-driven planning is the set of business processes, analytics, and technologies that enable companies to analyze, choose, and execute against the precise mix of customer, product, channel, and geographic segments that achieves their business objectives.

- Demand sensing is the translation of downstream data with minimal latency to understand what is being sold, who is buying the product (attributes), and how the product is impacting demand.

- Demand shaping enables companies to influence the future volume and profits by orchestrating a series of marketing, sales, and product tactics and strategies in the marketplace.
  - Companies believe that they are shaping demand but find that they are really just shifting demand (moving demand from one period to another).

- The next generation demand management process capability framework is made up of five key components.

1. Large-scale hierarchical statistical engine for forecasting hundreds of thousands of products up/down the business hierarchy.

2. Visualization analytics (VA) for monitoring, tracking, reporting, and exploration.

3. Post reconciliation of performance to determine why the statistical forecasts did not meet expectations based on the analytics and domain knowledge.

4. Executive alignment to support change management to gain sustainable adoption.

5. Continuous business process improvements.

FURTHER READING

Leonard, Michael, "Large-Scale Automatic Forecasting Using Inputs and Calendar Events," SAS Institute Inc. white paper, 2005, pp. 1–28.

CHAPTER **5**

Performance
Metrics

easuring forecast performance is one of the most important elements of the demand forecasting process, and the least understood when put into practice. As you know, what gets measured gets fixed, and what gets fixed gets rewarded. You cannot improve your forecast accuracy until you measure and benchmark your current forecast performance.

It is not unusual to encounter companies that have never truly measured the accuracy of their demand forecasts on an ongoing basis. Some measure forecast accuracy weekly, monthly, and quarterly at the most aggregate level in their product hierarchy with little focus on the lower levels—the stock-keeping unit (SKU) detail or internal mix within the aggregates. It is not uncommon to find many companies that have virtually no idea that their lower-level product forecasts at the brand, product group, and the SKU detail have extremely high forecast error (or very low forecast accuracy). This is usually attributed to the way they calculate forecast accuracy (or error). They normally do not measure forecast error in terms of absolute values. As a result, when they sum those error values to the aggregate levels, the plus and minus signs wash each other out, making the accuracy look much better than the lower level detail. In fact, most senior-level managers rarely use or understand the term *forecast error*. The burden of translating forecast error to more understandable forecast accuracy terms normally falls on the shoulders of the demand planners and process owner.

The two most discussed topics today in demand forecasting are *forecastability* and *process performance* (efficiency). The most common performance metric used across all industry verticals is MAPE (mean absolute percentage error), which pays little attention to the forecastability of demand and process efficiency. Furthermore, very few companies actually measure the touch points in their demand forecasting process before and after someone makes a manual adjustment (override) to determine if they have added value.

WHY MAPE IS NOT ALWAYS THE BEST METRIC

The most commonly used forecast accuracy measure for goodness of fit is the mean absolute percentage error (MAPE). MAPE is obtained by computing the average absolute percent error for each time period. The actual formulation is written as:

$$MAPE = \frac{1}{n}\sum_{t=1}^{n}\frac{|(A_t - F_t)|}{A_t} \times 100$$

As a percentage, this measure is a relative one, and thus it is preferred to most other forecast accuracy measures. In other words, MAPE is similar to MAE (mean absolute error) except that it is dimensionless, which makes it helpful for communication purposes and in making comparisons among forecasts from different scenarios. However, MAPE is biased toward estimates or forecasts that are below the actual values. Therefore, you are penalized less if you overachieve your forecast than if you underachieve. This becomes obvious when you look at the extremes. For example, a forecast of zero can never be off by more than 100 percent, but there is no limit to errors on the high side. When working with judgmental forecasts, it could become a problem in the event of an intentional biasing of the forecasts. Nevertheless, if this problem is not likely to occur in your situation, then you should use MAPE, as it is easily understood. Another major challenge with MAPE is that when actual demand is zero, it is undefined, or when actual demand is close to zero, the value can explode to a huge number and, when averaged with the other values, can give a distorted image of the magnitude of the errors. This can happen across time for a single series or across products in a single time bucket. A final consideration with MAPE is that it allocates equal weight to each period. In other words, it is scale dependent. This is fine when measuring error across periods of time, but not for measuring error across SKUs for one period of time. For example, when measuring mean forecast error across a group of items for a given period of time, say, March 2016, you need to consider using a method that accounts for each item's proportional weight to the total.

An innovative method that addresses the issue of scale dependence is called weighted absolute percentage error (WAPE), which is sometimes referred to as weighted MAPE (WMAPE). It is preferred over MAPE because it accounts for each product's contribution to the total error by weighting the impact of the individual item value of each product within the group as it is related to the total. As you can see in Table 5.1, if we were measuring SKU accuracy for a given point in

Table 5.1 Example of SKU Demand Metrics for a Large Company

(1)	(2)	(3)	(4)	(5)	(6)	(7)	(8)
SKUs	Sales ($0 00)	Forecast	% Attainment	Error	Absolute Error	Absolute Percentage Error	Weighted Absolute Percentage Error
t	A_t	F_t	$A_t/F_t \times 100$	$A_t - F_t$	$|A_t - F_t|$	$\dfrac{|A_t - F_t|}{A_t} \times 100$	$\sum(|A_t - F_t|) \div \sum(A_t) \times 100$
P1	10	10	100	0	0	0.0%	0.0%
P2	9	10	90	−1	1	11.1	11.1
P3	20	18	111	2	2	10.0	7.7
P4	40	35	114	5	5	12.5	10.1
P5	30	40	75	−10	10	33.3	16.5
P6	100	90	111	10	10	10.0	13.4
P7	10	20	50	−10	10	100.0	17.3
P8	7	11	64	−4	4	57.1	18.6
P9	13	7	186	6	6	46.2	20.1
P10	20	32	63	−12	12	60.0	23.2
Sum	259	273	94.98 [a]	−14	60	340.2	
Mean				−1.4	6.0 [9][b]	34.0 [10][c]	
Weighted							23.17 [d]

*Mean Absolute Deviation (MAD)
**Mean Absolute Percentage Error (MAPE)
***Weighted Absolute Percentage Error (WAPE)
****Forecast Attainment

130

time, each corresponding SKU would affect the outcome based only on its contribution or unit volume proportion within the group.

The actual formulation can be written as:

$$WAPE = \left[\sum_{t=1}^{n} |(A_t - F_t)| + \sum_{t=1}^{n} (A_t) \right] \times 100$$

Although WAPE is a good alternative to MAPE, it is only a small innovation in performance metrics. It doesn't address forecastability or process efficiency.

The commonality of these algebraic measures is that they all relate to the difference between the actual value and the forecasted value. As such, these measures have intuitive appeal in a business environment. Subsequently, if we are serious about increasing forecast accuracy, it is desirable for each of these measures to be close to zero. However, in reality, it is almost impossible to have zero error or 100 percent accuracy. Unfortunately, many companies tend to set forecast accuracy (error) targets too high, particularly in the initial stages of implementation. For example, once they establish actual accuracy (error) across the organization, which might range from 50 to 100 percent error, they immediately set their accuracy targets at 25 to 35 percent error based on benchmarking surveys published in forecasting journals or established by other companies in the same industry vertical. Such accuracy levels may be unattainable, given the nature of their demand patterns. The first step is to establish the current forecast error and then set an improvement percentage of, say, 5 to 10 percent in the first year rather than setting an arbitrary target that may not be achievable.

WHY IN-SAMPLE/OUT-OF-SAMPLE MEASUREMENT IS SO IMPORTANT

Another performance metric rarely used or discussed is when fitting models to actual demand historical data (e.g., fitting a mathematical model to the actual demand history to determine how well the model will forecast). The model may fit very well (low error) but do a terrible job forecasting actual demand. In other words, a model that fits actual demand history with an error close to zero does not imply that it will do a good job forecasting future demand. This problem can be remedied by measuring true in-sample/out-of-sample forecast error. Out-of-sample measurement starts by separating your demand history into two data sets: an initial modeling set, also known as the in-sample data set, and a test data set, or out-of-sample data set (holdout periods).

The modeling in-sample data set is used to estimate any parameters (e.g., trend, seasonality, cycles, and/or relationship factors) and initialize the method. Then you create and compare demand forecasts against the out-of-sample test data set.

Since the test data set was not used as part of the model-fitting initialization using the in-sample data set, these forecasts are actual projections created without using the values of the observations. The error calculations are measured only for the out-of-sample test data set. For example, if you have 156 weekly periods of demand history, you may decide to hold out the most current 13 weeks of history as your out-of-sample test data set and fit your model to the oldest 143 weekly periods. Then you would forecast the 13 most recent periods, comparing the forecasts to the out-of-sample test data set to see how well the model is forecasting. This method provides a better reflection of how well a statistical model is able to forecast demand.

Using a consumer product data set of roughly 156 weeks (data points), we can create an out-of-sample data set using the most current 13 weeks, and then use a Holt-Winters exponential smoothing method to model the in-sample data set. We can then forecast out against the out-of-sample test data set so that we can compare the forecasts to actual demand to see how well the model is forecasting. In Figure 5.1, we see that the model fitted MAPE to the in-sample data set is 15.10 percent on average, and the out-of-sample data set MAPE is 17.19 percent on average. As you can see, the out-of-sample (or holdout) data set has a higher MAPE than the in-sample data set. This is not unusual.

Table 5.2 details the out-of-sample error for this consumer product data set using the latest 13 weeks of demand history as the out-of-sample test data set. Although the average forecast error is 17.19 percent across the 13-week out-of-sample test data set, there are periods in which the error is much higher. The actual error ranges from 1 percent to as high as 34 percent. However, all but three weekly predictions are within the upper/lower limits at a 95 percent

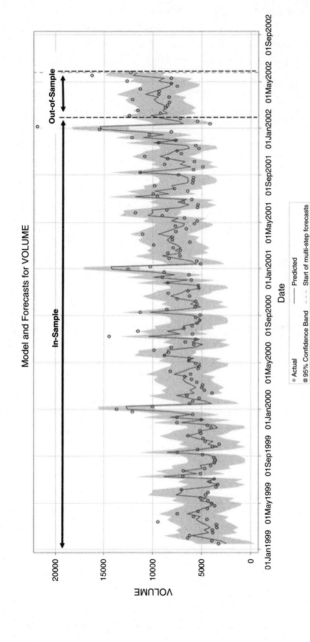

Figure 5.1 In-sample/out-of-sample test for forecast accuracy.

133

Table 5.2 In-Sample/Out-of-Sample Weekly Actuals versus Forecast

Holdout	Actual	Forecast	ME
Week 1	11516	9009	21.76
Week 2	8295	9132	10.09
Week 3	12083	9857	18.42
Week 4	8341	9482	13.67
Week 5	9416	10755	14.22
Week 6	9354	9845	5.24
Week 7	11283	10104	10.44
Week 8	7551	8293	9.82
Week 9	8125	8204	0.97
Week 10	12628	9421	25.39
Week 11	8129	8887	9.32
Week 12	16282	10957	32.70
Week 13	12269	16476	34.28
MAPE			**17.19**

confidence level (see Figure 5.1 graph areas above/below forecast for the 13-week out-of-sample data set), which is very good.

It is always best to view the out-of-sample error both graphically as well as in a table to see if there are any periods that are abnormally high or low, which indicates the need for additional relationship factors, such as intervention variables, to calculate sales promotion lifts, specific marketing events, and others. It is also very important to determine if any forecasts fall outside the upper/lower confidence limits. Those forecasts are critical in identifying unexplained error associated with possible relationship factors. Although they might be due purely to randomness, those higher-than-normal errors usually are associated with an event like a sales promotion—in this case, possibly a sales promotion, marketing event, or other related factors.

Conducting an out-of-sample test is essential for determining the likely accuracy of a quantitative method. The statistical fit to the in-sample data set alone is not enough to determine the value of the method, as the in-sample fit may have little relationship to the accuracy of its future forecasts. It is also good practice to use 13 periods (a quarter) or more as your out-of-sample test data set for weekly data and a minimum of 156 periods for weekly data for your in-sample data set. Using three complete annual cycles will allow you to see how well the method predicts seasonality, trend, cycles, and other relationship factors. You should have at least 36 monthly, or 156 weekly periods of demand history for your in-sample data set. Three complete years of historical demand are recommended to truly capture the effects of seasonality. However, you can capture seasonality with only two years (24 months or 104 weeks) of historical demand. Three years is preferable unless it is not available. Otherwise, two years will be sufficient. Also, providing an upper/lower range for predicted values is more important than a single point estimate of forecasted demand. At a 95 percent confidence level, 19 out of 20 of your forecasts should be within the upper/lower confidence limits. Always provide upper/lower confidence limits with all your forecasts, so the upstream planning functions can utilize the ranges to determine safety stock and other plans for possible swings in demand. Some feel a 95 percent confidence level may be too tight (less realistic), and might recommend lowering the confidence limit to 90 percent to provide a more realistic upper/lower range. In that case, the upper/lower range would be greater, thus protecting against larger variations in demand.

FORECASTABILITY

The topic of forecastability is becoming the focal point for many articles and research as companies are realizing that not all their products are forecastable, given the data constraints and variability in demand. As more companies begin to deploy more statistically based methodologies, they are quickly realizing that you cannot push a forecast "Easy" button and obtain immediate forecast accuracy within an 85 to 95 percentage range.

In most cases, forecast accuracy is less than 50 percent. As a result, companies are asking themselves what is forecastable and what is not. In addition, they want to know how they can segment their products to get the most accuracy across the product portfolio. The best way to answer this question is to conduct an assessment of the data to determine if there are any forecastable patterns, assess the degree of accuracy when forecasting a given time series, and estimate the expected range of error when deploying basic time series methods.

According to Mike Gilliland (author of *The Business Forecasting Deal*), using the coefficient of variation (CV) to measure forecastability is a quick-and-easy way to make that determination in typical business forecasting situations. He suggests computing the CV based on sales for each data series being forecast over some time frame, such as the past year. He explains, if an item sells an average of 100 units per week, with a standard deviation of 50, then CV = standard deviation/mean = 0.5 (or 50 percent).

It is useful to create a scatter plot relating CV to forecast accuracy achieved. In Figure 5.2, the scatter plot of data for a consumer product, there are roughly 5,000 points representing 500 items sold through 10 distribution centers (DCs). Forecast accuracy (0 percent to 100 percent) is along the vertical axis, and CV (0 percent to 160 percent—truncated) is along the horizontal axis. As you would expect, with lower sales volatility (CV near 0), the forecast is generally much more accurate than for item/DC combinations with high volatility.[1]

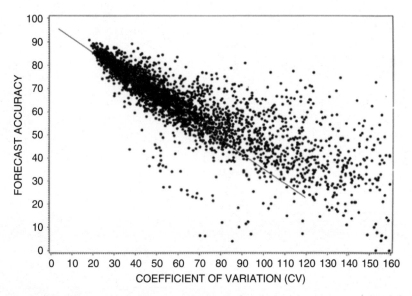

Figure 5.2 Coefficient of variation comparisons.[2]

The line through this scatter plot is not a best-fit regression line. It can be called the *forecast value added line*, and shows the approximate accuracy you would have achieved using a simple moving average as your forecast model for each value of CV. The way to interpret the graph is that for item/DC combinations falling above the FVA line, this organization's forecasting process was adding value by producing forecasts more accurate than would have been achieved by a moving average. Overall, this organization's forecasting process added four percentage points of value, achieving 68 percent accuracy versus 64 percent for the moving average. The plot also identifies plenty of instances where the process made the forecast less accurate (those points falling below the line), and these would merit further investigation. Such a scatter plot (and use of CV) doesn't answer the more difficult question—how accurate can we be? However, the surest way to get better forecasts is to reduce the volatility of the behavior you are trying to forecast. While we may not have any control over the volatility of our weather, we actually do have a lot of control over the volatility of demand for our products and services.

Why should a company consider forecastability when applying forecasting methods? Doesn't a company's technology solution conduct automatic diagnostics and apply the appropriate forecasting method? Experience dictates that all data are not the same. In fact, treating data the same may decrease the accuracy of the forecasts, as you might apply only one method across the product portfolio, not realizing that each group of products has different data patterns based on how they were sold and supported over the product life cycle. Applying methods prior to evaluating data might make the forecast difficult to understand and explain to senior management. In fact, using automatic *best pick* selection is not always the best approach.

FORECAST VALUE ADDED

Companies have been searching for a performance measurement that can effectively measure and improve the demand forecasting process, reduce cycle time, and minimize the number of touch points. The best approach a company can take is to implement a new methodology for measuring demand forecasting process performance and accuracy called forecast value added (FVA), or lean forecasting.

Forecast value added is a metric for evaluating the performance of each step and each participant in the forecasting process. FVA is simply the change in forecast accuracy before and after each touch point in the process based on any specific forecast performance measurement, such as percentage error (PE), absolute percentage error (APE), mean absolute percentage error (MAPE), or weighted absolute percentage error (WAPE).

FVA is measured by comparing the forecast accuracy before and after each touch point or activity in the demand forecasting and planning process to determine if that activity actually added any value to the accuracy of the demand forecast. Using the statistical baseline forecast as a standard or benchmark, companies should measure each touch point in the demand forecasting process, and compare it to the accuracy of the statistical baseline forecast. If the activity increases the accuracy of the statistical baseline forecast, then that activity should remain in the process. However, if the activity does not improve the accuracy of the statistical baseline forecast, it should be elimi-nated, or minimized (simplified), to reduce cycle time and resources, thereby improving forecast process efficiency (see Table 5.3). FVA is a common-sense approach that is easy to understand. The idea is really simple—it's just basic statistics. What are the results of doing something versus what would have been the results if you hadn't done anything? According to Mike Gilliland, FVA can be either positive or negative, telling you whether your efforts are adding value by making the forecast better, or whether you are making things worse. FVA analysis consists of a variety of methods that have been evolving through industry practitioners' applications around these new innovative performance metrics. It is the application of fundamental hypothesis testing to business forecasting.

H_0: YOUR FORECASTING PROCESS HAS NO EFFECT

FVA analysis attempts to determine whether forecasting process steps and participants are improving the forecast—or just making it less accu-rate. It is good practice to compare the statistical forecast to a naïve forecast, such as a random walk or seasonal random walk. Naïve fore-casts, in some situations, can be surprisingly difficult to beat; yet it is

Table 5.3 Performance Metrics Comparisons

Products	FORECASTS			Actual Demand (units)	APE		
	Statistical (units)	Marketing Adjustment (units)	Sr. Mgmt. Override (units)		Statistical	Marketing Override	Sales Override
Product Family X	1,831	2,030	2,675	1,993	8.1%	1.9%	34.2%
Product A	1,380	1,400	1,800	1,450	4.8%	3.4%	24.1%
Product B	228	320	400	290	21.4%	10.3%	37.9%
Product C	165	230	350	185	10.8%	24.3%	89.2%
Product D	58	80	125	68	14.7%	17.6%	83.8%
WAPE					**12.3%**	**12.7%**	

very important that the software and statistical modeler improve on the naïve model. If the software or modeler is not able to do this—and you aren't able to implement better software or improve the skills of the modeler—then just use the naïve model for the baseline forecast. A naïve forecast serves as the benchmark in evaluating forecasting process performance. Performance of the naïve model provides a reference standard for comparisons. In other words, is the forecasting process adding value by performing better than the naïve model?

FVA is consistent with a lean approach identifying and eliminating process waste, or non-value adding activities that should be eliminated from the process. Non-value adding resources should be redirected to more productive activities that add value to the company. However, the flaw is that we don't know whether these observed differences are real (i.e., are they a result of a step in the process?); they might be due to chance. This is another reason why a more rigorous statistical test is needed to identify the real differences. Table 5.4 illustrates the results of a typical demand forecasting process using FVA.

MAPE is the most popular forecasting performance metric; but by itself, it is not a legitimate metric for fully evaluating or comparing forecast performance. MAPE tells you the magnitude of your error, but it does not tell you anything about the forecastability of your demand. It does not tell you what error you should be able to achieve. Subsequently, MAPE, by itself, gives no indication of the efficiency of your

Table 5.4 An Example of an FVA Report[3]

Process Step (1)	MAPE (2)	Naïve (3)	Statistical (4)	Override (5)	Consensus (6)
Naïve	50%	–	–	–	–
Statistical Forecast	45%	5%	–	–	–
Analyst Override	40%	10%	5%	–	–
Consensus Forecast	35%	15%	10%	5%	–
Approved Forecast	40%	5%	5%	0%	–5%

Notes:

1. Column 2 gives MAPE of each set of forecasts. For example, 50% MAPE is of Naïve Forecasts, 45% of Statistical Forecasts, and so on.

2. Other columns give percentage point improvement made by one set of forecasts over the other. For example, Statistical Forecasts improved over the Analyst Override by 5 percentage points, and 10% over the Consensus Forecasts.

Table 5.5 Which Demand Forecasting Is More Accurate?[4]

Analyst	MAPE
A	20%
B	30%
C	40%

forecasting process. To understand these things, you need to use FVA analysis. FVA can also be used as a basis for performance comparison. Suppose you are a forecasting manager and have a bonus to give to your best forecast analyst. The traditional way to determine which analyst is best is to compare their forecast errors. Table 5.5 is based on this traditional analysis, which clearly indicates that Analyst A is the best forecaster and deserves the bonus. But is this traditional analysis the correct analysis?

What if we consider additional information about each analyst, and the types of products they are assigned to forecast. Although Analyst A had the lowest MAPE, the types of products that were assigned to him/her were steady-state (long-established mature) items, with some trend and seasonality, no promotional activity, no new items, and low demand variability. In fact, an FVA analysis might reveal that a naïve model could have forecast this type of demand with a MAPE of only 10 percent, but Analyst A only made the forecast less accurate (see Table 5.5). On the other hand, Analyst B had more difficult demand to forecast, with some added dynamics of promotional activities and new items that make forecasting even more challenging. FVA analysis reveals that Analyst B added no value compared to a naïve model, but he/she did not make the forecast less accurate. What this FVA analysis reveals is that Analyst C deserves the bonus. Even though Analyst C had the highest MAPE of 40 percent, he/she actually had very difficult items to forecast—short life cycle fashion items with lots of promotional activity and high demand variability. Only Analyst C actually added value compared to a naïve model, by making the forecast more accurate than a naïve model.

This simple example reveals another factor to be wary of in traditional performance comparison, as you see in published forecasting benchmarks. Don't compare yourself or your company to what others are doing. The company that achieves best-in-class forecast accuracy may be best because it has demand data that are easier to forecast, not because its process is worthy of admiration. Also, you can't compare model fit indices for models based on different underlying data. The proper comparison is your performance versus a naïve model. If you are doing better than a naïve model, then that is good. And if you or your process is doing worse than a naïve model, then you have some challenges to overcome.

The FVA approach is meant to be objective and analytical, so you must be careful not to draw conclusions unwarranted by the data. For example, measuring FVA over one week or one month is just not enough data to draw any valid conclusions. Period to period, FVA will go up and down, and over short periods of time, FVA may be particularly high or low just due to randomness and/or variability of the data. When you express the results in a table, as shown in Table 5.6, be sure to indicate the time frame reported, and make sure that the time range has enough historical points to provide meaningful results.

The best results would occur with a full year of data from which to draw conclusions. If you've been thoroughly tracking inputs to the forecasting process already, then you probably have the data you need to do the analysis immediately. You should consider computing FVA with the last year of statistical forecasts, analyst overrides, consensus forecasts, executive approved forecasts, and actuals. Naïve models are always easy to reconstruct for the past, so you can measure how well a naïve model would have done with your data from the past year. While a full year of historical data is nice, if you are just starting to collect forecast data, you may not have to wait a full year to draw conclusions. Graphical presentation of the data, using methods from statistical process control, can be a big help in getting started with FVA. However, a thorough and ongoing FVA analysis will require the ability to capture the forecast of each participant in the process at every touch point (or step), for all of your item and location combinations, in every period. This will quickly grow into a very large amount of data to store and maintain, so companies will need software with sufficient scalability and capability. This is definitely not something you can do in Excel.

Table 5.6 Performance Metrics Comparisons

Analyst	Item Type	Item Life Cycle	Seasonality?	Promotions?	New Items?	Demand Volatility	MAPE	MAPE (Naïve Forecast)	FVA
A	Basic	Long	No	None	None	Low	20%	10%	–10%
B	Basic	Long	Some	Few	Few	Medium	30%	30%	0%
C	Fashion	Short	High	Many	Many	Hight	40%	50%	10%

143

FVA is truly an innovation in business forecasting that is being widely accepted as part of a company's standard performance metrics. The FVA performance metrics are a proven way to identify waste in the forecasting process, thus improving efficiency and reducing cycle time. By identifying and eliminating the non-value-adding activities, FVA provides a means and justification for streamlining the forecasting process, thereby making the forecast more accurate.

SUMMARY

Measuring forecast performance is critical to improving the overall efficiency and value of the demand forecasting process. There are two distinct purposes for measuring forecast accuracy: (1) to measure how well we predicted the actual occurrence or outcome, and (2) to compare different statistical models to determine which one fits (models) the demand history of a product and best predicts the future outcome. The methods (e.g., MAE, MPE, MAPE, and WAPE) used to calculate forecast error are interchangeable for measuring the performance of a statistical model, as well as the accuracy of the prediction.

When it comes to fitting a model to the actual historical data, the model may fit very well (low MAPE), but do a terrible job forecasting actual demand. In other words, the fact that a model fits actual demand history with an error close to zero does not mean that it will do a good job forecasting future demand. This problem can be remedied by measuring true out-of-sample forecast error. This is a more meaningful test of how well a statistical model can predict demand. Finally, FVA measures the change in forecast accuracy before and after each touch point in the demand forecasting process to determine if that activity actually added any value to the accuracy of the demand forecast.

The primary purpose for measuring forecast accuracy is not only to measure how well we predicted the actual occurrence but also to understand why the outcome occurred. Only by documenting the design, specifications, and assumptions that went into the forecast can we begin to learn the dynamics associated with the item(s) we are trying to predict. Forecast measurement should be a learning process, not just a tool to evaluate performance. You cannot improve forecast accuracy unless you measure it. You must establish a benchmark by measuring current forecast performance before you can establish a target for improvement. However, tracking forecast error alone is not the solution. Instead of only asking the question, "What is this month's forecast error?" we also need to ask, "Why has forecast error been tracking so high (or low) and is the process improving?"

The results in any single month may be due purely to randomness. You should not jump to conclusions or even spend time trying to explain a single period's variation. Rather, you should be reviewing the performance of the process over time and determining whether you are reducing error. Ongoing documentation of the specifics that went into each forecast is actually more important if you are truly dedicated to improving your forecast performance. Unfortunately, as forecast practitioners, we will always be judged based on forecast error or accuracy alone.

KEY LEARNINGS

- You cannot improve your forecast accuracy until you measure and benchmark your current forecast performance.
- Most companies only measure forecast accuracy at the aggregate (highest) level of the product hierarchy, with little attention to the lower-level mix.
  - The most important level of the product hierarchy to measure forecast error is at the lower-level mix.
- The two most discussed topics today in demand forecasting are forecastability and process performance (efficiency).
- The most common performance metric used across all industry verticals is MAPE (mean absolute percentage error).
- An innovative method that has become popular to address the issue of scale dependence is called weighted absolute percentage error (WAPE), which is sometimes referred to as weighted MAPE (WMAPE).
- Using in-sample/out-of-sample model testing is the best way to determine the forecastability of a mathematical model.

- FVA (forecast value added) is truly an innovation in business forecasting that is being widely accepted as part of a company's standard performance metrics.

- FVA is a performance measurement that can effectively measure and improve the demand forecasting process, reduce cycle time, and minimize the number of touch points in the process.

- FVA is consistent with a lean approach identifying and eliminating process waste, or non-value-adding activities that should be eliminated from the process.

NOTES

1. Michael, Gilliland. 2010, *The Business Forecasting Deal: Exposing Myths, Eliminating Bad Practices, Providing Practical Solutions* (New York: John Wiley & Sons, 2010), pp. 1–266.
2. Ibid.
3. Ibid.
4. Ibid.

FURTHER READING

"Innovations in Business Forecasting," *Journal of Business Forecasting* 33, no. 1 (Spring 2014), pp. 29–34.

Chase, Charles W. Jr., *Demand-Driven Forecasting: A Structured Approach to Forecasting*, 2nd ed. (Hoboken, NJ: John Wiley & Sons), pp. 1–360.

Gilliland, Michael, "Is Forecasting a Waste of Time?" *Supply Chain Management Review* (July/August 2002), pp. 16–23.

CHAPTER **6**

The Analytics

I f the demand planners (or demand analysts) at your company are using advanced statistical models like ARIMA, ARIMAX, and dynamic regression using causal factors (i.e., price, intervention variables to capture sales promotion lifts, and outliers, along with other causal factors), then you are among a handful of companies that are doing true demand-driven forecasting and planning using advanced statistical modeling. It is amazing that in 2016, according to an *Industry Week* study, 77 percent of demand forecasters still use Excel, and the number one mathematical method being deployed is moving averaging.[1] This is embarrassing to say the least for demand forecasting and planning. With all the data collection, processing, and technology advancements over the past two decades, companies would rather use buffer inventory stock to protect against demand variability than invest in new skills, analytics, and technology to improve their demand management process. In fact, companies are still cleansing their demand history manually to separate baseline and promoted volume due to the restrictions of their legacy ERP systems as a result of the limited array of statistical methods (moving averaging and exponential smoothing methods) available in their model repositories. Those methods can only model patterns associated with trend, seasonality, and cycles.

As we discussed in Chapter 3, companies can holistically model the baseline trend, seasonality, correct for outliers, and model the effects of price and sales promotions using ARIMAX and dynamic regression models without cleansing the historical data. Furthermore, we can do it automatically up/down a company's business hierarchy for hundreds of thousands of products by geography, market, channel, brand, product group, product, SKU, demand point, and key account (customer).

UNDERLYING FUNDAMENTS OF STATISTICAL MODELS

When it comes to quantitative methods, it is not that difficult to predict or forecast the continuation of an established pattern or relationship. The difficulty is forecasting change related to a specific pattern or relationship, the timing of the change, and the magnitude of the change. This is the real test of a forecasting method and/or process. Although both quantitative and judgment methods operate based on the principles of identifying existing patterns and relationships, the real difference lies in the method by which information is captured, prepared, and processed. Quantitative methods require systems to access, store, and synchronize information (data). Then, using mathematical equations (models), they identify and model those patterns and relationships. Once the patterns are identified and quantified, the quantitative methods can predict the changes in those patterns and relationships. This is written algebraically as:

$$\text{Forecast} = \text{Pattern(s)} + \text{Randomness}$$

This simple equation shows that when the average pattern of the underlying data has been identified, some deviation will occur between the forecasting method applied and the actual occurrence. That deviation is called *randomness,* or unexplainable variance. The objective is to maximize the ability to identify patterns and minimize the unexplained variance. Given this is the true nature of this simple equation, we can rewrite it as:

$$\text{Forecast} = \text{Pattern(s)} + \text{Unexplained Variance}$$

When it comes to ways of identifying patterns and predicting those patterns into the future, most methods determine patterns as four specific elements: trend, seasonality, cycle, and randomness (or unexplained variance). The identification of past patterns over time is called *time series analysis.* This means that the patterns are directly associated with the passing of time.

We can rewrite our forecasting equation to:

$$\text{Forecast} = \text{Trend}_{t-1} + \text{Seasonality}_{t-1} + \text{Cycle}_{t-1}$$
$$+ \text{Unexplained Variance}$$

where $t = $ time

Figure 6.1 is an example of time series components of a CPG product identified using a statistical times series model to identify trend, seasonality, cycle, and irregular (or unexplained randomness) patterns.

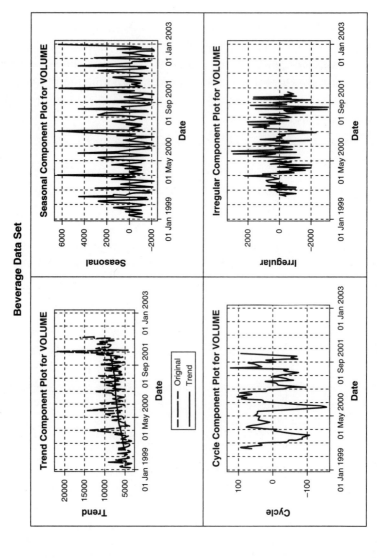

Figure 6.1 Three key times series components and unexplained randomness (or irregular component).

Figure 6.1 indicates that there is definitely a trend associated with these data, and it is positive. However, the trend has slowed slightly over time and appears to be accelerating in recent periods (see the upper-left-hand trend plot). There is also a significant amount of seasonality associated with this data set (see the upper-right-hand seasonality plot), with December being a key seasonal period as well as April, June, July, and September. There is some possible cyclical influence, but it is not consistent from year to year (see the lower left-hand cycle plot). Finally, there is a consistent amount of irregular (or unexplained) randomness that is not being explained by the trend, seasonality, and cycle components. The irregular component could be related to some other relationship (influence) factors, such as price, advertising, sales promotions, and/or competitor activities (see the lower-right-hand irregular plot). Or, as is often the case, the irregular component could be due simply to randomness. When the trend is removed from the data, the seasonality, cycle, and irregular components (unexplained variance) become much more apparent when plotted. This finding will be critical when applying more sophisticated quantitative methods.

In contrast, the identification of relationships is generally associated with causal impacts that occur over the passage of time, where a change in a particular factor directly affects the demand for the item forecasted. Adding causal factors to our model may explain away some, or a large percentage, of the unexplained variance. We can rewrite our equation to accommodate those causal factors that can further enhance our ability to predict the outcome of demand. By doing so, our forecasting equation now becomes:

$$\text{Forecast} = \text{Trend}_{t-1} + \text{Seasonality}_{t-1} + \text{Cycle}_{t-1} + \text{Causal Factor(s)}_{t-1}$$
$$+ \text{Unexplained Variance}$$

The most significant advantage that quantitative methods provide is their ability to sense and predict demand based on those fundamental elements that tend to make up demand over time, such as trend, seasonality, cycle, and unexplained randomness, in a very objective and systematic manner. Furthermore, trend, seasonality, and cycle components can be modeled and extrapolated with a relatively high degree of accuracy. Although randomness by definition translates to unpredictability, it can be isolated, measured, and summarized to determine the degree of variance in the predictions. In other words, unexplained randomness helps to identify not only uncertainty but also the amount of demand (or variance) that is not being explained by the trend, seasonality, and cyclical elements. If the unexplained randomness is high, then it makes sense to identify, collect, and integrate relationship or influence (or causal) factors to explain away the high level of variance. However, doing this requires more advanced forecasting methods, such as dynamic regression, autoregressive integrated moving average (ARIMA), and autoregressive integrated moving average with causal variables (ARIMAX).

Judgmental methods are not as robust as quantitative methods when it comes to sensing and predicting the trend, seasonality, and cycle elements, particularly across thousands of products in a business hierarchy, even when ample data exist and established patterns are constant over time. Unfortunately, judgmental techniques are still the most widely used forecasting methods in business today. Such methods are applied by individuals or committees in a consensus process to gain agreement and make decisions. Although many larger companies use quantitative methods on a limited basis, the vast majority of the inputs and adjustments (overrides) are conducted using judgment, rather than using what-if scenario analysis using quantitative methods.

Furthermore, judgmental methods tend to be biased toward the individual or committee developing the forecast. They are *not* consistently accurate over time due to the subjective nature of their development. In some cases, executives may not really understand the firm's sales situation, since they are too far removed from the actual marketplace. Finally, judgmental methods are generally not well suited for firms with a large number of products or stock-keeping units. In these situations, the scope of the forecasting task is simply too large. As a result, forecasts tend to be top-down, rather than bottom-up, or middle-out requiring labor-intensive disaggregation using Excel by the demand planning team.

Senior-level managers and forecast practitioners must realize and accept that there will always be some level of unexplained variance in the predictions generated by both quantitative and judgmental methods. Forecasting is not an exact science that can be estimated within a one-hundredth degree of tolerance, like other sciences. For example, we can predict the reentry of a spacecraft into the Earth's atmosphere within a few meters, but may only be able to predict the demand for a product within a ±25 percent error (or 75 percent accuracy). During the last two decades, quantitative methods have been proven to outperform judgmental methods in many cases due to their structured unbiased (objective) approach. Judgmental methods tend to add variance to statistical baseline forecasts due to the biased nature of the individuals applying their judgment. Experience indicates that the best way to integrate domain knowledge (judgment) into a demand forecast is by creating a hypothesis, locating and accessing the data, and conducting the analysis to validate or invalidate the hypothesis (assumptions). It has been proven that arbitrarily making judgmental overrides based on biased notions that somehow those adjustments will improve the accuracy of a quantitative forecast tends to not improve the accuracy.[2]

HOW PREDICTABLE IS THE FUTURE?

There are situations in which certain events with distinct patterns can be easily predicted with a high degree of accuracy over a time horizon, such as trend or seasonal patterns. Other situations are less predictable when using traditional trend, seasonality, and cyclical techniques to uncover patterns in the data. Nevertheless, these situations can be predicted using causal factors, such as price, advertising, sales promotions, or economic activities such as disposable income, consumer price index, and other related factors. However, in other cases, there may be very little data available, or the demand for the product is so random that it is completely unpredictable. Such cases often are the result of sporadic or intermittent demand caused by erratic ordering practices or other factors related to the product and/or marketplace. This situation occurs frequently in industries (such as automotive and appliances) that require service parts, as service part failures can appear to be random in nature. Here, too, over time you can begin to see distinct patterns related to certain part failures and use that information to predict future part replacements. Traditional time series methods such as exponential smoothing are not sophisticated enough to include causal factors. In these situations, more advanced methods are required, such as multiple linear regression and ARIMA models with intervention variables.

A prerequisite for all forms of forecasting, whether quantitative or judgmental, is that a pattern or relationship exists that can be identified and modeled (measured). Once modeled, we can project the pattern into the future, assuming the relationship will continue into the future. Each pattern or relationship must be correctly identified and measured before you can create a forecast. When such patterns or relationships do not exist, it is almost impossible to forecast, even with some prior assessment of past events using quantitative or judgmental methods. In some cases, the patterns and relationships coexist with random noise (unexplained variance) and can change unpredictably over time.

The primary cause of this unpredictability can be linked directly to human behavior, such as shifts in attitudes associated with trends in the marketplace and self-fulfilling prophecies related to human intervention that influence the outcomes or change the patterns and relationships. The longer the time horizon or sales history of a product or service, the greater the possibility a pattern or relationship can be observed, as human behavior and attitudes do change over time. There is also more time to adjust forecasts and shape demand using what-if analysis to achieve the desired results. Finally, a fundamental shift in the marketplace may occur that will change the entire market environment, such as a technology discovery like the introduction of digital photography. This is a revolutionary change with no historical time horizon that makes it almost impossible to predict prior to its introduction.

Contrast the introduction of digital photography with the introduction of an ice cream flavor like slow churned chocolate ice cream, which is actually evolutionary (line extension). In this situation, we can use chocolate ice cream as a surrogate or like product using its historical time horizons to forecast the introduction of slow churned chocolate ice cream. Simply stated, revolutionary new products are the hardest to predict, as there are no historical patterns or relationships to identify, measure, and predict the outcome.

Fortunately, based on prior experience, roughly 85 to 95 percent of new product launches are evolutionary, including product line extensions, which allow forecasters to borrow the launch history of like products or surrogates to forecast the new product. Granted, there will always be minor differences, but those differences can be adjusted using domain knowledge and other causal factors that can affect the launch, such as sales promotions and marketing support activities.

Some general factors can systematically affect or influence the fore-castability of any product or group of products: size or volume of the forecast, data aggregation, data stability, and competitiveness.

Size or Volume of the Forecast

For example, the larger the amount of an item's volume you are fore-casting, the lower the unexplained variance in comparison to the actual volume being forecasted, thus the lower the error. The statistical law of large numbers tells us that the size of the forecasting error decreases as the number or size of the item's volume being forecast increases. The opposite occurs as the number of items or size decrease.

For example, if we forecast 1,000 and sell 900, our error is 100, which is a 10 percent error (or 90 percent accuracy rate). Subse-quently, if we forecast 10 and sell 5, our variance is 5, but our forecast accuracy is 50 percent. Although the size of the variance and the actual volume are small, the error increased significantly. The reverse occurs when the volume forecasted is large. Although variances may be large, they are offset by the sheer size of the volume, thus reducing the error.

Given the statistical law of large numbers, it is more accurate to forecast the demand for the number of 8-ounce servings of carbon-ated soft drinks sold in a week than it is to forecast the number of service repair parts needed to service failures in the field for a partic-ular appliance in a week. The sheer number of 8-ounce servings is in the millions compared to the service repair parts, which are in the hun-dreds. Percentage error is more relevant for business purposes as it is unit independent and more scale dependent, making it more appeal-ing. It is true that percentage error can explode when dealing with very small (or zero) volumes. It is still more practical to use percentages, but with the understanding that the percent error associated with smaller numbers tends to skew the error.

Aggregation of Data

The more aggregated the data, the more accurate the forecasts, and the less aggregated the data, the less accurate the forecasts. In other words, it is more accurate to predict the trend or seasonality across a multiple of products or regions aggregated (summed) than to predict trend and seasonality across individual products or regions. For example, forecasting demand for a particular consumer product in the grocery channel in a specific demographic area of a region could be more challenging than trying to predict the demand for several consumer products aggregated to the brand level within an entire channel (e.g., grocery, mass merchandising, drug, gas and convenience, or wholesale club) for all demographic areas, as each channel and demographic market may be too granular with a lot of outliers, causing higher unexplained variance. Yet combining channels in market areas could distort the trend and seasonality associated with those individual channels and market areas. However, aggregating products within those channels and market areas almost always improves the ability to model and predict trend and seasonality.

Demand Stability

In some cases, the more stable or inelastic demand for the item being forecast, the more accurate the forecast. For example, the demand for lower-priced living necessities that are purchased regularly can be forecast with a higher degree of accuracy than the demand for luxury items that are less frequently purchased. In other words, milk and bread, which are necessities, have more stable historical demand patterns associated with the buying patterns of consumers, making it easier to predict future demand. The demand for premium cookies that are purchased less frequently is more difficult to forecast, as these cookies have less priority (or are purchased less frequently), creating a less stable demand history. The more stable the data with consistent purchasing patterns, the more accurate the forecasts, and the less stable the data, the more inaccurate the forecasts.

Cycles also play into the stability of demand. Luxury items tend to be more sensitive to cycle changes as people prioritize their purchases during downturns and tend to spend more on luxury items during upturns, when they have more disposable income. Those items that are less stable during downturns are harder to predict, as they are very elastic (or sensitive) to changes in business cycles and other influencing factors. More stable products, such as milk and bread, are less sensitive to cycles, as consumers consider them necessities, making them easier to forecast.

Competitiveness of the Environment

It is more difficult to predict demand in highly competitive environments because competitors influence the demand patterns, which compromises the forecaster's ability to sense and predict demand due to the unstable nature of the marketplace.

IMPORTANCE OF SEGMENTATION OF YOUR PRODUCTS

Forecast practitioners developing demand forecasts on a large scale across their company's product portfolio can choose from among all the forecasting methods available in their demand forecasting systems (e.g., exponential smoothing—nonseasonal and seasonal, ARIMA, ARIMAX, or dynamic regression). Unfortunately, all of these methods are not equally effective for any given situation. When forecasting on a large scale, demand planners need to consider segmenting brands and products based on their value to the company, the availability of data and information, and forecastability. *Forecastability* is the measure of the degree to which something may be forecast with accuracy.

Forecast practitioners must assess and segment their product portfolio and apply the appropriate forecasting methods in conjunction with one another to achieve the optimal performance across the entire product portfolio. Unfortunately, many forecasting solutions and practitioners use one methodology to forecast all their products, resulting in poor performance, rather than applying the appropriate method(s) in concert with one another depending on the situation and availability of data and information, as well as forecastability.

The topic of forecastability is becoming the focal point for many articles and research as companies are realizing that not all their products are forecastable, given the data constraints and variability in demand. As more companies begin to deploy more statistically based methodologies, they are quickly realizing that you cannot push a forecast easy button and get immediate forecast accuracy within 85–95 percent. In many cases, the forecast accuracy is less than 70 percent. As a result, companies are asking themselves what is forecastable and what is not, and how can they segment their products to get the most accuracy across their product portfolio. The best way to answer the question of forecastability is to conduct an assessment of the data to determine if there are any forecastable patterns, assess the degree of accuracy when forecasting a given time series, and estimate the expected range of error when deploying basic time series methods.

Why should a company consider forecastability when applying forecasting methods? Doesn't a company's demand forecasting system conduct automatic diagnostics and apply the appropriate forecasting method? Experience dictates that all data are not the same. In fact, treating data the same may decrease the accuracy of the forecasts, as you might apply only one method across the product portfolio, not realizing that each group of products has different data patterns, based on how they were sold and supported over the product's life cycle. Applying methods prior to evaluating data may make the forecast difficult to understand and explain to senior management. In fact, using automatic best pick selection is not always the best approach. A good example is when demand planners cleanse the historical demand history of a product; they cleanse not only the sales promotional lifts but also the seasonality. The result: Their ERP system demand management module only picks moving averaging and nonseasonal exponential smoothing models. If the data are not cleansed, the statistical forecasting engine using best pick selection might have selected seasonal exponential models for over 80 percent of the products. This may improve forecast accuracy by as much as 10 percent on average across their product portfolio. In addition, periodic evaluations should be conducted to ensure that the best method is being applied to the data. The best place to start is decomposing each data set by product group or brand to identify and determine the magnitude of trend, seasonality, cyclical, and unexplained variance.

It is important to establish the level and magnitude of the four core patterns to determine whether there is a need to introduce additional causal factors (data) and information.

Time series analysis can provide the understanding required to uncover demand patterns. When segmenting demand to determine what methods are appropriate for brand, product group, and product efforts, you should focus on four key areas:

1. Low value, low forecastability
2. Low value, high forecastability
3. High value, low forecastability
4. High value, high forecastability

It is important to highlight demand inconsistencies and identify appropriate time series forecasting technique(s). It is also important to educate senior managers in the company on forecast accuracy expectations based on data availability, value set by the company, and method chosen. When evaluating forecast data, we look at two key factors: (1) value to the company and (2) forecastability. Let us take this conceptual design further and consider a company's product portfolio as falling into four quadrants:

1. *Slow-moving* products with fragmented data across targeted markets and consumers.

2. *New products* with little historical sales data (revolutionary new products) or with similarities with existing products (evolutionary products or line extensions). Also, short life-cycle products like fashion jeans, which normally have six-month life cycles.

3. *Fast-moving* products that are highly correlated to sales and marketing causal factors, requiring the collection of causal data and information.

4. *Steady-state* products with long stable historical demand with distinct time series patterns.

A company can begin to segment its products to determine how forecastable they are and what methods it should apply, given the strategies surrounding each brand based on market dynamics associated with consumer buying habits, competitive activities, and others.

Figure 6.2 expands on the four segment areas using product portfolio management principles to help define each product segment.

Slow-Moving Products

The slow-moving products quadrant in the lower left-hand corner of Figure 6.2 represents those brands and products that are offered in smaller regional niche markets and in some cases specialty brands and products target specific consumers based on age, gender, ethnicity, and/or socioeconomic status. Specialty brands can also target non-traditional retail channels, such as the Internet. These products are sometimes used to maintain specific consumers who may otherwise leave the franchise if the specialty products are discontinued. Although many specialty products have low volumes, they are almost always profitable. They normally have fairly extensive demand history but in some situations have very little seasonality and virtually no cyclical patterns that can be modeled using traditional forecasting methods. Due to the nature of specialty products, demand can have high unexplained variance requiring more information regarding causal factors to explain away the unexplained variance. However, causal factors may not be available or collected due to the limited investment by companies in collecting the data and information, particularly if the specialty product is sold in nontraditional retail channels. In recent years, there has been more investment in collecting demand data and information from the Internet to help improve the forecast accuracy of specialty products.

New Products

The new products quadrant in the upper-left-hand corner of Figure 6.2 can be broken down into three subcategories: (1) line extensions or evolutionary new products, (2), new product introductions that are revolutionary, and (3) short-life-cycle products.

Evolutionary New Products

Line extensions on average represent about 5 to 10 percent of a company's product portfolio and account for about 95 percent of all

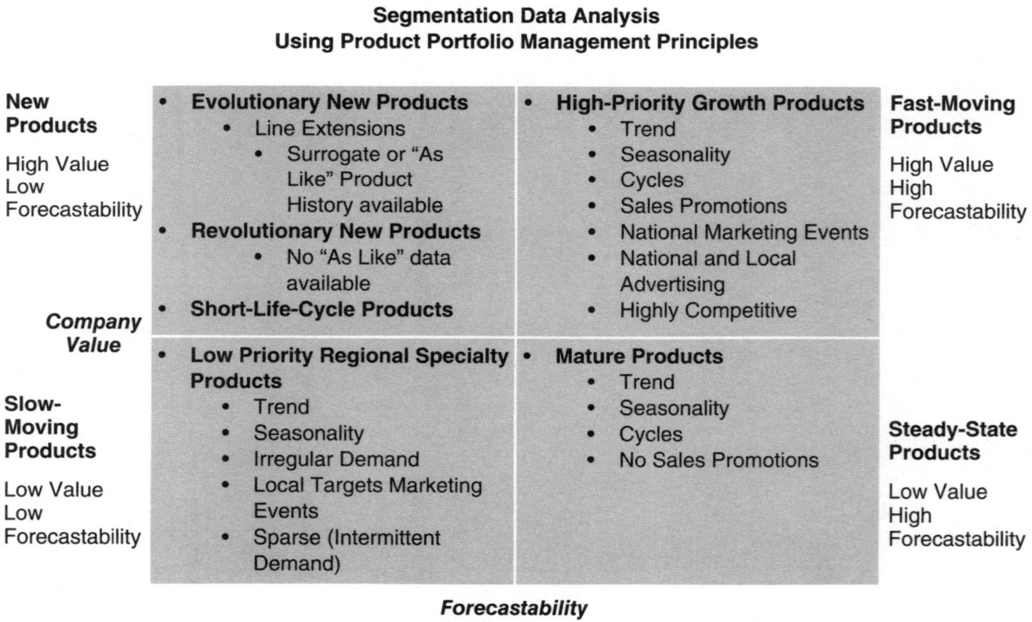

Segmentation Data Analysis
Using Product Portfolio Management Principles

New Products

High Value
Low Forecastability

- **Evolutionary New Products**
  - Line Extensions
    - Surrogate or "As Like" Product
    - History available
- **Revolutionary New Products**
  - No "As Like" data available
- **Short-Life-Cycle Products**

Fast-Moving Products

High Value
High Forecastability

- **High-Priority Growth Products**
  - Trend
  - Seasonality
  - Cycles
  - Sales Promotions
  - National Marketing Events
  - National and Local Advertising
  - Highly Competitive

Company Value

Slow-Moving Products

Low Value
Low Forecastability

- **Low Priority Regional Specialty Products**
  - Trend
  - Seasonality
  - Irregular Demand
  - Local Targets Marketing Events
  - Sparse (Intermittent Demand)

Steady-State Products

Low Value
High Forecastability

- **Mature Products**
  - Trend
  - Seasonality
  - Cycles
  - No Sales Promotions

Forecastability

Figure 6.2 Four segmentation quadrants using product portfolio management principles.

the new product launches. These products usually are associated with existing brands and can be affiliated with past line extensions. As such, they can be forecasted using like products or surrogates. Using data-mining techniques and analysis, the forecast practitioner can mine internal and/or external data for like products based on similar attributes and characteristics. This is referred to as *structured judgment*. The uptake or launch curves (data) can be used to forecast the line extension. Additional causal factors can be added to determine the magnitude and degree of the demand velocity for the new product during the initial 4 to 13 weeks of the launch. As actual demand is captured it can be used to adjust the forecasts. Once enough demand history is established, the new product line extension can be forecast using its own past demand history.

Revolutionary New Products

These new products create new markets and brand segments that did not exist prior to the launch, such as digital photography. In many cases, the new product represents breakthrough technology that changes the landscape and dynamics of current markets and industry verticals. Unfortunately, there is no like product or surrogate data available to predict and forecast the demand for these new products. In most cases, it requires the creation of primary research data and the collection of information based on surveys, questionnaires, focus groups, and a great deal of domain knowledge and understanding regarding the product and the dynamics of the marketplace.

Short-Life-Cycle Products

Such products are prominent in the apparel industry with designer fashion clothing but can also occur in other industries where products are phased in/out of the marketplace on a regular basis. The historical demand for such products is usually less than a year and on average six months, particularly with fashion-designer clothing. However, these new products can be handled in the same way line extensions are forecast, using like products as surrogates. The difference is that the historical demand for the like products is very short, making it more difficult to sense seasonality and cyclical patterns.

Fast-Moving Products

The fast-moving products quadrant in the upper-right-hand corner of Figure 6.2 represents those brands and products that are designated as the primary growth engines of the business. These particular brands and products have the most potential for generating the needed unit volume and profit required to meet the company's short- and long-term objectives and shareholder targets. For the most part, there is enough demand history to uncover trends, seasonality, and some indications of cyclical patterns. However, there is a great deal of unexplained variance in the data as a result of all the sales and marketing activities being deployed. These activities enhance seasonality with sales promotions, and influence the trend with other various marketing activities such as advertising, merchandising vehicles, and retailer incentives. Although it is fairly easy to sense trend and seasonal patterns, they tend to have high degrees of variance as the manufacturers are enhancing the seasonality with other programming, such as sales promotions. In these situations, influence or causal factors are required to explain away the high unexplained variance.

Steady-State Products

Finally, the steady-state products quadrant in the lower-right-hand corner of Figure 6.2 represents those products that have been designated as high profit and low growth. They have established trends and seasonality, and have been sold for years providing long demand histories with distinctive trend, seasonality, and cyclical patterns that can be easily modeled and forecast. Although steady-state products are not considered fast-moving products they deliver consistent profit year after year, which is transferred to fund the sales and marketing efforts to drive incremental volume and profit for fast-moving products.

Understanding the strengths and limitations of quantitative and qualitative forecasting methods, we can plot forecasting methods into quadrants accordingly, as shown in Figure 6.3. We can use a combination of data mining, clustering, statistical, and judgmental methods for the new products quadrant; moving averaging, sales force composites, and intermittent demand methods for the slow-moving products quadrant; causal methods for the fast-moving products quadrant, and time series methods (e.g., exponential smoothing methods) for the steady-state products quadrant. We diagnose and segment our products based on the four quadrants, and then match appropriate forecasting methods to address our forecasting needs. Now we can apply the forecasting methods to the products with the best class of methods, thus improving our ability to forecast those products more accurately. As can be seen, given the diversity of our product portfolio, multiple forecasting methods will be required to accurately predict demand for our brands and products (see Figure 6.3).

Now we have a segmentation format to plot our brands and products in the corresponding quadrants and apply the appropriate methods to determine what data resources will be required to maximize our forecast accuracy across our product portfolio.

Although we can use time series methods to segment our demand history for a brand or product into trend, seasonality, cycles, and unexplained randomness, we still need more sophisticated methods, such as causal models (e.g., ARIMA, ARIMAX, multiple regression), to address the unexplained patterns. Simple time series methods cannot model relationships with causal factors. Causal factors (e.g., price, advertising, sales promotions, marketing activities, competitive activities, etc.) should be introduced to explain away the majority of unexplained variance to minimize the error. By segmenting products based on the four quadrants related to product portfolio management, those brands and products that require more sophisticated methods can be isolated, and relationship factors can be identified to explain away the unexplained variance resulting in improved forecast accuracy.

Finally, it has been found that on average 10 percent of a company's product portfolio falls in the slow-moving product quadrant, 5 percent in the new product quadrant, 35 percent in the fast-moving product quadrant, and 50 percent in the steady-state product quadrant (see Figure 6.4). This means we can forecast close to 50 percent of a company's product portfolio using simple time series methods, like Holt-Winters Three-Parameter Exponential Smoothing, ARIMA, and others. Thus, we can automate a large percentage of the company's product portfolio. This frees up a demand analyst's time to focus on the 35 percent fast-moving products with more sophisticated methods like ARIMA, ARIMAX, and multiple regression.

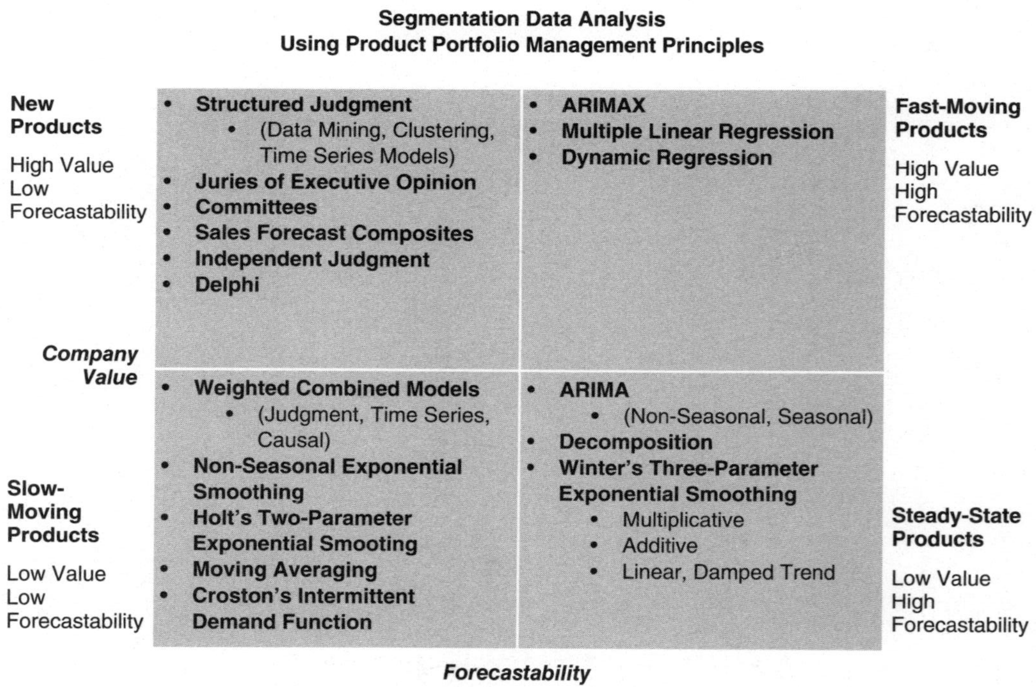

Segmentation Data Analysis
Using Product Portfolio Management Principles

New Products
High Value
Low Forecastability

- **Structured Judgment**
  - (Data Mining, Clustering, Time Series Models)
- **Juries of Executive Opinion Committees**
- **Sales Forecast Composites**
- **Independent Judgment**
- **Delphi**

Fast-Moving Products
High Value
High Forecastability

- **ARIMAX**
- **Multiple Linear Regression**
- **Dynamic Regression**

Company Value

Slow-Moving Products
Low Value
Low Forecastability

- **Weighted Combined Models**
  - (Judgment, Time Series, Causal)
- **Non-Seasonal Exponential Smoothing**
- **Holt's Two-Parameter Exponential Smooting**
- **Moving Averaging**
- **Croston's Intermittent Demand Function**

Steady-State Products
Low Value
High Forecastability

- **ARIMA**
  - (Non-Seasonal, Seasonal)
- **Decomposition**
- **Winter's Three-Parameter Exponential Smoothing**
  - Multiplicative
  - Additive
  - Linear, Damped Trend

Forecastability

Figure 6.3 Plotting statistical methods based on segmentation and portfolio management principles.

Segmentation Data Analysis
Using Product Portfolio Management Principles

New Products

High Value
Low Forecastability

Fast-Moving Products

High Value
High Forecastability

Evolutionary New Products
- Line Extensions
  - Surrogate or "As Like" Product
  - history available

5%

Revolutionary New Products
- No "As Like" data available

Short-Life-Cycle Products

High-Priority Growth Products
- Trend
- Seasonality
- Cycles
- Sales Promotions
- National Marketing Events
- National and Local Advertising
- Highly Competitive

35%

Company Value

Slow-Moving Products

Low Value
Low Forecastability

Steady-State Products

Low Value
High Forecastability

Low-Priority Regional Specialty Products
- Seasonality
- Irregular Demand
- Local Targets Marketing Events
- Sparse (Intermittent Demand)

10%

Mature Products
- Trend
- Seasonality
- Cycles
- No Sales Promotions

50%

Forecastability

Figure 6.4 Percentage of products that fall in each quadrant.

166

The main reason why ERP demand management modules haven't delivered on their promise of creating a more accuracy forecast is the fact that they only use simple times series methods to address the 50 percent of products in the lower-right-hand steady-state product quadrant. They are not designed to address the 35 percent of the product portfolio that falls in the upper-right-hand fast-moving product quadrant, nor the upper-left-hand new product quadrant. So, close to 40 percent of a company's product portfolio is not being addressed with the appropriate statistical methods. As a result, they rely on gut-feeling judgment to forecast those products.

Today, best-in-class demand management solutions are designed to address all four quadrants, with the appropriate statistical methods automatically on a large scale up/down a product hierarchy. These same best-in-breed solutions can run side-by-side in the same environment with the ERP transactional systems to complement their demand management (DM) modules, and/or replace them. These same best-in-class DM solutions tend to run two thirds faster across the company's product portfolio with greater accuracy at the lower level product mix.

CONSUMPTION-BASED MODELING

Integrating consumer demand into the demand forecasting and planning process to improve shipment (supply) forecasts has become a high priority in the consumer packaged goods (CPG), automotive, pharmaceuticals, OTC (over-the-counter) drug products, appliances, and high-tech industries, as well as in many other industries over the past several years.

Until recently, many factors, such as data collection and storage constraints, poor data synchronization capabilities, technology limitations, and limited internal analytical expertise have made it impossible to integrate consumer demand with shipment forecasts. Consumer demand data includes point-of-sale (POS) data and syndicated scanner data from Nielsen/Information Resources Inc. (IRI)/Intercontinental Marketing Services (IMS). A process called multi-tiered causal analysis (MTCA) links consumer demand to supply (downstream data to upstream data), using a process of nesting advanced analytical models. Although this process is not new in concept, it is new in practice. With improvements in technology, data collection and storage, processing, and analytical knowledge, companies are now looking to integrate downstream consumer demand with their upstream shipment (supply replenishment) forecasts to capture the impact of marketing activities (sales promotions, marketing events, in-store merchandizing, and other related factors) on supply. In-store merchandizing includes primarily floor displays, features, feature/display, in-store circulars, and temporary price reduction—TPR. MTCA is a process that considers marketing (demand signal) and replenishment (supply signal) strategies jointly rather than creating two separate forecasts (i.e., one for consumer demand and another for shipments). MTCA has implications for sales and marketing to participate in the sales & operations planning (S&OP) and integrated business planning (IBP) processes.

CONSUMPTION-BASED MODELING USING MULTI-TIERED CAUSAL ANALYSIS

MTCA is a process that links downstream and upstream data together using a series of advanced quantitative methods. The first step in the MTCA process is to identify and model those factors that influence consumer demand (POS/syndicated scanner data). Then, using the demand model parameters execute various what-if scenarios to shape and predict future consumer demand. Finally, linking consumer demand to supply (sales orders or shipments) using the consumer demand historical data and shaped future forecast as a leading indicator in a shipment model, thus linking consumption to supply, rather than using gut feelings.

In those industries where downstream data are available, consumption-based modeling is used to model the push/pull effects of the supply chain by linking a series of quantitative models together based on marketing investment strategies and replenishment policies to retailers. The theoretical design applies in-depth causal analysis to measure the effects of sales and marketing programs on consumer demand at retail (pull), and then links it, via consumer demand, to supply (push). This is known as a two-tiered model. In the case of companies with more sophisticated distribution networks, a three-tiered (or more) model could incorporate wholesalers (i.e., consumer to retailer to wholesaler to manufacturer) and/or distributors.

Once the causal factors that influence consumer demand are determined, and those business drivers of consumption are sensed (measured) and used to shaped future demand, a second model is developed using consumer demand as the primary explanatory variable (or leading indicator) to link consumer demand to supply (shipments). The supply model can also include such factors as trade promotions, wholesale gross price, cash discounts (or off-invoice allowances), co-op advertising, and seasonality to predict supply (shipments). In many cases, consumer demand is pulled forward one or more periods to account for the buying (replenishment) patterns of the retailers. For example, mass merchandisers, such as Wal-Mart, buy in bulk prior to high periods of consumer demand, usually one or more periods (months or weeks) prior to the sales promotion. Other retailers, such as Publix, carry large varieties of products and hold small inventories. This shortens their purchase cycle, and requires them to purchase products more frequently with virtually no lag on consumer demand when introduced into the supply model. Other variables, such as price and advertising, also need to be lagged and transformed to account for the lagged decay rate and cumulative aspects of consumer awareness using transfer functions. With that, if retail consumer demand (D) of Product A is:

$$\textbf{Demand}(D) = \beta_0 \text{Constant} + \beta_1 \text{Trend} + \beta_2 \text{ Seasonality} + \beta_3 \text{ Price}$$
$$+ \beta_4 \text{ Advertising} + \beta_5 \text{ Sales Promotion}$$
$$+ \beta_6 \% \text{ ACV Feature} + \beta_7 \text{ Store Distribution}$$
$$+ \beta_8 \text{ Competitive price} + \dots \beta n$$

(Distribution is percentage of stores in which product will be sold.)

then Product A's supply (S) would be:

$$\textbf{Supply}(S) = \beta_0 \text{ Constant} + \beta_1 \text{ D(lag}_{1+n}) + \beta_2 \text{ Trend} + \beta_3 \text{ Seasonality}$$
$$+ \beta_4 \text{ Gross dealer price} + \beta_5 \text{ Factory rebates}$$
$$+ \beta_6 \text{ Trade discounts} + \beta_7 \text{ Co-op advertising}$$
$$+ \beta_8 \text{ Trade promotions} + \dots \beta_n$$

In the case of consumption-based modeling, some of the explanatory variables (key business indicators, KBIs) are held static while others are changed to simulate the impact of alternative marketing strategies on consumer demand, using what-if scenario analysis. The impact of the selected scenario is linked to supply (shipments). The goal here is to simulate the impact of changes in those key performance indicators (shaping future demand) such as price, advertising, in-store merchandising, and sales promotions (or other events) that can be changed; determine their outcomes (predict future consumer demand); and choose the optimal strategy that produces the highest volume and revenue (return on investment, ROI). The key assumption is that if all things hold true based on the model's parameter estimates when the level of pressure on any one or group of explanatory variables is changed, it will have X impact on future consumer demand, resulting in Y change in supply (shipments). The most difficult explanatory variables to simulate are those related to competitors as well as to factors such as weather, economy, and local events, over which companies have little or no control.

CONSUMPTION-BASED MODELING CASE STUDY

Step-by-Step Process

This step-by-step process is an actual application of MTCA to sense, shape, and predict demand. Then, link downstream (POS/syndicated scanner) data to upstream (shipment) data, thus synchronizing demand and supply for a large CPG manufacturer. A brand manager, demand analyst (statistical modeler), and demand planner all work together to evaluate the efficiency and productivity of the company's sales and marketing efforts (sense the demand signal by measuring the impact of those key business drivers that influence demand), take actions (shape future demand) with the goal of driving more profitable volume growth, and proactively predict future consumer demand (POS/syndicated scanner data). Then, link predicted demand to supply to create a supply plan (shipment forecast). The brand manager has the domain knowledge of the market, category, channel, brand, products, SKUs, and marketplace dynamics; the demand analyst has the statistical experience and knowledge to apply the appropriate quantitative methods; and the demand planner has the demand planning (supply planning) expertise. This raises three major questions:

1. What tactics within the sales and marketing programming are working to influence the demand signal within the retail grocery channel? Identifying and measuring the KBIs that influence demand is called *sensing demand*.

2. How can they put pressure on those KBIs to drive more volume and profitability using what-if analysis? In other words, what alternative scenarios can be identified to maximize their market investment efficiency? This is *shaping* future demand.

3. How does the final shaped demand influence supply replenishment (shipments)?

MTCA Six-Step Process

Step 1: Gather the Pertinent Data for Consumer Demand and Shipments

In the example here, POS syndicated scanner data (153 weeks, starting January 2009) were downloaded from the IRI (Information Resources Inc.) database at the total U.S. market, grocery channel, brand, product group, product, package size, and SKU level. This example focuses on the product group weekly case volume (consumption), average price per unit, in-store merchandising vehicles (displays, features, features and displays, and temporary price reduction—TPR), and weighted distribution percentages by product, which were downloaded along with major competitor information. The marketing events (sales promotions/marketing events) calendar from the sales and marketing plan were also downloaded. Finally, weekly supply volumes (shipments) were downloaded along with wholesale price, case volume discounts (off-invoice allowances), trade promotions/events, and local retailer incentives being offered by the CPG manufacturer.

It was decided that it made more sense to model at the product group level (middle-out), which is four levels deep into the product hierarchy (see Figure 6.5) rather than at the individual SKU level (bottom-up), and disaggregate the product case volumes down to the

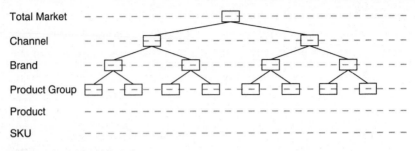

Figure 6.5 Product hierarchy.

individual SKU level, using the bottom-up statistical demand forecasts to build in the trends associated with the lower level product/SKU mix. This particular CPG brand is nationally distributed with several size and package configurations.

The product group unit/case volume projections will be disaggregated down across all the lower levels to the SKUs based on their historical demand (syndicated scanner data) and supply (shipments), including any trends established using basic time series methods (e.g., Holt-Winters Exponential Smoothing, and others). The SKU forward forecasts will provide a mechanism to build in trends associated with those lower Product/SKU levels, while the brand level forward projections will reflect sales and marketing investment activities and seasonality. In other words, we will build models at every level (bottom-up), but run our what-if scenarios at the middle-out product group level. Finally, use the lower-level SKU forecasts to disaggregate the middle-out product group forecast volumes down to the SKU level. This method of disaggregation builds in the lower-level trends, creating a more dynamic result, which is more accurate than using a static disaggregation.

Finally, reconcile the entire hierarchy to make sure that all levels add up to the total (top level) including the middle-out disaggregated levels. So, any changes related to the middle-out disaggregated forecast will have an impact on the total. This requires large scale automatic statistical forecasting technology. You cannot do this using Excel.

Step 2: Build the Demand Model

Build the consumer demand (consumption) model using downstream data to sense demand. The demand analyst runs the company forecasting system to create the business hierarchy, and then investigates all the data to create statistical consumer demand forecasts at all levels of the hierarchy using time series and causal models—in this case, using the IRI syndicated scanner data from their demand signal repository. DSR is a centralized database that stores, harmonizes, and normalizes data attributes and organizes large volumes of demand data—such as POS data, wholesaler data, electronic data interchange (EDI) 852 and 867, inventory movement, promotional data, and customer loyalty data for use by decision support technologies, category management, account team joint value creation, shopper insight analysis, demand planning forecast improvement, inventory deployment, replenishment, and transportation planning. Then, at the product level in the hierarchy, create consumer demand models to sense, shape, and predict future demand (D), which is the first tier in the MTCA process. Demand drives supply, not the reverse, so it is important to model demand before supply. The demand forecast serves as the primary leading indicator or explanatory variable in the supply (S) model. The model chosen is an ARIMAX model (ARIMA model with causal variables) that uses causal factors that are significant in influencing demand.

See Table 6.1 for model results.

Step 3: Test the Model

Test the predictive ability of the model using out-of-sample data. The model was tested with a 13-week out-of-sample forecast (holdout sample). Overall, the predictability of the model is very good, with a fitted MAPE of 4.23 percent, and a holdout MAPE of 5.12 percent. Even on a week-to-week basis, the model is fairly good (well below the industry average of 22 to 35 percent, based on benchmarking surveys published in the *Journal of Business Forecasting*). If the demand analyst finds a week(s) in the holdout sample test that is outside the 95 percent-confidence level range, the brand manager may know what happened and can identify additional inputs that need to be added to the model. This is where domain knowledge, not gut feeling, can help.

The ARIMA model is holistically modeling the demand history at the brand level without cleansing the data. The model is capturing the trend, seasonality, irregular shifts, and four causal

Table 6.1 CPG Product Level Consumption Model Fit

CPG Product Consumption Model (IRI Syndicated Scanner Data) ARIMA (3,1,0) (0,0,0)					
$R^2 = 88.79$			Fitted MAPE = 4.23%		
Adj $R^2 = 88.26$			Out-of-Sample MAPE = 5.12%		
Component	Parameter	Estimate	Standard Error	t-Value	P-Value
Demand	AR1	−0.68731	0.12369	−5.56	0.0001
Demand	AR2	−0.34503	0.1469	−2.35	0.0217
Demand	AR3	0.02187	0.012784	0.17	0.8647
ACVDisplay	SCALE	47365.9	11416.3	4.15	0.0001
ACVDisplay	NUM1	−3282	10636.5	10.31	0.7586
ACVDisplay	NUM2	−18236.7	10896.3	−1.67	0.0987
ACV Wghtd Distribution	SCALE	247.88	59.82	4.14	0.0001
ACV Wghtd Distribution	NUM1	170.57	69.18	2.47	0.0161
ACV Wghtd Distribution	DEN1	0.36025	0.04838	7.45	0.0001
ACV Wghtd Distribution	DEN2	−0.84716	0.04296	−19.72	0.0001
TPR	SCALE	446.31	303.13	1.47	0.1463
TPR	NUM1	32.13	286.55	0.11	0.911
Avg Price per Unit	SCALE	−3232	613.71	−5.27	0.0001
Avg Price per Unit	NUM1	1607.5	1977.8	0.81	0.4191
Avg Price per Unit	DEN1	−0.83102	0.55307	−1.5	0.1375
Avg Price per Unit	DEN2	−0.28308	0.21145	−1.81	0.0743

factors (store distribution, displays, price, and a sales promotion). These factors are significant in predicting future consumer demand. The parameter estimate for the sales promotion is the actual lift factor (12,917.3 incremental cases per week), which is separated from the trend and seasonality. The demand analyst may identify additional explanatory variables that may be incorporated into the model, or identify additional sales and marketing events that may have been overlooked. In our example, each of the holdout-sample forecasts were within the 95 percent confidence level. This is not uncommon for consumer demand models. This is because most of the POS/syndicated scanner data at the aggregate level are very stable.

Plus, there was no change in the customers' inventory replenishment policies. The core reason why shipment data are unstable is due to changes in replenishment policy, and/or month and/or quarter end load-in practices by the manufacturer.

Step 4: Refit the Model

Refit the model using all the data. After identifying and verifying the consumer demand model parameter estimates for all the explanatory variables and testing the model's predictive capabilities, the modeler refits the model with the 13-week out-of-sample data (using all 153 weeks of data). See Figure 6.6 for the final model fit, forecast, and comparison to shipments using the entire data set including the 13-week out-of-sample. As you can see, consumer demand and shipments at the product group level are highly correlated with no lag associated with consumption and shipments. This is normal in the grocery channel as they order frequently (three to five days) and carry more SKUs. However, in other channels, for example, the Mass Mechanizing and Club channels (e.g., Wal-Mart, K-Mart, Sam's, BJ's, and others), they replenish less frequently (three to four weeks), but buy in large quantities. In these channels, there could be a one- to four-week lag (positive lag) between consumption and shipments, requiring the demand analyst to pull forward consumption history and forward forecast in the shipment (supply) model.

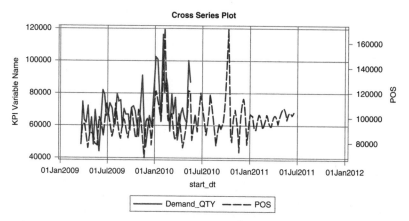

Figure 6.6 CPG product-level consumption model fit with forecast versus shipments.

Step 5: Run a What-If Scenario

Run what-if scenarios to shape future demand. Using the consumer demand model, the product manager can shape future demand by conducting several what-if simulations by varying future values of different explanatory variables that are under his/her control. Upon completion of the simulations, the product manager chooses the optimal scenario that generates the most case volume and profitability, which then becomes the consumer demand future forecast for the next 52 weeks. The optimum model can be selected in a matter of minutes with the right technology. Once the optimal scenario (model) is chosen based on available marketing spend, document the assumptions.

In many cases, the marketing budget constraints play a key role in the number and the type of sales promotions the company can execute. Finance also plays a role in assessing the financial impact on a revenue and profitability basis. It is recommended that post analysis assessments be conducted prior to updating the model and regenerating a new forward consumer demand forecast to identify opportunities and weaknesses in the sales and marketing investment plan. In other words, a post reconciliation of the actual execution of the final scenario should be conducted after each weekly or monthly update to determine the deviation of actual from the forecast so that corrective action can be taken.

Step 6: Link Demand and Supply

Link the consumer demand forecast to supply (shipments). The process just described is now applied to develop a model for supply (shipments) using demand (D) as the key leading indicator (independent variable) along with its forward forecast based on the final scenario chosen by the product manager in the demand-shaping phase of the process. As a result, the demand analyst links the first tier (demand) to the second tier of the supply chain (supply) by incorporating consumer demand (D) as one of the explanatory (predictor) variables in the supply (S) model. The results in Table 6.2 show demand along with trend, seasonality, and a trade promotion are influencing supply. One of the most significant variables in the supply model is consumer demand (parameter estimate = .5663), which indicates that for every 10 cases shipped into the grocery channel, 5.663 cases are being pulled through

Table 6.2 CPG Product Level Shipment Model Fit

CPG Product Shipment Model				
R² = 78.84		Fitted MAPE = 11.40%		
Adj R² = 78.40		Out-of-Sample MAPE = 12.37%		
Component	Parameter	Estimate	Standard Error	t-Value	P-Value
Shipment	MA1	−0.84648	0.02967	−28.53	0.0001
Shipment	MA52	0.31001	0.13235	2.4	0.0182
Demand	Scale	0.56635	0.08779	6.45	0.0001
Demand	NUM1	−0.1477	0.08863	−1.67	0.1012
Trade Promotion	Scale	44740.3	10977.7	4.08	0.0001

the grocery channel by consumer demand at the product group level. Conversely, roughly 4.3 cases (10 − 5.67 cases = 4.3 cases) are being pushed through the channel by offering trade incentives to retailers. This indicates some loading is occurring at the retailer, as the CPG Company is shipping in more than the retailer is selling through to the consumer. This will eventually lead to higher inventory at the retailer's distribution centers. Another key variable in the shipment model is the trade promotion parameter estimate that indicates the volume lift (44,740.3). In this case, whenever the CPG Company runs this trade promotion, it generates an incremental 44,740.3 cases per week. That is the trade promotion lift above the trend and seasonality; as in the ARIMAX model, we have accounted for both the trend and seasonality. You cannot decompose the historical volume in this manner using exponential smoothing models.

Also, it is interesting to note that fitted MAPE for supply is 11.4 percent and the 13-week out-of-sample MAPE is 12.37 percent, which is well below the industry average of 15.0 to 25.0 percent. Keep in mind the industry average is based on one-month-ahead monthly forecasts, while the MTCA model is of 1 to 13 weeks ahead. These results are not uncommon using the MTCA process.

The demand planner then uses the supply model to create 52-week forward forecasts for supply. Additional supply shaping can take place by the demand planner using what-if analysis with different values of future explanatory variables. Figure 6.7 is the final supply forecast (shipment plan). Prior to the pre-S&OP meeting,

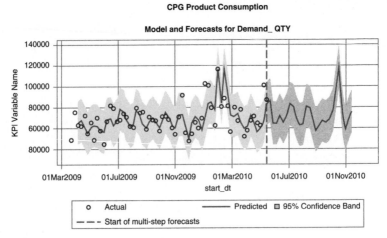

Figure 6.7 CPG product-level shipment model fit with forecast.

the demand planner disaggregates the product group level supply forecasts down across all the member SKUs, and reconciles the supply forecast business hierarchy using the company's demand forecasting and planning system. Using the middle-out product supply forecasts, disaggregate them down the hierarchy to the SKU level mix, and then summarize the results to make sure the entire supply forecast is in sync (summarized and balanced) up/down the business hierarchy.

Consumption-based modeling using the MTCA approach is a simple process that links a series of causal models—in this case, two ARIMAX models—through a common element (consumer demand) to model the push/pull effects of the supply chain. It is truly a decision support system that is designed to integrate statistical analysis with downstream (POS and/or syndicated scanner) and upstream (shipment) data to analyze the business from a *holistic supply chain* perspective. This process provides both brand management and demand planners with the opportunity to make better and more actionable decisions from multiple data sources (e.g., POS/syndicated scanner, internal company, and external market data). The purpose of the process is to provide a distinct opportunity to address supply chain optimization through the nesting (supply chain distribution tiers) of causal models to sense demand signals, and then use what-if simulations based on alternative business strategies (sales/marketing scenarios) to shape and predict future demand. Finally, the objective is to link consumer demand to supply replenishment (shipments) using a structured approach that relies on data, analytics, and domain knowledge rather than gut feelings and manual manipulation (manual overrides). The key benefit of consumption-based modeling using the MTCA process is to capture the entire supply chain by focusing on sales and marketing strategies to shape future consumer demand, and then link demand to supply using a holistic framework. These relationships are what truly define the marketplace and all marketing elements within the supply chain.

SUMMARY

Today, technology exists to enable demand analysts to leverage their data resources and analytics capabilities as a competitive advantage, offering a true, integrated supply-chain management perspective to optimize the demand-driven value chain. Relying on a traditional demand (supply) model is like taking a picture of inventory replenishment through a narrow angle lens. Although you can see the impact within your own supply replenishment network (upstream) with some precision, the foreground (downstream) is either excluded or out of focus. As significant (or insignificant) as the picture may seem, far too much is ignored by this view. To capture the full picture of the supply chain, consumption-based modeling using the MTCA approach provides a wide-angle telephoto lens to ensure clear resolution of where a company is and where it wants to go.

There are no longer challenges preventing companies from moving to this new demand management approach. Today, the data collection, storage, and processing are no longer a challenge; scalable technology can run millions of data series in a matter of a few hours; and advanced analytics are able to run hundreds of iterations using a broad array of methods up/down a business hierarchy automatically. Universities now teach advanced analytics as required courses in most undergraduate and graduate business programs. It is simply a matter of investing in people (advanced analytical skills), process (horizontal processes), analytics (predictive analytics), and technology (scalable demand-driven technology).

KEY LEARNINGS

- Statistical forecasting methods are designed to model patterns in the demand history. Those basic patterns are trend, seasonality, and cycle.

- In many cases, other factors are influencing demand. In those situations, more advanced statistical methods are required, like ARIMA, ARIMAX, and multiple regression, which can also measure the effects of causal factors, like price, sales promotions, advertising, and in-store merchandising (i.e., displays, features, display/features, temporary price reductions (TPR), and others).

- When forecasting on a large scale, demand planners need to consider segmenting brands and products based on their value to the company, the availability of data and information, and forecastability.
  - *Forecastability* is the measure of the degree to which something may be forecast with accuracy.

- When segmenting demand to determine what methods are appropriate for brand, product group, and product efforts, you should focus on four key areas:
  1. Low value, low forecastability
  2. Low value, high forecastability
  3. High value, low forecastability
  4. High value, high forecastability

- When evaluating forecast data, we look at two key factors: (1) value to the company and (2) forecastability. This conceptual design can be taken further to consider a company's product portfolio as falling into four quadrants:
  1. *Slow-moving* products with fragmented data across targeted markets and consumers.
  2. *New products* with little historical sales data (revolutionary new products) or with similarities with existing products (evolutionary products or line extensions). Also, short-life-cycle products like fashion jeans, which normally have six-month life cycles.

3. *Fast-moving* products that are highly correlated to sales and marketing causal factors, requiring the collection of causal data and information.

4. *Steady-state* products with long stable historical demand with distinct time series patterns.

■ Consumption-based modeling using MTCA is a process that links downstream and upstream data together using a series of advanced quantitative methods.

  ■ The theoretical design applies in-depth causal analysis to measure the effects of sales and marketing program effects on consumer demand at retail (pull), and then links it, via consumer demand, to supply (push).

■ Consumption-based modeling is designed to integrate statistical analysis with downstream (POS and/or syndicated scanner) and upstream (shipment) data to analyze the business from a *holistic supply chain* perspective.

  ■ This process provides both brand management and demand planners with the opportunity to make better and more actionable decisions from multiple data sources (i.e., POS/syndicated scanner, internal company, and external market data).

NOTES

1. "Demand-Driven Forecasting and Planning Research Study," *Industry Week/SAS* (2014), p. 9.
2. Robert Fildes and Paul Goodwin, "Good and Bad Judgment in Forecasting: Lessons from Four Companies," *Foresight: The International Journal of Applied Forecasting* 8 (Fall 2007), pp. 5–10.

FURTHER READING

Chase, Charles W. Jr., "Using Downstream Data to Improve Forecast Accuracy," *Journal of Business Forecasting* 34, no. 1 (Spring 2015), pp. 21–29.

Chase, Charles W. Jr., *Demand-Driven Forecasting: A Structured Approach to Forecasting,* 2nd ed. (Hoboken: John Wiley & Sons, 2013), pp. 253–282.

CHAPTER 7

The Demand Planning Brief

The next generation demand management process is more than just creating an accurate demand forecast. It is a business analytics function embedded downstream in the sales and marketing organization, providing analytics support to drive demand generation. As such, demand analysts working closely with sales and marketing provide predictive analytics support to validate and justify sales tactics and marketing strategies that drive the final demand response. Demand-driven is more than just being responsive, it is about being interactive with the goal of optimizing market investment (spend) in support of the unconstrained demand forecast.

The challenge for supply chain executives is to gain commitment from sales and marketing through improved processes, metrics, and technologies, while addressing the question, "What's in it for sales and marketing?" It's a journey, with a series of steps required to encourage sales and marketing to take ownership, and more importantly, accountability. Although sales plays a significant role in providing inputs, it is marketing that influences demand, and that has a direct impact on the unconstrained demand forecast. The best way for an organization to build trust and accountability is by providing proven analytical support and becoming a trusted adviser to the commercial organization. Embracing downstream data, learning how to provide valued insights through predictive analytics, and most of all, collaborating in a meaningful way are the keys to getting sales and marketing to take ownership in the demand planning process.

Sponsorship and leadership play significant roles in the involvement of sales and marketing within the monthly demand planning, as well as the sales and operations planning (S&OP) processes. The demand planning team must become an integral member of the commercial team to gain alignment to drive the business strategy. A vision with an end state in mind, along with a roadmap that builds improvements over time, is a necessary ingredient to improve sales and marketing accountability for the unconstrained demand forecast.

The mistake that organizations make is that either they request a forecast of everything sales and marketing plans to sell, or they are not held accountable for providing any forecast. Neither approach is correct nor serves to hold sales and marketing accountable for forecast accuracy improvements.

Demand sensing and shaping capabilities not only provide the ability to predict demand more accurately, but also can uncover deep insights into customer/consumer behavior by identifying those key performance indicators that influence consumer demand and replenishment policies. These factors can be quantified (measured), and used to shape future demand based on sales and marketing tactics and strategies. As such, those tactics and strategies need to be tested and validated using predictive analytics and documented to maintain accountability and ownership. To that point, the demand planning process needs to support those activities using a combination of analytics and domain knowledge. The demand analyst has the analytics knowledge and the sales and marketing team has the domain expertise. It is all about accountability, ownership, and participation in the demand planning process. By hiring and embedding demand analysts (also, called *data scientists*) downstream in the commercial organization you begin to create a partnership and trust with sales and marketing becoming over time their analytic confidant.

The best way to build accountability and ownership of the unconstrained demand forecast is through sound testing using analytics, and documentation of the assumptions (tactics and strategies) that were used to justify the demand forecast. Then, get sign-off by the sales and marketing senior management team prior to the S&OP meeting. The best course of action is documenting the demand forecasting and planning process by implementing a monthly *demand planning brief* that outlines in detail what tactics and strategies were tested to validate the assumptions using data and analytics versus *gut feeling* judgment. Formalizing a process and documentation to capture this information not only provides a benchmark for justification of continuous improvement but also builds accountability and ownership.

DEMAND PLANNING BRIEF

The monthly demand planning brief is a living document that rolls across a weekly time horizon and allows the organization to continuously look ahead and plan based on sales tactics and marketing investment strategies. It contains the details and actions taken by the demand forecasting and planning team working closely with the sales and marketing organizations using feedback from actual execution to final demand response. This tight collaboration in maintaining this document between the demand forecasting and planning and sales and marketing organizations tends to create trust, accountability, and ownership. Here is a standard monthly demand planning brief template along with an embedded *analytic snapshot* report outlining the statistical methods evaluated, what-if scenarios executed, and recommendations.

To gain sales and marketing accountability for the unconstrained demand forecast means making the two organizations accountable for their role in the demand planning process. It starts with identifying and documenting the agreed-to inputs and responsibilities during the creation of the weekly demand plan so that sales and marketing clearly understands its role within the process. It also means actively revisiting input assumptions and testing their validity using proven analytic approaches based on sales tactics and marketing strategies that include sales promotions, in-store merchandizing, competitive activities, and market assumptions that influence revenue and profit goals. Most companies do not revisit these assumptions with regularity to identify forecast error and improve inputs from sales and marketing.

The purpose of the demand planning brief is not only to analyze and document assumptions, but also to conduct monthly *post-reconciliation* to determine what programs worked and what tactics did not meet expectations. It also puts the focus on whether sales executed against those assumptions, rather than blaming the forecast models for the poor results. It is about accountability against execution, with the intention to learn and take course-corrective actions.

To provide more perspective and understanding, here is an actual example of a demand planning brief for a winery.

The XYZ Winery
Demand Planning Brief

Monthly Demand Planning Brief
Template

Brands/Product Group/Products _____

Region ____ **Channel** _____

Forecast Cycle ____

Date: _____

Part 1

Executive Summary

Business Brief: Analytic Snapshot

Model Comparison Chart

Part 2

Forecasting Strategy Overview

What-If Scenarios (Demand Shaping)

Strengths & Weaknesses

Strategy Detail

Summary

Monthly Demand Planning Brief

The XYZ Winery Case Study

Executive Summary

OVERVIEW

The demand planning team has performed time series analysis in support of the sales and marketing teams to leverage historical wine demand data to achieve higher forecast accuracy and to increase revenue from pricing and sales promotion actions. More than three years of the winery's historical demand was analyzed to evaluate the effectiveness of sales promotions, create weekly forecasting models, and predict the effects of price increases across all products and markets.

BACKGROUND

XYZ Winery produces four wine varieties: Table Red, Table White, Value Red, and Vintage Red.

These wines are marketed in four regions of the United States: Northeast (Region 1), Central (Region 2), Southeast (Region 3), and West (Region 4). There are two sales promotions reflected in the historical demand data:

1. **May Promotion:** Buy one case of wine and get a 15 percent discount, starting the week of May 5, 2015, and lasting four weeks.

2. **December Promotion:** Buy one case of wine and get a 10 percent discount, run in 2013 and 2014. In 2013, the sales promotion started the week of December 25 and ran for one week. In 2014, the sales promotion started the week of December 31 and ran for one week.

RECOMMENDED FORECAST METHODOLOGY

We built a product hierarchical set of forecast models, including a top-level model that forecasts company-wide sales for the XYZ winery; sales demand on a per-region basis; and sales for each type of wine within each region. We used middle-out reconciliation, as this resulted in the lowest final MAPEs, and is consistent with our desire to make business decisions at the regional level.

The final top-level (total company level) model shown in Figure 7.1 has a final MAPE of 4.55 percent and shows forecasts continuing to increase through the end of 2015.

These models were built using the winery's sales promotion information, unit prices, and demand history. Of the original 21 system-generated models, 7 models were further revised to reduce

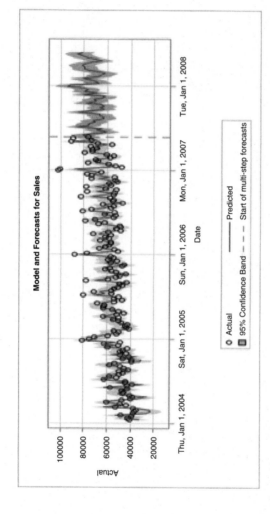

Figure 7.1 Demand forecast results at the top company level.

their out-of-sample (holdout) MAPE to meet the targeted goal of 14 percent. Overall recommendations regarding key findings about promotions, price increase strategies, and a quick view of the model summary (analytics snapshot) are captured in the following demand planning brief.

MODEL HIERARCHY

We were asked by the senior management team to determine the best models to deploy across regions and wine type, and in doing so it was felt that optimal business decisions could be made at the regional level. This is attributable to the evident variation among the regions; therefore, a middle-out forecast by region was selected as the reconciliation level in the hierarchy, as seen in Figure 7.2. Regions 1 (Northeast) and 2 (Central) make up for almost 88 percent of the total wine sales. Upper management would want to focus on these regions in particular to fine tune the models to inherently optimize sales demand.

MODEL SELECTION CRITERIA

Over the demand history (176 weeks), trends, seasonality, sales promotional events, holidays, and outliers were considered in optimizing the best possible model across the regions and types. To accurately

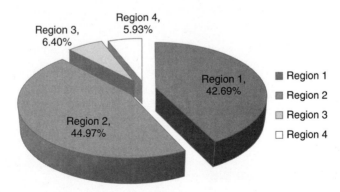

Figure 7.2 Wine sales by region.

capture the variability among the regions and wine types, we used ARIMA, exponential smoothing, and multiple regression models for each level of the product hierarchy.

For each level of the hierarchy, we used the holdout MAPE as our criterion for selecting a final best model from the set of candidate model types. We used a holdout sample of 13 weeks based on the following factors:

- We were asked to consider the impact of price increases through the remainder of 2015. This required us to use the models to generate forecasts for the next 31 weeks. We wanted to use an out-of-sample (holdout) for a minimum of one quarter, since this allows us to assess the models' forecasting accuracy on previously unseen data covering the company's agreed to frozen forecast horizon of three months.

- Wine sales demand follows an annual seasonal pattern, and we wanted to preserve at least three full seasons' worth of data when building and selecting our models. This requirement limited us to no more than 13 weeks of data to effectively test the models' accuracy. Three years of data is the minimum required to capture the full effect of seasonality.

Only one model, the overall model for the Northeast Region-2 was *not* selected based on the lowest holdout MAPE. The holdout MAPE for the final Northeast Region overall ARIMA model, accounting for seasonality and differencing (capture trend effects) with base price, was only 2 percent greater than the best system-generated exponential smoothing model. However, the ARIMA model yielded predictions that closely track the known seasonality of the data. Therefore, we determined it was worthwhile to select the model that yields more useful predictions over a model with mean-based predictions and only a slightly better holdout MAPE.

Once our initial models were built, we focused on improving the accuracy of system-generated models with a final MAPE of >14 percent. Most of these could be improved upon, even if by a few percent.

In addition to the promotional events that we were asked by senior management to assess, we also added holiday events into our models.

These events were only kept if they proved significant. Additionally, an outlier analysis was performed. One example of a model that uses outlier events is the Northeast region Vintage wine model. This ARIMA system-generated model determined August 14, 2004, to be a significant outlier. By adding this event into the model, 1,735 cases of wine were accounted for during this week. We are working closely with the sales and marketing teams to uncover any local events that may have taken place to better explain the outlier.

SUPPORTING INFORMATION

It is worth mentioning some general patterns/consistencies across all the models. Selection of the exponential smoothing models was predominant for the table red and white wines in all regions. Holt-Winters Additive Exponential Smoothing models chosen at the region/type level for table red and white present both a trend/cycle and a seasonal component, which makes the Holt-Winters Three-Parameter model the optimal model in this case. Vintage wine models could not be explained by only trend, seasonality, and cyclical elements. Vintage models were greatly improved upon by using ARIMA models with base price as an independent variable. As seen in Table 7.1, vintage wines' sales demand in all regions and price are highly correlated; therefore, integrating a causal (influence) factor such as price into the models explained more of the variation in demand.

Value wines make up only 11 percent of the total wine sales, and are typically less affected by seasonality and sales promotions keeping

Table 7.1 Correlation between Sales and Price for Each Region/Wine Type

	Table Red	Table White	Value	Vintage
Region 1	0.36	.036	−0.39	−0.91
Region 2	0.35	0.35	0.39	−0.80
Region 3	0.36	0.36	0.39	−0.90
Region 4	0.38	0.38	0.38	−0.97

them significantly stable compared to the other wines primarily due to the low volume of sales. Some caution should be used when reviewing the value wine models, particularly in the Northeast region. The trends of the value wine sales demand appear to be exponential, linear downward as time increases, which explains the selection of the Linear Holt ES models for Regions 1, 3, and 4. Forecasts produced by this model are smoothed and less sensitive to past swings in demand. The Northeast region was best modeled by an ARIMA seasonal model using base price as an influence factor. This situation lead to additional questions since the low volume of sales should have made the value wine models consistent across the regions. We further investigated the data for value wine and found the average price for value wine was higher than table red and white wines (see Figure 7.3). We further subset the data to only look at base price of value wines by region and found that the Northeast region was extremely different from the other regions.

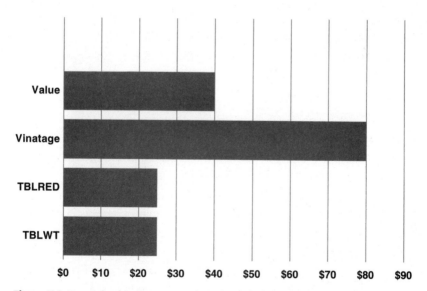

Figure 7.3 Base price for wine types: value priced higher than red/white.

ANALYTIC SNAPSHOT

Models Evaluated

ARIMA, Exponential Smoothing, and Dynamic Regression models were created using the middle-out method as the best method of hierarchical forecasting. Based on adjusted R-square values, model fit statistics, interpretability, and forecasting charts the optimal models for each region and type of wine were selected in order to forecast demand and plan promotions.

Model Summary

Overall, 21 models were system-generated. Using a holdout MAPE of under 14% as an acceptable cutoff point, there were 7 models requiring additional attention to improve accuracy and predictability.

"What If" Scenarios

A 5% price increase per case across the board will result in:

■ 4.5% drop in unit sales

■ 0.3% rise in revenue

Recommendation Methods

Due to the limited effects of an overall price increase, a more targeted price increase is recommended as below:

■ Strongly recommend a 5% price increase in Western value wines & white wines, and in Central region for all types.

■ Cautiously recommend a 5% price increase in Southeast for all types, and in Western vintage wines.

■ Do *not* recommend a price increase either in Northeast for all types, or in Western red wines.

Strengths

■ The December promotion (10% discount) was more effective for any given week than the May promotion (15% discount).

■ During the December promotion, the forecast showed an estimated 24.39% weekly increase in sales, with estimated forecasts in the Northeast and the Southeast regions with a higher increase of over 30%.

■ A one-week 10% discount promotion repeated four times throughout the year may be a better program for increasing sales than a single 15% discount with a four-week duration.

Weaknesses

■ Both the May and December promotions had limited effect in generating incremental sales demand for the Central region.

■ The May promotion was so recent that the forecast models could not be tested for accuracy once it was included in the model. However, based on the fitted model estimates the May promotion suggested a moderate increase in incremental sales demand.

Recommendations

■ Run quarterly promotions where the customer buys one case and gets a 10% discount in West, Northeast, and Southeast regions. Sales from these promotions would help counteract the negative effects on sales volume from the price increases taken, and would raise overall revenue.

  ■ Institute an ongoing process of updating and revising forecast models with newer sales data in order to better understand and shape demand.

Key Differentiators

■ Although the December sales promotion provided significant incremental sales demand due to the holiday (Christmas/New Year) there was a significant pantry load, which actually created a slight negative impact over sales for the two week period. However, running a 10% off sales promotion four times a year may have an overall positive impact generating significant incremental sales demand.

■ A 5% price increase per case across the board will result in:

  ■ 4.5% drop in unit sales

  ■ 0.3% rise in revenue

Methodology

Historical wine sales demand history starting from January 2014 to May 2015 were used to conduct the analysis. In order to accurately forecast demand and plan promotions and sales for the remainder of 2015, the process flow outlined in Figure 7.4 was adopted.

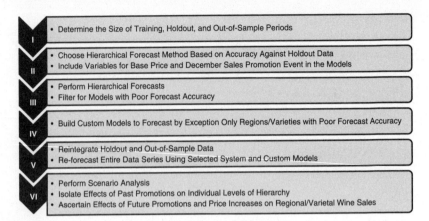

Figure 7.4 Demand forecasting and planning process flow.

As the winery's four-week-long promotion in May 2015 happened to occur at the tail end of the data series, determining the period of data to be set aside for model validation was the first and most crucial step in the aforementioned process flow. Including the unique sales behavior of those four weeks within the validation data would distort any accuracy statistics, as it would not be representative of the rest of the data series. Hence it was decided to split the series into three components as shown in Figure 7.5.

Demand historical data for a full three-year period was considered necessary to accurately model the forecasts. The remaining 13 weeks of data were further split into Holdout and Out-of-Sample components in such a way that the holdout data still captured a full quarter of a year, while data pertaining to the May 2015 promotion was left out of the original training data set and validation phases of the forecasting process flow.

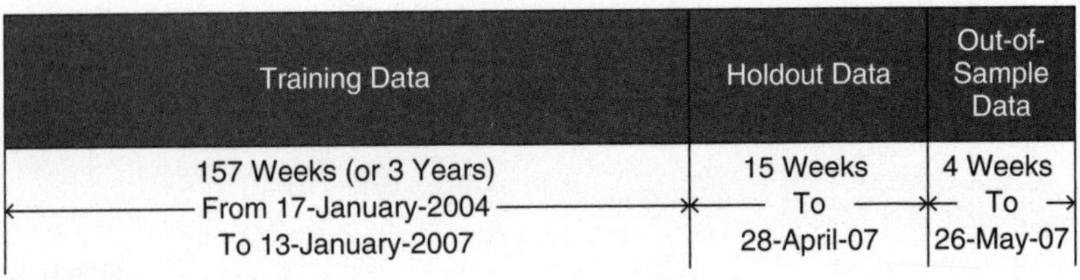

Training Data	Holdout Data	Out-of-Sample Data
157 Weeks (or 3 Years) From 17-January-2004 To 13-January-2007	15 Weeks To 28-April-07	4 Weeks To 26-May-07

Figure 7.5 Breakdown of the data series.

With the above training and holdout samples in place, weekly demand for the remainder of 2015 was forecast using all three hierarchical methods, top-down, middle-out, and bottom-up, and with causal factors for base price and the December sales promotion event (with two occurrences in 2013 and 2014). Table 7.2 summarizes the comparative qualities of the middle-out method, and highlights the system-generated forecast models and the mean absolute percent errors (MAPEs) at each level of the hierarchy. It is sorted in ascending order of the MAPE for the holdout portion of the historical demand data series.

It may be noted that the reconciled MAPEs of the entire data series were used in selecting the best method and level of hierarchical forecasting. Clearly, the middle-out method generated more accurate forecasts than the top-down method across all levels of the hierarchy. Although the bottom-up method proved more accurate at the varietal wine level, middle-out remained the preferred method for two reasons:

1. To avoid introducing too much noise at the granular level into higher level forecasts; and

2. Because that noise might be further accentuated by the unique sales behavior of the May 2015 sales promotion.

Once the appropriate hierarchical forecasting method was chosen, the holdout MAPE was the measure of interest and the agreed to benchmark MAPE to beat (14 percent), as it measures model accuracy against a representative subset of the data. As is evident from Table 7.2, the majority of the forecasts had a holdout MAPE under 10 percent. For instance, the overall model had a holdout MAPE of 5.91 percent; that is to say, it estimated the holdout data with over 94 percent accuracy. For the varietal forecasts with high holdout MAPEs, a MAPE under 14 percent was deemed satisfactory, especially since they accounted for a fairly small proportion of overall sales. The hierarchical levels that warranted further modeling in order to bring down the MAPE are highlighted in the box in Table 7.2. The custom models built to improve these MAPEs are evaluated and compared in the following section (Model Selection and Interpretation).

Table 7.2 System-Generated Hierarchical Forecasts with Corresponding Error Percentages

Region	Type	MAPE (%) Holdout ↓	Training + Holdout	Reconciled MAPE (%) Middle-Out	Top-Down	System-Generated Model
Central	All	0.19	0.52	0.52	0.92	ARIMAX (012) (100)
Central	Vintage	0.55	1.12	1.13	1.53	ARIMAX (012) (100)
Central	Table White	1.62	1.73	1.48	1.87	ARIMAX (012) (100)
Central	Table Red	1.63	1.80	1.50	1.90	ARIMAX (012) (100)
Central	Value	2.06	2.80	2.88	2.76	Smoothing (Linear Exponential)
Overall	All	5.91	15.13	14.79	15.13	ARIMAX (Intercept)
West	All	6.18	16.38	16.38	16.71	ARIMAX (100) (000)
Southeast	All	6.22	15.73	15.73	16.07	ARIMAX (100) (000)
Northeast	All	6.61	14.41	14.41	14.75	ARIMAX (Intercept)
Southeast	Vintage	6.70	15.13	18.38	18.72	ARIMAX (Intercept)
Northeast	Vintage	7.72	12.74	14.52	14.88	UCM
West	Vintage	9.23	16.81	20.74	21.07	UCM
Northeast	Table Red	12.81	13.63	15.74	16.07	Smoothing (Winters' Additive)
Northeast	Table White	12.99	13.86	16.17	16.50	Smoothing (Winters' Additive)
West	Table Red	14.26	13.43	17.46	17.79	Smoothing (Winters' Additive)
Southeast	Table Red	14.26	13.43	17.00	17.33	Smoothing (Winters' Additive)
West	Table White	14.26	13.43	17.46	17.79	Smoothing (Winters' Additive)
Southeast	Table White	14.26	13.43	17.00	17.33	Smoothing (Winters' Additive)
Northeast	Value	14.94	27.54	27.41	27.15	Smoothing (Linear Exponential)
West	Value	14.95	27.60	27.86	27.58	Smoothing (Linear Exponential)
Southeast	Value	14.95	27.60	27.53	27.25	Smoothing (Linear Exponential)

The custom models for these seven levels and the system-generated models for the remaining levels were then run again, this time including the out-of-sample data, as well as including an event variable for the May 2015 sales promotion. The following section also includes an interpretation of the results from these demand forecasts. Finally, what-if scenarios were constructed and compared to examine the effects of the two promotional events (December and May) and of a hypothetical price increase on overall sales as well as on sales in specific regions and of specific wine varieties (see Scenario Analysis).

MODEL SELECTION AND INTERPRETATION

Model Comparison and Building

Separate models were built via automatic selection for each variety of wine (vintage, value, table white, and table red) within each region of sales, for the individual sales regions, and on the entire combined dataset. The demand forecasting and planning system built exponential smoothing models (ESM), auto-regressive integrated moving average (ARIMA), and multiple regression models for each, and automatically selected the best models based on the lowest holdout MAPE. A cutoff level was set at 14 percent MAPE accuracy prior to modeling, which was deemed to be an acceptable error rate given the supply chain's ability to protect against a 14 percent swing in demand using safety (buffer) stock. Using this cutoff, seven models received additional attention to improve forecast accuracy. Table 7.3 shows the final model selections for each variety and region, as well as MAPEs and other measures of fit.

Value Wine: West, Northeast, and Southeast Regions

The models for value wines in the West, Northeast, and Southeast regions required further attention. Figure 7.6 shows the autocorrelation chart for the Western region (with the holdout sample):

The autocorrelation charts in Figure 7.6 show a significant spike at Lag 1 in the partial autocorrelation function (PACF) and the autocorrelation function appears to have exponentially decreasing values. These are characteristics that indicate a likely ARIMA

Table 7.3 Final Model Fit Statistics

Region	Type	Final Model	Holdout		Training + Holdout	All Data		
			MAPE	R-Squared	MAPE	MAPE	Reconciled MAPE	R-Squared
Overall	All	ARIMAX (Intercept)	6.39	0.60	15.13	6.46	6.25	0.88
Central (4)	All	ARIMAX (012) (100)	0.19	0.93	0.52	0.27	0.27	0.96
Central (4)	Vintage	ARIMAX (012) (100)	0.55	0.91	1.12	0.51	0.74	0.93
Central (4)	Table White	ARIMAX (012)(100)	1.62	-0.18	1.73	1.79	1.35	0.74
Central (4)	Table Red	ARIMAX (012) (100)	1.63	-0.18	1.80	1.84	1.39	0.73
Central (4)	Value	ARIMAX (1,1,1)	2.06	-0.01	2.80	2.50	2.78	0.26
North East (2)	All	ARIMAX (Intercept)	6.61	0.53	14.41	7.71	7.71	0.83
North East (2)	Vintage	UCM	7.72	0.73	12.74	10.09	14.52	-0.78
North East (2)	Table Red	Smoothing (Winters' Additive)	12.81	0.03	13.63	10.83	9.56	0.85
North East (2)	Table White	Smoothing (Winters' Additive)	12.99	0.02	13.86	10.79	9.38	0.85
North East (2)	Value	ARIMAX (1,1,1)	13.47	0.03	22.77	20.04	22.34	0.11
South East (3)	All	ARIMAX (100) (000)	6.22	0.62	15.73	6.61	6.61	0.88
South East (3)	Vintage	ARIMAX (Intercept)	6.70	0.73	15.13	7.59	13.50	0.63
South East (3)	Table Red	ARIMAX (1,1,1)	14.26	0.04	16.77	17.46	8.41	0.86
South East (3)	Table White	ARIMAX (1,1,1)	14.26	0.04	16.77	17.46	8.41	0.86
South East (3)	Value	ARIMAX (1,1,1)	14.95	0.03	22.92	20.13	33.01	-0.72
West (1)	All	ARIMAX (100)	6.18	0.61	16.38	6.46	6.46	0.89
West (1)	Vintage	UCM	9.23	0.39	16.81	7.63	11.43	0.67
West (1)	Table Red	ARIMAX (1,1,1)	14.26	0.15	16.00	17.50	8.96	0.85
West (1)	Table White	ARIMAX (1,1,1)	14.26	0.04	16.77	17.46	9.02	0.85
West (1)	Value	ARIMAX (1,1,1)	14.95	0.02	22.82	20.13	32.16	0.65

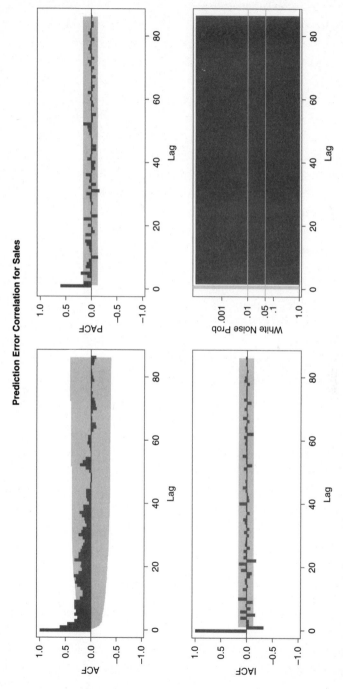

Figure 7.6 Autocorrelation panel for value wines in Western region.

(1,1,0) model. We added the price variable, which reflects the price of a case of value wine, to test if this affects the number of cases purchased. However, even with the price variable, there still remained an upward/downward trend and so differencing of the demand history was taken to capture (account) for the trend effects. After running the model, the residual errors were checked to verify if any seasonality remained or if there were any outliers. After careful study of the output, it was determined that the residual errors were inflated on the weeks of December 24, 2013, and December 30, 2014, which coincide with our promotions. Interestingly, the promotion had a positive effect on sales demand, which indicates that the promotion led to added incremental demand. With each of these factors included into the model, the overall MAPE based on the holdout sample decreased to 13.49 percent.

Multiple models were tested to verify that the holdout MAPE had been minimized, but we were ultimately unable to beat the afore-mentioned model. Exponential smoothing models were generated but have a minimum MAPE of over 14.95 percent. Other ARIMAs such as (0,1,1) and (0,1,2) were tested, but they did not predict the hold-out sample as accurately. Much effort was spent on building multiple regression models due to the increased interpretability available via such modeling techniques. However, this increased interpretability was not significant enough to offset the large increase in MAPE.

The MAPEs for value wine forecasts in the Northeast and South-east regions also fell outside of the filtering threshold. It was quickly apparent that the autocorrelation charts were very similar to the West-ern region. The same modeling methodology was used to build models for these regions, but the ARIMA (1,1,1) model with the December sales promotion (intervention variable) causal variable offered the low-est MAPE.

Table Red Wine: West and Southeast Region

For both of these regions, exponential smoothing models were auto-matically selected, but the MAPEs fell outside of the cutoff level. Using similar methods to above, various models were built to best fit the data. It was again noted that both of these regions' autocorrelation charts were very similar, implying that similar models could be employed for both regions. An ARIMA (1,1,1) model with the December sales promotion causal variable offered the best predictive power over the holdout sample period bringing MAPE under the 14 percent threshold.

Table White Wine: West and Southeast Region

Table white wines in the West and Southeast regions had MAPEs over the cutoff level under the automatic model selection. As with each of the earlier sets of models, the autocorrelation charts for these two levels of the hierarchy were very similar, and thus similar models were likely to minimize both MAPEs. Models were built manually using similar methods to those used on the earlier levels, and again the ARIMA (1,1,1) model with the December sales promotion causal variable proved the most accurate. This model decreased the holdout MAPE for both models to 13.98 percent.

The original exponential smoothing model offered a relatively similar holdout MAPE. However, the ARIMA (1,1,1) model had a substantially higher Adjusted R-squared value of 0.784 versus 0.346 for the ESM. Additionally, the increased interpretability of the ARIMA model and the ability to add event variables made the decision straightforward. ESM models offer limited interpretation, and are primarily used to maximize forecast accuracy when interpretation of other factors like sales promotions is not needed.

Overall Model

The overall model was autogenerated with the middle-out hierarchical settings and selected an ARIMA model with a holdout MAPE of 5.91 percent, well below our cutoff level. Additional analysis was not necessary due to the strong predictive strength of the model. The final model selected was reconciled, which included the base price, the December sales promotions, the May sales promotion, and an outlier variable for the week of December 18, 2013.

Figure 7.7 shows the parameter estimates for the final overall model. There appears to be trend and seasonality associated with wine sales. The estimate for base price implies that for each dollar increase

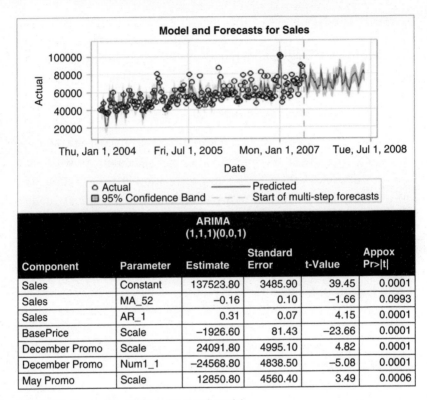

Figure 7.7 Parameter estimates for overall model.

in price, with all else held constant, sales would decrease by approximately 1,926.6 cases per week. The December sales promotion, which offered 10 percent off every purchase during the last week of 2013 and 2014, increased weekly sales on average by 24,091.8 units. However, there was a negative effect that occurred the week after the December sales promotion, which decreases sales by 24,568.8 units. These lower sales could be a result of customers' pantry loading additional wine anticipating the holiday with family and friends visiting and for gifting purposes. The May sales promotion, on the other hand, increased weekly sales by approximately 12,850.8 cases on average with little if any pantry load effects.

SCENARIO ANALYSIS

The Implications of a 5 Percent Price Increase

An across-the-board price increase of 5 percent per case would result in an estimated 4.47 percent drop in sales for the XWZ Winery as a whole, while raising total revenues by an estimated 0.3 percent because the effects of this price increase are not uniform across all regions and products, it is believed that a more targeted price increase would have a stronger positive effect on revenues. Figure 7.8 shows the drop in sales after a 5 percent increase in price.

As Table 7.4 shows, the Northeast region has the largest projected loss of sales, with an estimated reduction of 63,511 cases sold, a loss of 6.54 percent of regional sales volume. Since this results in a projected revenue loss of 1.86 percent once the price increase is also taken into effect, a price increase in Northeast is not recommended. In contrast, the Central region shows a strong projected revenue increase, with the price increase more than making up for the slight loss of sales. The Southeastern region shows a slight increase in projected revenue, but the difference is small enough that other business considerations should be taken into account when deciding whether to take a price increase.

On the face of it, the Western region appears similar to Southeast. But when further subdivided by type of wine, as shown in Table 7.5, only red wine sales in the Western region cannot sustain the price increase. An increase in price for the other types of wine would result in a stronger projected growth of revenues.

Final Recommendations

Given these results and analysis, our final recommendation related to whether to proceed with a 5 percent price increase across regions/types is as follows:

- **Increase prices in the Central region, but not for the other types of wine as it would result in a stronger projected growth of revenues.**

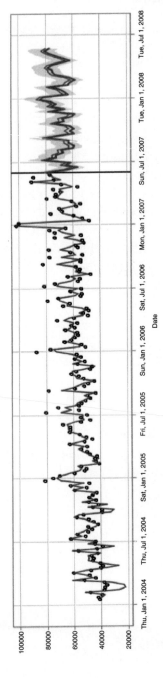

Figure 7.8 Nationwide sales projections for 2015, with and without a price increase.

Table 7.4 Projected Change Due to 5% Price Increase

Projected Change in Remaining 2007 Sales Due to 5% Price Increase					
	Overall	West (1)	Northeast (2)	Southeast (3)	Central (4)
Total Change/Volume	−96652	−42596	−63511	−5477	−430
Percent Change/Volume	−4.47%	−4.59%	−6.54%	−3.91%	−0.40%
Percent Change/Income	0.30%	0.18%	−1.86%	0.90%	4.58%
Recommendation		Limited Increase	Do Not Increase	Possible Increase	Increase

Table 7.5 West Region Projected Change in Sales Volume & Income by Type

Western Region Projected Change in Remaining 2007 Sales Due to 5% Price Increase				
	Vintage	Red	White	Value
Percent Change/Volume	−1.78%	−7.79%	0.20%	−1.04%
Percent Change/Income	0.18%	−3.18%	3.13%	5.21%
Recommendation	Possible Increase	Do Not Increase	Increase	Increase

Pros

▪ **Lower unit loss:** Total units loss, under our recommended scenario, will be **2,082 units** (compared to a potential 44,964 unit loss if prices were increased across all regions).

▪ **Substantial additional profits for the Central region**: Given that the expected decrease in units for Central region is very low (only 0.2 percent), we believe that the price increase will turn out beneficial for XYZ Wines in terms of profit. To support this insight, we conducted a hypothetical P&L analysis (see Table 7.6) under the following assumptions for the Central region.

Another final assumption, not shown in Table 7.6, is related to the cost structure of the Central region. We assumed a cost structure of 80 percent fixed costs, and 20 percent variable costs.

Table 7.6 P&L Analysis Assumptions

Variable	Assumption	Source
Average Price, Region 2	$54	WineData
Units (June–December, 2007)	971,679	Forecast Model for Region 2
Profit Margin (%)	17%	Industry Benchmark: Beverages – Wineries & Distillers, Yahoo! Finance (http://biz.yahoo.com/p/347mktd .html)

P&L Analysis: Actual versus Scenario

Overall, XYZ Winery will potentially add **$2,530,765** to its bottom line by increasing prices 5 percent in the Central region. Bear in mind that the Central region (Region 2) is the most influential region for the company, as it accounts for 45 percent of total sales. These figures could be subject to significant improvement by the financial department, but we believe they signal the potential for increasing profits for the company if we were to make this move.

Cons/Risks

■ **Unexpected decrease in units for Region 2, Central:** Our price/volume sensitivity analysis was performed under the assumption that the past relationship between price and volume holds for our demand forecast in Region 2 (Central). See Table 7.7. To assess the risk of a volume decrease different from the forecasted 0.2 percent, we used the same financial model of the previous section. Based on this model, we established a maximum unit decrease **threshold of 5.7 percent**. This

Table 7.7 What-If Analysis for 5% Price Increase in Region 2

	Actual	Scenario	Change
Price	$54	$57	5%
Units	971,679	969,736	−0.2%
Revenue	$52,470,666	$54,984,011	4.8%
Profit	$8,920,013.22	$11,450,778.38	28.4%
Profit Mrg.	17.0%	20.8%	3.8%

is, if demand in Region 2-Central decreases above this level, then the price increase will be detrimental for the region in terms of profit (less profit than the expected under the no price increase scenario). This threshold, we believe, could be used to monitor the demand response for the first few weeks of the price increase and dampen the risk of an unexpected variation in volume.

In an attempt to analyze the effects of known sales promotions, interventions were created and applied up and down the hierarchy for the three events outlined by senior management. These events were as follows:

1. **May sales promotion:** Buy a case and get a 15 percent discount.

   a. The sales promotion started the week of May 5, 2015, and ran for four weeks.

2. **December sales promotion:** Buy one case and get a 10 percent discount.

   a. The sales promotion was a test promotion the week of December 31, 2013 and 2014, and ran one week.

In addition to the sales promotion events, we also selected pre-defined holiday events from the event repository to run against our models. It is important to note that only one of the sales promotions was used in the final models to help explain variation in the data. The December 31, 2013, promotion appears in five of the forecasting models as either a pulse or temporary change event. Additionally, a few highly significant outlier events were detected and applied to the appropriate models to account for additional variation in the wine sales demand data. We are currently working closely with the sales and marketing teams to uncover any local events run by retailers during those times.

Cons/Risks

■ The December sales promotion, which offered 10 percent off every purchase during the last week of 2013 and 2014, increased weekly sales on average by 24,091.8 units. However, there was a negative effect that occurred the week after the December sales promotion, which decreased sales by 24,568.8 units. This sales promotion on the surface does not appear very effective when applied across all regions and products as consumers appear to be pantry loading due to the holiday in anticipation for additional consumption during the holiday, and gifting. However, running this promotion multiple times (four times) over the year could significantly increase volume, thus reducing pantry loading.

■ We are interested in investigating further with senior management the possibility of running the December sales promotion during the weeks prior to and during Valentine's Day as we found two outlier events were significant in the weeks of February 21 and February 28 in 2004. The spike in sales demand during these two weeks accounts for around 30,000 cases of wine sales.

■ In the Southeast region, a highly significant outlier event was detected during the week of August 14, 2012. This spike accounts for 17,350 cases of wine sold in the Northeast region of the United States. Perhaps there was a back to school sales promotion? Or perhaps this surge in sales is directly correlated with Hurricane Sandy, which made landfall in South/North Carolina and in the next day moved up the east coast. Maybe people in the Northeast stocked up on wine for the storm. Either way, further investigation is needed to understand this event.

Final Recommendation

Based on our analysis, although the December promotion was the more effective for any given week, the depth of the promotion and seasonal timing encourage consumers to pantry load. This situation actually decreases sales over the two-week period. The larger percent discount (15 percent) proved better for the company's bottom line in May 2015, and weekly incremental sales rose by a larger amount overall (12,850.8 units). The May event did last longer (three weeks) than the December event, thus increasing total demand more than the shorter event, but we believe there may be an opportunity to

Table 7.8 Estimated Change in Sales due to Promotions

Estimated Change in Sales Due to Promotions					
	Overall	West (1)	Northeast (2)	Southeast (3)	Central (4)
Estimated Weekly Increase During December Promotion	23500	10513.3	10615.6	1565.2	Not significant[1]
Estimated Weekly Percent Increase During December Promotion	24.39%	24.94%	30.59%	30.34%	Not significant
Estimated Weekly Increase During May Promotion	12850.8	6231.2	5570.5	906.6	Not significant
Estimated Weekly Percent Increase During May Promotion	15.55%	17.02%	14.92%	16.50%	Not significant

offset these effects by having 4 one-week 10 percent discount events spaced throughout the year, realizing the higher weekly benefit of the December event with similar benefits to the longer duration of the May event. We also do not recommend running any promotions in the Western region. See Table 7.8.

Giving a 10 percent-off, one-week, December-style promotion spaced throughout the year could be the vehicle for generating additional sales. The increased sales from the sale promotion could be enough to counteract any sales lost due to the price increase. It was found that instituting a 5 percent price increase across the board together with a quarterly one-week 10 percent-off promotion would result in an estimated 1.21 percent reduction in sales by volume and a corresponding 2.10 percent increase in revenues. On the other hand, by instituting the price increase only for those regions and types of wine recommended in the previous section, and offering the quarterly discount only in the Central, Northeast, and Southeast regions, significantly higher revenues would be expected.

SUMMARY

The monthly demand planning brief allows companies to continuously look ahead and plan based on sales tactics and marketing investment strategies. It contains the details and actions taken by the demand forecasting and planning team working closely with the sales and marketing organizations using feedback from actual execution to final demand response. This tight collaboration in maintaining this document between the demand forecasting and planning and sales and marketing organizations creates trust, accountability, and ownership.

As seen through the winery example, the next generation demand management process is more than just creating an accurate demand forecast. It is a business analytics function embedded downstream in the sales and marketing organization providing analytics support to drive demand generation. As such, demand analysts working closely with sales and marketing provide predictive analytics support to validate and justify sales tactics and marketing strategies that impact the final demand response.

Demand sensing and shaping capabilities not only provide the ability to predict demand more accurately, but also can uncover deep insights into customer/consumer behavior by identifying those key performance indicators that influence consumer demand and replenishment polices. These factors can be quantified (measured) and used to shape future demand based on sales and marketing tactics and strategies. As such, those tactics and strategies need to be tested and validated using predictive analytics and documented to maintain accountability and ownership.

Implementing a monthly demand planning brief is the best way to build accountability and ownership of the unconstrained demand forecast through sound testing using analytics and documentation of the assumptions (tactics and strategies) that were used to justify the demand forecast. Then, get sign-off by the sales and marketing senior management team prior to the S&OP meeting. The monthly *demand planning brief* outlines in detail what tactics and strategies were tested to validate the assumptions using data and analytics versus gut feelings.

KEY LEARNINGS

- Implementing a monthly demand planning brief is the best way to build accountability and ownership.

- The monthly demand planning brief outlines in detail what tactics and strategies were used to create the final demand response.

- Demand sensing and shaping capabilities provide the ability to not only predict demand more accurately, but also uncover insights that influence future demand. Those insights are driven through the use of downstream data and collaboration between demand planning and sales and marketing.

- The next generation demand management process will require new analytics skills and the hiring of demand analysts (data scientists) who need to be embedded in sales and marketing closer to the customer/consumer to support demand generation.

CHAPTER **8**

The Strategic Roadmap

The purpose of this chapter is to outline the demand planning self-assessment, identify gaps, and create a strategic roadmap to the next generation demand management, which is a journey that requires investment in people, process, analytics, and technology. The roadmap will guide supply chain leaders in determining the sequence of actions required to bring all four dimensions of the demand planning process into focus, along with a step-by-step strategic roadmap.

CURRENT STATE VERSUS FUTURE STATE

Transitioning from current state to future state demand planning seldom evolves slowly over time naturally. Companies that have successfully moved from current state to future state are dedicated to focusing their efforts on improving their demand planning capabilities by investing in people, process, analytics, and technology. Future state brings structure to the demand planning function, with the goal of bringing more consistency to the overall process with emphasis not only on improving forecast accuracy but also on providing actionable insights through predictive analytics to support demand generation. At this level of process capabilities, companies are able to integrate downstream consumption (true demand) data with upstream shipments (supply) data from their demand signal repositories, and ERP transaction systems to identity demand patterns and to produce calculated fact-based forecasts that are driven by consumer demand where statistically feasible. Higher accuracy across the product mix requires the capability to produce middle-out demand plans based on validated sales tactics and marketing strategies, disaggregating them down to SKU/demand point with automatic generated reconciliation for hundreds of thousands of products using large-scale hierarchical forecasting technology. The goal is visibility through demand sensing to the end product demand down to the SKU level detail proactively shaping future demand based on data, analytics, and domain knowledge.

Regardless of the industry, every company supplying a product or service has long supply lead times—in many cases, longer than their customer's lead times. According to feedback from global CPG companies, demand volatility is increasing, and there is no foreseen decline. In fact, many companies see demand variability increasing over the next two to three years as changes in consumer preferences continue, and channel purchases move to the IoT. Meanwhile, legacy siloed demand planning processes, simple statistical methods, and ERP technologies have been unable to accurately predict future demand across their vast complex supply chains. Companies that are working in the current state have become overwhelmed by ever increasing volatility of demand, which they are unprepared to handle. This has led to erosion of volume growth, profitability, and customer service performance by having the wrong mix of products in the wrong locations at the wrong time.

Current state suggests that there is very limited or little formalized demand planning discipline in the business. This is not to say that demand planning is not occurring, but rather the process is usually siloed with little if any horizontal connection between the supply and demand functions. The supply chain, the locations in the value chain, functional groups, organizations, and even individuals within those organizations all develop their own future plan requirements for their operational needs. Usually, these fragmented demand plans are generated based on untested and invalidated sales tactics, marketing strategies, and financial objectives. Furthermore, there is very little linkage to actual end-consumer preferences and customer demand outlook (see Figure 8.1).

To transition from current state to future state, the first requirement is that business leaders understand the strategic importance of demand planning. This can only be achieved by assigning a champion, preferably someone at the C-level who can address the change management challenges and get the full support of the senior

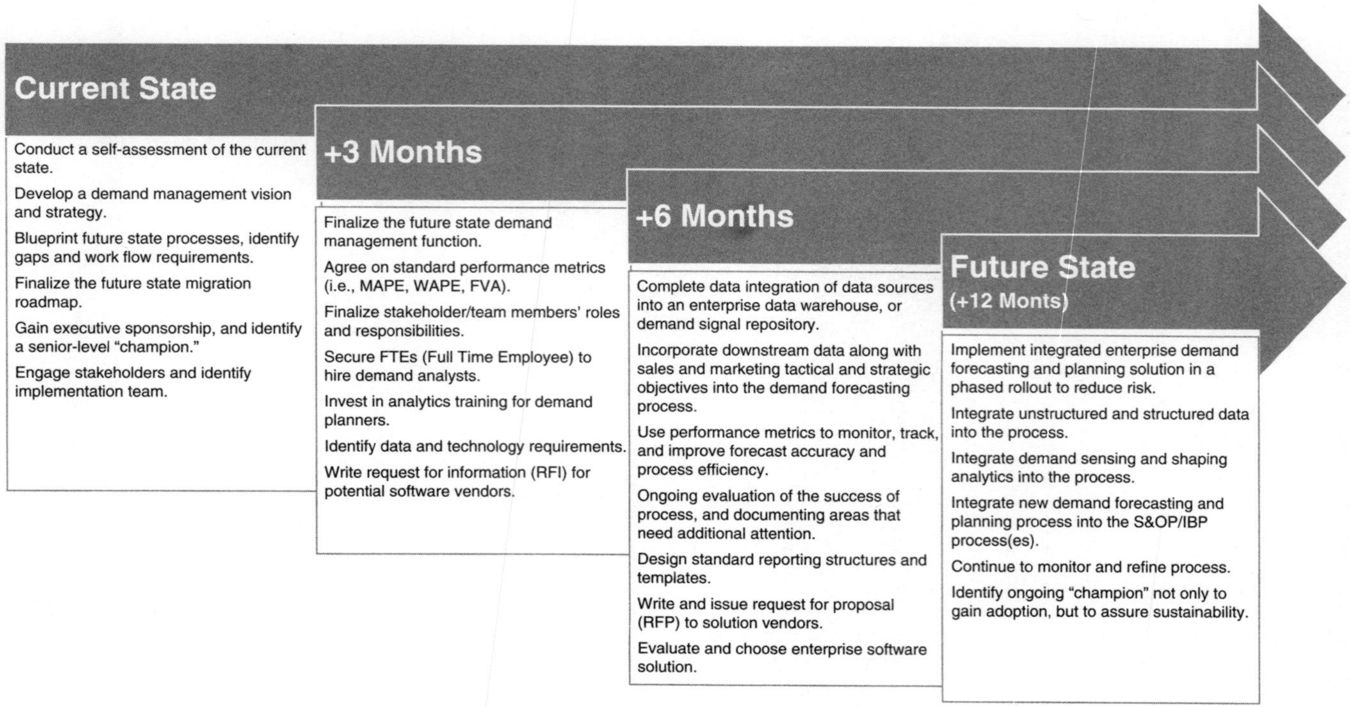

Current State

Conduct a self-assessment of the current state.

Develop a demand management vision and strategy.

Blueprint future state processes, identify gaps and work flow requirements.

Finalize the future state migration roadmap.

Gain executive sponsorship, and identify a senior-level "champion."

Engage stakeholders and identify implementation team.

+3 Months

Finalize the future state demand management function.

Agree on standard performance metrics (i.e., MAPE, WAPE, FVA).

Finalize stakeholder/team members' roles and responsibilities.

Secure FTEs (Full Time Employee) to hire demand analysts.

Invest in analytics training for demand planners.

Identify data and technology requirements.

Write request for information (RFI) for potential software vendors.

+6 Months

Complete data integration of data sources into an enterprise data warehouse, or demand signal repository.

Incorporate downstream data along with sales and marketing tactical and strategic objectives into the demand forecasting process.

Use performance metrics to monitor, track, and improve forecast accuracy and process efficiency.

Ongoing evaluation of the success of process, and documenting areas that need additional attention.

Design standard reporting structures and templates.

Write and issue request for proposal (RFP) to solution vendors.

Evaluate and choose enterprise software solution.

Future State
(+12 Monts)

Implement integrated enterprise demand forecasting and planning solution in a phased rollout to reduce risk.

Integrate unstructured and structured data into the process.

Integrate demand sensing and shaping analytics into the process.

Integrate new demand forecasting and planning process into the S&OP/IBP process(es).

Continue to monitor and refine process.

Identify ongoing "champion" not only to gain adoption, but to assure sustainability.

Figure 8.1 Strategic roadmap from current state to future state.

Note: Timeline indicates when each stage in the migration roadmap begins.

218

management team (see Figure 8.1). Only with senior leadership support and a champion driving the necessary change management activities will adoption and sustainability of the future state take place within the company. The demand planning process owner working closely with the champion will need to build a strategic roadmap identifying the necessary process capabilities to successfully implement the next generation demand management organization across the four dimensions of demand planning (people, process, analytics, and technology).

Transforming your demand management organization from current state to future state will be a journey requiring commitment and continuous investment in people, process, analytics, and technology. Although many organizations start by focusing on projects to improve processes and implement enabling technology, the greatest gains will be achieved by investing in people skills and predictive analytics, and addressing corporate cultural behavior. Changing corporate behavior is the hardest thing to do, and it takes the longest amount of time and commitment.

The journey starts with an assessment of the current state to establish a benchmark to measure the progress of the future state. The journey follows a logical structured flow, which is explained by expanding on the content outlined in Figure 8.1. First, the company must be convinced that moving to the future state is essential to support long-term growth and profitability. This will basically answer the *why* question: Why should the company embark on this journey? Next, the organization will detail the *what*: What is the end state, and what are the intermediate steps needed to reach it? With the organization's buy-in and support, the next challenge will be to clarify the *how*: How can the company progress from current state to future state?

The purpose of this chapter is to delve deep into Table 8.1 by providing a more detailed explanation of the *why* by reviewing the current state, and then, expanding on those key points identified in Figure 8.1. Finally, provide a step-by-step roadmap regarding people, process, analytics, and technology of the *how*. Let's begin with an assessment of the current state.

Table 8.1 Strategic Roadmap from Current State to Future State.

		Strategic Road Map		
	Current State	Future State	Gap	Migration Path
People	▪ Demand planners using system-generated basic time series methods used in a "black box" approach ▪ No use of downstream data ▪ No investment in analytics training	▪ Advanced statistical skills using predictive analytics ▪ Understanding downstream data ▪ Companies are now hiring demand analysts with advanced analytics knowledge to provide demand planners with more accurate statistical forecasts	▪ Demand planners have no advance analytics skills ▪ Using basic times series methods ▪ Demand planners need to transition from managers of data to demand analysts with a focus on predictive analytics ▪ No investment in demand analysts with more advanced analytics skills	▪ Hire demand analysts (data scientists) and embed them in the sales and marketing organizations to provide analytics support to develop the final demand response ▪ Embed demand analysts in sales and marketing to provide analytic support with a focus on uncovering insights to drive demand generation ▪ Send demand planners to forecasting certification program ▪ Train demand planners in the use of downstream POS/syndicated scanner data along with sales and marketing tactics and strategies
Process	▪ Supply centric operation planning oriented ▪ Forecasting shipments or sales orders ▪ Not using POS/syndicated scanner data (true demand) ▪ Many people making manual overrides ▪ Not using FVA/Lean Forecasting to monitor and track touch points	▪ Demand-driven supply chain focused on customer excellence ▪ Forecasting true consumer demand using downstream (POS/syndicated scanner data) ▪ Sensing demand signals and shaping future demand using "What-If" Scenario analysis	▪ Strategic importance of demand planning is not understood by senior management ▪ Siloed attempts to predict future demand using shipments ▪ Sales and Marketing not participating in S&OP process ▪ Forecasting shipments (supply) or sales orders (replenishment) with no integration with consumption ▪ Weak collaboration with Sales and Marketing	▪ Redefine SCM to include the downstream commercial teams creating a "holistic supply chain" linking demand and supply ▪ Horizontal supply chain process ▪ Identify and secure a "champion" preferably at the C-Level to address the change management challenges of the migration to future state ▪ Introduce FVA/Lean Forecasting to improve forecast accuracy and increase process efficiency by eliminating touch points in the process ▪ Invest in demand-driven forecasting process that is more demand centric

(continued)

Table 8.1 (Continued)

Strategic Road Map

	Current State	Future State	Gap	Migration Path
	▪ Forecast is top-down ▪ Collaborative planning is politically driven with minimal accountability ▪ Performance metrics are focused on aggregate level	▪ Demand shifting only occurs during the S&OP/IBP process upon adding supply constraints ▪ Implementing FVA to improve forecast accuracy and efficiency ▪ Focusing on the lower product mix, not only the aggregate level ▪ Using Demand Planning Brief with "Analytics Snapshot" to test, validate, and document sales tactics and marketing strategies	▪ Lack of data integration with POS/syndicated scanner data and shipments ▪ Not sensing demand signals and shaping future demand using "What-If" Scenario analysis ▪ Too many people touching the forecast ▪ Not using FVA to minimize touch points adding accuracy and efficiency to the process ▪ Top-down forecasting driven by politically motivated goals and objectives ▪ Performance metrics are focused on aggregate versus the lower level product mix	▪ Integrate downstream POS/syndicated scanner data into the process ▪ Introduce demand sensing and shaping capabilities ▪ Segment data to apply appropriate methods ▪ Focus advanced analytics on fast-moving products using consumption based forecasting using the MTCA process ▪ Focus on measuring forecast accuracy at the lower levels of the product mix ▪ Introduce hierarchical forecasting with top-down, middle-out, and bottom-up forecasting ▪ Introduce "Demand Planning Brief" to document, test, and validate sales tactics and marketing strategies to build trust, accountability, and ownership
Analytics	▪ Simple statistical methods used (e.g., moving averaging and exponential smoothing)	▪ Using advanced statistical methods (e.g., ARIMA, ARIMAX, Dynamic Regression) ▪ Incorporate "What-If" Scenario Analysis (Demand Shaping) ▪ Consumption based forecasting using the MTCA process	▪ No advanced predictive analytics being used (e.g., ARIMA, ARIMAX, dynamic regression) ▪ No demand sensing and shaping being conducted ▪ No understanding of consumption based forecasting using the MTCA process	▪ Conduct hierarchical forecasting ▪ Introduce more advanced analytics (i.e., ARIMA, ARIMAX, dynamic regression) for demand sensing and shaping ▪ Integrate consumption based modeling using the MTCA process where appropriate for fast-moving products

(continued)

Table 8.1 (Continued)

| | Strategic Road Map | | |
	Current State	Future State	Gap	Migration Path
Technology	■ Primarily Excel (77%) ■ No demand sensing and shaping capabilities ■ Descriptive reporting only ■ Little integration across supply chain ■ No real centralized enterprise data repository or warehouse ■ Fragmented data marts supporting local applications ■ Unable to explore "Big Data" to uncover actionable insights using predictive analytics ■ Manually cleansing demand historical to accommodate short-comings of analytics methods deployed in technology—exponential smoothing	■ Large scale technology with demand sensing and shaping capabilities ■ Descriptive (reporting) and Predictive (statistical) Analytics capabilities ■ Control Tower/Dashboard reporting capabilities ■ Manage "Big Data" using parallel, grid processing, and in-store memory	■ Still using first generation ERP demand management solutions ■ ERP DM module requires cleansing of demand history into baseline and promoted ■ Unable to do "holistic" modeling ■ Excel is the technology of choice due to poor flexibility of legacy systems and lack of advanced analytics ■ No demand sensing and shaping capabilities ■ Poor BI capabilities with basic dashboards ■ Unable to handle "Big Data" due to first generation ERP solutions	■ Invest in demand-driven forecasting and planning best-in-class technology ■ "Large Scale Automatic Hierarchy Forecasting" engine ■ Advanced analytics model repository ■ MTCA technology for consumption based forecasting ■ Scalable to "Big Data" ■ Collaborative planning with workflow using Excel as interface ■ Introduce "holistic" modeling ■ Eliminate data cleansing ■ Invest in demand signal analytics (DSA) technology with control tower/dashboard and exploration capabilities using visual analytics (VA)

222

CURRENT STATE

Current state companies view the demand planning process from a supply-centric orientation that focuses completely on operational excellence, rather than customer excellence. It is vertically aligned with emphasis solely on reducing costs with little if any attention to demand generation. They view forecasts as always wrong. As a result, their strategy is to use buffer stock (inventory safety stock) to protect against demand variably. In their overall view, since companies' supply lead times exceed customers' lead times, some sort of demand planning has to occur in the supply chain. This leads to the function reporting into upstream operations planning far removed from the customer/consumer. Furthermore, as companies try to minimize out-of-stocks (OOS) and maximize on-time delivery to their customers in the short-term all the functions along the supply chain develop their own forecasts for future requirements hedging against the demand plan. The most commonly used information source for predicting future demand is historical unit volumes. This leaves the supply chain operating with a number of disconnected predictions of future demand. Those predictions are commonly optimized against the functional and department objectives, resulting in an overall sub-optimized supply chain.

Goals and Objectives

- A formalized demand planning process that is tactical with a focus on creating a shipment-based (supply-based) forecast that is not seen as a strategic planning process reflective of true demand by the commercial business teams.

- A short-term unit volume forecast is developed using the shipments (supply history) and/or sales orders (replenishment history). The planning horizon is based on an operational (one- to three-month frozen) planning view.

- S&OP process (bridge) is designed to close and explain the gaps between the current view of demand and the annual operating plan (budget) with the goal of setting sales targets to close the gaps.

People

- Demand planners' primary role is the management of information and data with the goal of creating a final shipment forecast (supply plan).

- Data cleansing and information management take up 80 percent or more of the demand planners' time during each planning cycle.

- Demand planners report upstream to the operations planning organization, with ownership and accountability falling primarily on the demand management team.

- Demand planners use system-generated basic time series methods (e.g., moving averaging and non-seasonal exponential smoothing)—a *black box approach*—to create the statistical baseline forecasts.

- Little if any investment is made in updating demand planners statistical skills.

- There is little use and little knowledge of downstream data.

Process

- Simple statistical methods, primarily moving averaging and nonseasonal exponential smoothing, are used to create a statistical baseline forecast. Promotions and outliers are cleansed from the historical demand history (shipments and/or sales orders), and adjusted and passed to the commercial teams for manual input.

- Little if any ownership or accountability for commercial overrides to the promoted volumes, which are manually layered back to the baseline forecast volume by the demand planners.

- The collaboration planning process is politically charged with minimal accountability for those who make manual adjustments to the statistical baseline forecasts.

- S&OP process is vertically aligned and tactical in nature with a focus on creating a three month frozen supply plan. No perceived benefits for the commercial teams to participate in the process. It is a top-down process with a focus on OP (operations planning) with no integration of downstream data, or accountability for financial plugs designed to close the gaps between the financial plan (budget) and current demand forecast.

Analytics

- Lights-out black box approach using simple statistical methods (e.g., moving averaging and nonseasonal exponential smoothing) to create the baseline demand forecasts. No use of predictive analytics.
- Some descriptive analytics are used for reporting purposes.
- The primary performance metric is MAPE focused on the aggregate level of the business hierarchy. Little if any attention to the lower-level mix MAPEs.
- Not using FVA/lean forecasting to monitor and track value-added and non-value-added activities in the process.

Technology

- Excel spreadsheets are the dominant tool for capturing and analyzing forecast information. They also are the resources for sharing information and data across the organization.
- Manually cleansing demand history into baseline and promoted volumes to accommodate shortcomings of the analytics methods deployed in their ERP demand management technology.
- Many times companies attempted to buy their way into demand planning competency by purchasing demand planning software before their processes, data, and organizations are developed and ready to become demand-driven. In other words, they purchase demand planning solutions and then twist and bend them to fit their existing process. This not only sub-optimizes the technology, but also the process, with poor results. This results in failure and expensive software not being used.

- Demand planning is based on ERP (enterprise resource planning) transactional data. ERP systems capture numerous amounts of detailed data, and the large volume of transactions complicates and slows down the process. Data downloads often take a very long time, and developing meaningful information from hundreds of thousands or more transactions is very tedious, complicated, and prone to errors.

- No real centralized enterprise data repository or warehouse to store information and data. Information and data are fragmented across the organization in data marts supporting local applications. As a result, unable to explore big data to uncover actionable insights using predictive analytics.

- The biggest challenge is converting massive amounts of data into actionable (or usable) information that the organization can absorb, understand, and use effectively to make better-informed decisions.

FUTURE STATE

Companies who begin the next generation demand management journey from current to future state start to consider the demand planning process as not only a tactical but also a strategic capability. Investments are made in creating a more structured fact-based process using data and predictive analytics. This requires further investment in dedicated demand analysts who have advanced analytics skills, rather than demand planners who manage data and information. Over time, the demand analysts and planners tend to acquire strong analytical skill sets and domain knowledge, adding more value to the demand plans instead of acting merely as data information manipulators.

The demand plans based on future state are based on sales tactics and marketing investment strategies predicting unit volumes, and then translated into revenue and profit. The company's objective is to reach a consistent rolling 18-month planning horizon (with a tactical planning horizon ranging between 6 and 13 weeks). At this stage, companies have the ability to measure forecast accuracy, and they can identify the primary sources of error using FVA (forecast valued added) with the goal of making significant improvements in forecast accuracy as well as process efficiency by eliminating nonvalue added activities.

Goals and Objectives

- *There is executive-level sponsorship required to assure adaption and sustainability of the new process design.* The initial executive level support for demand planning usually comes from the senior supply chain leadership team who sponsors, supports, and becomes the champion of the new demand planning process. The sponsor has a vested interest in the outcome of each demand plan update, and interacts with its business cross-functional peers (sales, marketing, and finance) to improve decision making process to drive revenue growth and profit. However, that does not mean a C-level manager from sales and/or marketing should not be given the opportunity to champion the new generation demand management process, as it is not just about reducing costs. In fact, given that downstream data, sales tactics, and marketing strategies play a key role in the process, it makes more sense to have a C-level manager from the commercial side of the business champion the future state.

- Preferably, a committee/board made up of C-level managers represented by sales, marketing, finance, and operations should be established as the overseer of the process by which the stakeholder (champion) reports. Any challenges related to change management and other related activities requiring approvals (i.e., hiring, training, technology purchases, and others) will require sign-off by the oversight committee/board. This cross-sectional board over time will better understand the value and benefits creating accountability and ownership of the process.

- The unconstrained consumer demand forecast is generated using downstream POS/syndicated scanner data (where appropriate), sales orders, and shipment history supported by internal consumer/trade insights. The demand planning process relies on historical customer/consumer demand in developing both the short-term tactical and long-term strategic plans. Most companies usually leverage only the historical data from customer sales orders and shipments in order to get a view of historical demand patterns. Emerging collaboration with sales and marketing teams provides valuable consumer insights for future demand forecasts. So, it is imperative that information regarding sales promotions, pricing, and other related factors is identified to sense and shape future demand, including customer sales orders and/or shipments where POS/syndicated scanner data are not available or do not make sense.

■ *The main objective is to generate a unit volume unconstrained demand plan as an input into the S&OP/IBP process.* Since one of the main uses for demand forecasts is supply planning, the forecast should reflect unit volumes. Also, translation from units to revenue is more accurate than the reverse due to pricing changes. Therefore, it is recommended to always create the demand plan in units, then convert it to revenue. The final demand plan is developed at the SKU/location level, and the resulting data are uploaded to upstream operations planning systems.

■ Demand planning is a tactical and strategic supply chain process that can no longer be compiled in a vacuum upstream in the operations planning area. The demand forecasts of the next generation demand management process provide valuable input to sales and marketing to support demand generation as well as operational execution. If dollars, profit margins, and other related versions of the future demand forecast are required, it is necessary to invest in new demand-driven technology that can convert the unit volume forecast into those unit measures on the fly through a conversion table to support all planning requirements. However, it is critical that the initial demand forecast be derived in units, then converted to dollars, profit, pallets, and others to maintain continuity and accuracy across the organization. There should always be one version of the truth (most up-to-date unconstrained demand forecast) that all participating departments can view on demand.

People

- *Dedicated demand planners supported by demand analysts who are embedded in the commercial organization.* Companies are investing in centers of forecasting excellence at the corporate level, and are staffing those centers of excellence with demand analysts, not demand planners. Demand analysts are responsible for creating the statistical baseline forecasts for all the regions/divisions. Once those statistical forecasts are tested and validated, working closely with the regional/divisional demand planners, the forecasts are turned over to the demand planners, who work closely with the local commercial business teams to make adjustments based on local sales and marketing activities, such as sales promotions and other related marketing programs.

  The skill sets of these newly created demand analyst positions are different in that those individuals have advanced statistical skills and strong business acumen. They also have strong collaboration skills as they work closely with the regional demand planners. The regional demand planners are in a true planner role, rather than statistical forecasters working with the local commercial business teams to make adjustments to the statistical forecasts based on local sales/marketing activities (i.e., sales promotions, pricing actions, and others).

- *Companies are realizing the value of analytics and the positive impact it has on demand planning.* Companies are hiring dedicated demand analysts to provide more structure and analytics to the demand planning organization. The ratio of demand analysts to the number of demand planners depends on the size and complexity of the business. It is very common for global companies to assign a lead demand analyst at the global level to support each demand planning team at the regional level. The new role of demand planners is more of a coordinating role supporting demand planning, rather than manipulation of the statistical baseline forecast.

- *The demand planning role is moving from its traditional supply chain origins to the sales and marketing organizations.* The demand planner roles were initially established under the supply chain organization, but now companies are slowing realizing that demand planners need to be closer to the customer/consumer in order to improve forecast accuracy. Reporting into the supply chain puts demand planners too far upstream, removed from the customer, to understand those program vehicles that influence demand. Working downstream in the process supporting the commercial business, who are responsible for demand generation, demand planners are better positioned to translate those sales/marketing programs into viable inputs into the statistical unconstrained demand forecast. These new organizational changes allow demand planners to collaborate closely with the commercial team. Companies are finding a strong correlation between a centralized demand analyst structure supporting a decentralize regional demand planning organizational tends to improves forecast accuracy.

Process

■ *Formalizing the demand planning processes.* With dedicated demand planning resources trained and in place, the demand-planning process becomes standardized across the entire supply chain including sales and marketing. The best practices are propagated across the different demand channels. New-product life cycle management planning plays a key role and needs to be included in the next generation demand management process.

■ *Statistical methods are deployed to create the unconstrained demand forecast.* A holistic approach to statistical forecasting requires more advanced methods (e.g., ARIMA, ARIMAX, multiple regression) to develop holistic statistical baseline forecasts that are reflective of the sales and marketing tactics and strategies along with traditional time series methods (exponential smoothing) to address the different product segments (slow moving, new products, fast moving, and steady state). Although the most common platform for demand forecasting is Excel spreadsheet applications, they are not scalable, nor do they have the depth and breadth of predictive analytics to forecast bottom-up, middle-out, or top-down at the SKU/location level of granularity. This requires an enterprise data warehouse with large-scale automatic forecasting technology that can take advantage of information that resides in the company's demand signal repository.

■ *Tactical and strategic forecasts are required to support short- and long-term supply chain requirements.* Future state companies are extending their planning horizons past the comfort of customer order lead times. This is why companies extend their demand forecasts out to 18 months to execute against the strategic plan. However, they also require a 6- to 13-week forecast for tactical executional purposes. It is still common, however, for the fiscal year-end period to form a threshold beyond which the quality of forecast detail begins to diminish.

■ *Cross-functional collaboration is a key part of the process.* Internal cross-functional communication and collaboration take place between the customer-facing teams (sales, marketing), providing domain knowledge into the demand planning process. They review the results of the statistical unconstrained demand forecasts and provide insights into any significant upcoming marketing events, whether it is internal trade promotions or changes to regular customer/consumer demand patterns. At this stage, the customer-facing teams use the statistical model output to run what-if scenarios at the middle-out forecast levels to test and validate tactical and strategic programs to determine which programs drive not only incremental unit volume but also growth and profitability. Collaborating across the commercial organization and working closely with demand analysts, the cross-functional commercial teams as well as finance finalize the unconstrained demand forecast.

■ *Unconstrained demand forecasts and financial plans are compared to identify gaps.* The unconstrained demand forecasts (demand response) are compared to the financial plan that is usually expressed in unit volumes, and the financial plan, which is usually expressed in revenue terms to identify gaps. In order to make a fair comparison, it is especially important to have the capability to express both the unconstrained demand forecast and financial plan in both units and revenue. Once those gaps are identified and additional programs are validated and funded the future unconstrained demand forecast then becomes an input into the S&OP/IBP processes. Although the unconstrained demand forecast and financial plan are independently developed to ensure that the demand forecast and financial plan are directionally in sync, they are compared with each other during the S&OP process where upside/downside risks are documented, and a final supply plan is created based on supply constraints. Many companies refer to the final supply plan as either the shipment forecast or constrained demand forecast. It is actually a supply plan that is derived from the unconstrained demand forecast.

Analytics

- *More advanced analytics methods will be integrated into the demand planning process.* Demand analysts (or data scientists) will be hired who have advanced statistical knowledge and can apply more advanced models like ARIMA, ARIMAX, and multiple regression using causal factors (i.e., price, intervention variables to capture sales promotion lifts and correct for outliers, along with other causal factors).

- *Holistic modeling will replace data cleansing.* Companies will holistically model the baseline trend, seasonality, correct for outliers, and model the effects of price and sales promotions using ARIMAX and multiple regression models without cleansing the historical data. Furthermore, they will do it automatically up/down a company's business hierarchy for hundreds of thousands of products by geography, market, channel, brand, product group, product, SKU, demand point, and key account (customer). This will require investment in new demand-driven technology.

- *Segmentation of the products will be required to determine appropriate methods to deploy across the company portfolio.* When forecasting on a large scale, demand analysts will consider segmenting brands and products based on their value to the company, the availability of data and information, and forecastability. When segmenting demand to determine what methods are appropriate for brand, product group, and product efforts, demand analysts will focus on four key areas:

1. Low value, low forecastability
2. Low value, high forecastability
3. High value, low forecastability
4. High value, high forecastability

- When evaluating forecast data, companies will look at two key factors: (1) value to the company and (2) forecastability. This conceptual design can be taken further to consider the company's product portfolio as falling into four quadrants:

  1. *Slow-moving* products with fragmented data across targeted markets and consumers.

  2. *New products* with little historical sales data (revolutionary new products) or with similarities with existing products (evolutionary products or line extensions). Also, short life-cycle products like fashion jeans, which normally have six-month life cycles.

  3. *Fast-moving* products that are highly correlated to sales and marketing causal factors, requiring the collection of causal data and information.

  4. *Steady-state* products with long stable historical demand with distinct time series patterns.

- The company will begin to segment its products to determine how forecastable they are and what methods they should apply, given the strategies surrounding each brand based on market dynamics associated with consumer buying habits, competitive activities, and others.

- *Using downstream data to improve forecast accuracy.* Consumption based modeling using the MTCA process will be used to link downstream and upstream data using advanced quantitative methods. Consumption-based modeling is designed to integrate statistical analysis with downstream (POS and/or syndicated scanner) and upstream (shipment) data to analyze the business from a *holistic supply chain* perspective. This process provides both brand management and demand planners with the opportunity to make better and more actionable decisions from multiple data sources (i.e., POS/syndicated scanner, internal company, and external market data).

■ *In the future, measuring forecast performance is viewed as critical to improving the overall efficiency and value of the demand forecasting process.* There are two distinct purposes for measuring forecast accuracy:

1. Measure how well predicting the actual occurrence or outcome, and

2. Comparing different statistical models to determine which one fits (models) the demand history of a product and best predicts the future outcome.

■ The methods (e.g., MAE, MPE, MAPE, and WAPE) used to calculate forecast error are interchangeable for measuring the performance of a statistical model as well as the accuracy of the prediction.

■ *The primary purpose for measuring forecast accuracy is not only to measure how accurately the actual occurrence was predicted, but also to understand why the outcome occurred.* Only by documenting the design, specifications, and assumptions that went into the forecast will companies begin to learn the dynamics associated with the item(s) they are trying to predict. Forecast measurement will be a learning process, not just a tool to evaluate performance. You cannot improve forecast accuracy unless you measure it. You must establish a benchmark by measuring current forecast performance before you can establish a target for improvement. However, tracking forecast error alone is not the solution. Instead of only asking the question, "What is this month's forecast error?" companies will also need to ask, "Why has forecast error been tracking so high (or low) and is the process improving?" These questions will become practice for those companies who successfully transition to the next generation demand management.

■ *The results in any single month may be due purely to randomness.* Companies will not jump to conclusions or even spend time trying to explain a single period's variation. Rather, they will be reviewing the performance of the process over time and determining whether they are reducing error. Ongoing documentation of the specifics that went into each forecast will be viewed as more important to improving forecast performance.

■ *FVA will become the most important approach the company can take to measure and evaluate the demand forecasting process.* FVA will become the most critical performance metric for evaluating the performance of each step and each participant in the forecasting process. FVA is consistent with a lean approach identifying and eliminating process waste, or non-value adding activities that should be eliminated from the process. Non-value adding resources will be redirected to more productive activities that add value to the company. The FVA performance metrics are a proven way to identify waste in the forecasting process, thus improving efficiency and reducing cycle time. By identifying and eliminating the non-value adding activities, FVA provides a means and justification for streamlining the forecasting process, thereby making the forecast more accurate.

Technology

■ *Next generation demand planning technology will offer an integrated suite of forecasting, analysis, visualization, reporting, and optimization workbenches built on a common data model along with data integration capabilities.* The technology will provide users of all types (i.e., sales, marketing, finance, and demand planning) the information they need through a set of common control towers, dashboards, and scorecards as well as dynamic performance reports.

■ Performance metrics including FVA, MAPE/WAPE, customer service, out-of-stocks (OOS), days of supply will be monitored, tracked, and reported daily, as well as sell through metrics to determine how well customer/consumer sales and marketing tactics are performing.

■ *The technology will be big data ready.* It will include the ability to extract value from nontraditional data sources (e.g., unstructured text from social media), which requires the combination of rich analytics and data management.

   ■ Included will be data integration applications/tools combined with parallel and grid processing technology to access and analyze big data.

   ■ These solutions will have the ability to access demand signal repositories where internal transactional data, POS data, syndicated scanner data, as well as other internal/external information reside.

■ *Large-scale automatic hierarchical forecasting engines with expanded model repositories with a complete array of advanced forecasting methods (i.e., ES, ARIMA, ARIMAX, multiple regression, and others) to model and forecast all products across a company's portfolio.* They will integrate consumer demand (pull), model it, and forecast it automatically using data access tools and predictive analytics. The depth and breadth of statistical capabilities will allow demand analysts to model and predict incremental lifts of sales volumes (demand sensing) associated with sales promotions, marketing events, and other related activities, as well as automatically identify and correct for irregular events (outliers) that affect demand. They will provide faster integrated simulation and scenario planning capabilities (demand shaping) that allow demand analysts and planners to test various scenarios using model parameter estimates to determine the impact on the future forecast up/down companies' business hierarchies for hundreds-of-thousands of products. Included will be top-down, bottom-up, and middle-out reconciliation.

■ *New product forecasting capabilities that combine analogies with sound judgment providing an objective basis for predicting new product demand using as-like or surrogate products based on a product profile.* The process will help validate user judgment and allow for the elimination of outliers to produce a better historical set of data for the new product launch.

- Included will be the capability to integrate unstructured data (i.e., social media, IoT, and others) with structured data supporting the new product launch using sentiment analysis to capture consumer preferences providing critical real-time information to adjust the supply chain inventories, capture future enhancements for sustainability, and monitor sales and marketing tactics.

- *Collaborative planning capabilities providing workflow reconciliation up/down the business hierarchy creating averaged or weighted consensus forecasts based on past performance and future projections.* Assessment routines can be performed against financial KPIs to determine the impact on revenue management:

  - Configurable workflow approval process with an easy to use Excel interface for users.

  - Planners can easily override forecasts at any level of the product hierarchy and instantaneously see the overall impact across geographies, markets, channels, brands, products, and SKUs down to key customers and demand points.

  - Utilizes FVA to track and measure touch points in the process to identify added value and nonvalue added adjustments.

GAPS AND INTERDEPENDENCIES

Demand planning process leaders who have conducted a demand-planning self-assessment and find some or all of the four dimensions outlined at the current state must address the following gaps before they can reach full future state maturity.

Goals and Objectives

- *Provide adequate support for demand planning.* One of the core challenges for companies moving from current state to future is inadequate executive sponsorship and support for demand planning. Business executives may not have experienced the benefits of a more mature demand planning process, and may not understand how to leverage the process in support of the company's business strategy. The end result, senior level managers view the demand planning process as an operations planning process that is required to manage lower level product mix, and such, inadequately supports the development of a demand plan. In fact, the unconstrained demand forecast and resulting demand plan should be viewed as the current market conditions. Also, demand analysts working with sales, marketing, and finance can sense demand signals and shape future demand to determine the appropriate programing to close gaps between the business plan and current market conditions.

■ *The demand plan aligns with the annual financial plan.* The annual financial plan is used as the ongoing operating business plan instead of using it to drive business objectives. Current state companies use the business plan as the locked-in overriding demand plan, regardless of current market conditions. Any demand planning activities are expected to always produce a demand plan that aligns with the annual financial plan. It is very common to close any gaps that develop during the year with unspecified stretch goals (sales targets), or financial plugs. Senior management uses those stretch goals to make adjustments to the current demand plan in hopes that by some miraculous event the sales team will close the gaps, putting the company back on plan.

■ *Operations planning focuses on short-term execution of supply and replenishment.* The demand plans that are produced supposedly reflecting future demand are seen as unreliable by the supply chain function and they are reluctant to make decisions within the tactical time horizon using such a demand plan. As a result, the plans are primarily used for avoiding short-term stock-outs and maximizing revenue.

People

- *Demand planners are managers of information and data.* Demand planners spend over 80 percent of their time managing information and cleansing data, rather than focusing on using analytics to model and forecast future demand. Many barely understand how to apply predictive analytics to historical demand to measure the effects of sales promotions, correct for outliers, and identify other related causal factors that influence demand. Most have very little knowledge of downstream data, and almost none understand how to integrate downstream (POS/syndicated scanner) data with upstream data (sales orders/shipments). They are essentially supply planners. Demand planners will need to transition from managers of data to demand analysts, with a focus on predicative analytics in the future state.

- *There has been little if any investment in training demand planners in the area of predictive analytics.* Many companies feel that the primary role of demand planners is to manage the demand planning process, which requires strong communications skills, rather than analytics skills. This has led to a process that is based solely on judgment with very little if any applied analytics. As mentioned in prior chapters the demand planning discipline has digressed over the past decade to managing information, cleansing data, and collaborating across the organization. Although strong communications and collaboration skills are important, analytics are as important if not more important.

- *There are no dedicated demand analysts.* No resources are assigned for producing a statistical demand forecast other than the system-generated *lights out* forecast. Demand planning is seen as a minor task of managing data and information that is assigned to a spreadsheet jockey (typically production planners, buyers/planners, or others) in each function that requires a demand forecast.

Process

- *Demand plans are developed in silos across the supply chain.* Different functions need a projection of future requirements. Without an agreed to demand plan for the business, the functional groups are using plans that they develop independently using the historical volumes that are available and they have supported.

- *The finance function plays a dominant role in the demand planning process.* The finance function dominates the demand planning process. Their directive is to hold to the financial plan at all costs. In fact, they practice a philosophy called *hold-n-roll*—hold to the annual plan and roll the miss forward into the next period. In addition, the plans are expressed in financial terms, and there is no effective conversion from revenue to unit volumes.

- *The operations planning team has too much influence in the decision-making process.* In many current-state companies the operations planning function tends to have a lot of influence in the decision-making process. They are supply-driven, operating in a push environment where the manufacturing plants set the production rates according to their absorption and utilization objectives. They are inside-out focused, pushing product into the channels of distribution based on optimizing production efficiencies, rather than building demand based on consumer preferences.

  - The results are the wrong mix of products, requiring sales and marketing to run discount programs (i.e., sales promotions, temporary price reductions on shelf, and other related merchandising) to pull products through the channels of distribution. This reduces profit margins, thus reducing revenue and profit, not to mention lost market share.

- *There is limited or no use of downstream data to uncover consumer behaviors that influence demand.* Current-state companies lack the analytic knowledge to use downstream data to provide sales and marketing with insights regarding consumer/customer demand and apply those insights in a meaningful way to show the effects across the supply chain. Current-state companies focus all their forecasting resources toward predicting historical shipment (supply) volumes. Those shipment forecasts are used as the basis for calculating the future supply requirements. However, this can be quite detrimental to supporting seasonal demand and calculating the lifts associated with sales promotions, not to mention predicting new product launches.

- *The sales & operations planning (S&OP) process has failed to deliver the benefits due to vertical alignment.* Most current state companies are actually doing OP (operations planning), rather than S&OP. The process is vertically aligned, managed by a demand planning team that reports into the operations planning organization with a focus on creating a supply plan (shipment forecast). The VP/director of supply chain management along with finance makes the final decisions as to the supply plan. This creates a supply-driven environment with little attention to downstream data, demand generation, and revenue and profitability. The key discussions are based on reducing inventory costs, customer service, and on-time delivery.

  Meanwhile, the commercial business (sales/marketing) is not in attendance. The *S*, which stands for sales and marketing, perceives no real benefits from attending, as their core responsibilities are demand generation and increasing market share, revenue, and profit. They rely almost exclusively on downstream data (POS/syndicated scanner) to manage the business. Plus, they have virtually no accountability for demand forecast accuracy.

- *There is no alignment between demand and supply.* There is limited or no capability to produce a truely integrated demand plan that can be synchronized across the supply chain. As a result, companies tend to have unbalanced inventories that are based solely on historical supply (shipments), rather than true demand.

Analytics

■ *There is limited capability to improve demand forecast performance.* This is because of the lack of analytics skills and statistical methods available in the company's first generation ERP systems. Demand forecasting and planning are seen more as an art than a science, with multiple touch points in the process where adjustments are made completely based on judgment. There are no performance metrics capable of using accuracy measurements to improve process efficiency.

■ *There is no standard forecast accuracy measurement process other than MAPE.* The forecast accuracy is measured on an ad hoc basis, and the calculation methods vary between the businesses, regions, and functions.

Technology

■ *There is a lack of standardization and flexibility within companies' first-generation ERP solutions.* The demand management modules lack advanced statistical methods (e.g., ARIMA, ARIMAX, multiple regression), and were not designed to integrate downstream data into the process. They lack the capabilities to sense demand signals, shape future demand, and link demand to supply using consumption based modeling. This is due to the inflexibility of their technology for gathering source data requiring cross-referencing and mapping, restructuring, and scrubbing before it can be used for analysis and planning. This is also due to the lack of advanced predictive analytical methods that can do *holistic* modeling. As a result, demand planners spend 80 percent of their time managing data and analytics. This leads to islands of Excel spreadsheets driven by individual departmental purposes creating different views of the same data.

■ *Several systems contain data that could be valuable for improving the demand planning process.* These systems (e.g., ERP systems, data warehouses, data marts, and business intelligence (BI) systems) may be globally dispersed into regional data centers or perhaps even local servers, with no single group or function having a clear picture of what information is available and where.

■ *Processing information is slow and fragmented across the organization, making it difficult to utilize standard templates.* Reporting is Excel based, with varying degrees of detail and virtually no drilldown capabilities. The entire process is manual with many people burning the midnight oil to gather all the appropriate information and enter it into their ERP systems for processing.

As companies start developing the future roadmap to address the gaps identified, some interdependencies must be taken into consideration. Moving from current state to future state will require improvements in the demand planning process, as well as the resulting demand forecasts alone will not produce significant business benefits. The demand planning efforts must be closely aligned with the following adjacent areas:

■ *Demand planning:* The demand planning process must be able to integrate downstream data as well as consumer information into the demand forecast. Demand planning process improvement must be coordinated not only with supply planning requirements but also those commercial requirements so that the demand forecast can be translated into information that is relevant and usable across the entire supply chain. In this definition, supply chain includes sales and marketing. It is strongly recommended that the demand management transition be placed in parallel to sales and marketing tactical and strategic initiatives. Transferring accountability and ownership to the commercial organization will be essential to fully engage the commercial organization. This is a radical change in the process that will require a champion to lead the change management process. Corporate behavior changes by the commercial, supply chain, finance, and executive management organizations will take time and require small changes to gain adoption. Over time, the changes need to become part of the new corporate culture to assure sustainability.

■ *Pretechnology roadmap: As companies migrate from current state to future state with their demand management initiatives, one of the first requirements that arises is the need for new demand planning technology.* In reality, companies who are in current state of their demand planning process are often not ready to define the specific requirements for an integrated technology solution, nor are they able to effectively use advanced planning analytics. The best course of action is for the demand planning continuous improvement activities to focus on the process design by assessing the current state and blueprinting the future state. During the interim, investment in statistical skills training, and implementing FVA will begin to improve forecast accuracy and add efficiency to the process. Data integration and investment in an enterprise data warehouse along with the necessary technology (i.e., servers, grid processing, in memory processing, and others) is necessary before investing in a new demand management solution. These are necessary prework efforts that are required not only to identify specific data sources and technology gaps in the demand planning process but also to collaborate with the IT team to find the right technology foundation layer to support solution upgrades or acquisitions.

■ *Alignment of performance metrics and objectives.* One of the core reasons for siloed planning across the organization is due to independently set objectives created by each department involved in the process. When the functional objectives across the supply chain are set in silos for different purposes, or intent, it causes conflict and political posturing. Due to the conflicting performance targets, and because each group creates its own bias forecasts in order to meet those different objectives, no single plan will enable all the participating groups to achieve their goals. In support of the demand planning initiative, the business and finance leaders must plan for horizontal cross-functional metrics alignment that will support a one-consumer-based forecast from which all plans can be created. Shipment forecasts are supply plans, not a forecast.

■ *Horizontal alignment of the S&OP process.* Not only does there need to be horizontally aligned performance metrics, but the inclusion of the commercial teams (sales and marketing).

According to the demand management book written by Oliver Wight (Crum, Palmatier 2003), companies cannot synchronize demand and supply without sales and marketing participation. Integrating downstream data, embedding demand analysts in the commercial organization, and introducing consumption based modeling will not only create accountability and ownership of the unconstrained demand forecast, but will provide rationale for the sales and marketing organizations to participate in the S&OP process. Although demand planning is a foundational part of the S&OP process it can only be effective if aligned with sales and marketing and tasked to create an unconstrained demand forecast reflective of sales and marketing tactics and strategies, not with the intent to create a supply plan. The supply plan should be created by the operations planning team (e.g., supply planners). As companies move to future state the demand planning process needs to be more aligned to sales and marketing, not operations planning. Ideally, the demand planning team should report into a neutral organization in order to be unbiased to properly support the horizontal S&OP process roadmap. The unconstrained demand forecast is constrained through the S&OP process to create the final sales, marketing, and supply plans. Even more so, as companies transition from S&OP to IBP (integrated business planning).

STRATEGIC ROADMAP

As companies start their demand planning improvement journeys they should first conduct a self-assessment of their current process to determine where they are in relation to the current state. Upon completing the self-assessment use the migration roadmap to create a project plan to move to future state. It is very important that companies address all four dimensions outlined in Table 8.1 (e.g., people, process, analytics, and technology). All the dimensions need to be implemented with equal priority over the course of the journey as companies begin moving forward. No one dimension should receive higher priority during the migration roadmap than those that may already have higher maturity. The priorities in the migration roadmap in Figure 8.1 are considering all four dimensions. Companies should expect it to take 12 to 18 months to move to current state across all four dimensions, if starting universally at current state.

The most important parts of the demand planning process improvement journey are a clear strategy and vision, with key milestones identified along the way. The strategic roadmap outlined in Figure 8.1 is intended to be the demand management team's (stakeholder) guide for developing the migration path forward to the future state.

Goals and Objectives

■ *It is very important to develop a clear strategy and vision for the goals of the demand planning process.* The overall demand management vision does not need to be an exact plan, but rather, a strategy of how the end-state demand planning process can add value to the overall business strategy. As you develop the demand planning strategy, include all the relevant changes in people, process, analytics, and technology required to form an overall demand planning vision for your business.

■ *Develop a migration path for demand planning that demonstrates a clear roadmap from current state to future state with milestones, risks, and benefits.* Once leadership commitment is confirmed to support and sponsor the development of the new demand planning process, start developing a formal project plan outlining the timing, work, and responsibilities with milestones. In the plan, set the overall end objective to future state across all four dimensions of demand planning with clearly defined goals and objectives. Gain executive and business leaders' support building a business case to show the value of the new demand planning process. While forecast and demand planning errors and disconnects affect most business metrics, the best place to start building the business case benefits is around demand generation, revenue, and profit improvements, not just improved customer service levels, and inventory costs reductions, waste, and working capital.

- *Take a phased approach starting with a small subsector of your business to pilot the new process, analytics, and technology to show a quick win.* Identify a product line or business unit that is most manageable because of the size, limited complexity, cooperative leadership, and/or because it has the best potential for a quick win. Furthermore, start with high revenue (fast-moving) products that are considered growth products where there is sufficient internal data, POS/syndicated scanner data coverage, and causal factors. Those products not only are high volume, but are also fairly stable with high value.

People

- *Establish the benefits and secure approval to hire demand analysts (data scientists) to support demand sensing and shaping activities to complement the demand planners.* The business case for these new analytics roles should emphasize the advantage of enhanced statistical forecast accuracy due to the introduction of causal information, as well as the integration of consumption based modeling in support of demand generation, sales tactics, and marketing strategies. This strategy has been shown to improve inventory performance and customer service levels, thus lowering costs and improving revenue and profit.

- *Create more structured demand analyst and demand planner roles and responsibilities across the organization.* Place more emphasis on creating unconstrained demand forecasts and write new job descriptions for the two roles. Also, invest in analytics training for all the demand planners.

- *If no one is doing demand analysts activities, then consider recruiting and hiring several experienced professional demand analysts with strong statistical skills.* The average ratio based on recent experience is one demand analyst per four demand planners. Also, consider creating a COE (center of excellence) organization, to which demand analysts would report.

Process

- *Design a structured demand planning process that includes the commercial side of the business that encourages accountability and ownership.* Develop a process roadmap with detailed descriptions of the process steps, workflow, required inputs, roles and responsibilities, and expected outcomes. Clearly outline how demand planning and the S&OP/IBP process(es) integration are aligned with defined roles and responsibilities.

- *Determine the maximum and minimum data requirements.* This is both to get the process started and to not underestimate data collection, processing, and storage capabilities. However, scope your technology requirements to the maximum data requirements, so as not to underestimate the size of the server(s).

  This happens quite often with initial implementations. Once the data requirements are known, find out whether the required data are currently available. If available, then find out where the data are located, and if not, where they can be found. This is also key to data integration, Extract, Transform, and Load requirements, and sizing of the data model.

- *Identify the A products (SKUs) for the first phase of the new demand planning process.* For the purposes of the initial demand planning process setup, the A items are those that make up roughly 20 percent of the product portfolio, but 80 percent of the revenue. As you demonstrate, the demand planning capabilities of the A items add SKUs to the planning process over phases that are digestible for the organization.

- *Develop a demand forecast for the chosen businesses.* Where appropriate, use POS/syndicated scanner data, linking it to sales orders (or shipments) as they are closer to true demand. In either case, it makes sense to develop forecasts by geography, market, channel, brand, product group, product, and SKU levels in a hierarchical format. Hierarchical forecasts tend to be more accurate and easier to manage with the right enabling technology. The best place to start may be with sales orders (or shipments) alone, but with the intentions of including causal factors to measure promotion lift factors, correct for outliers, and forecast future sales orders. Comparing it to actual sales orders (or shipments) as a starting point could be a good way to defuse resistance to change from the operations planning group, but begin the transition to consumption-based forecasting where data are available and make sense. This will begin to draw in the commercial team to the demand planning process, as well as provide rationale to participate in the S&OP/IBP process(es).

■ *Start engaging the sales, brand/product management, and/or other customer facing teams in the process.* Once you have the initial unconstrained demand forecast developed, highlight a manageable number of key brands/products and causal factors. Then, encourage the sales and marketing teams to review the list and provide feedback on the chosen products and causal factors to be integrated into the consumption-based forecasts. It is important to emphasize the benefits of improved demand planning in support of demand generation to the sales and marketing teams. As demand forecast accuracy improves, the entire supply chain (including commercial) will be able to better support sales promotions, adhere to customer delivery commitments, plan for new business, and, due to increased customer collaboration, improve the company's credibility with the customer base.

Analytics

■ *Consider segmenting the company product portfolio into four categories.* These categories are (1) slow-moving products, (2) new products, (3) fast-moving products, and (4) steady-state products. Start by using time series methods (e.g., exponential smoothing—seasonal/nonseasonal, ARIMA—seasonal/nonseasonal models) to model and predict future demand for the steady-state products. Then, introduce ARIMAX (ARIMA with intervention and causal factors) to model the fast moving growth products capturing the effects of sales promotions, price, and other causal factors. Finally, address the slow-moving new products. Show small analytics wins (successes) to gain confidence and trust in the analytics.

■ *Use performance metrics to monitor, track, and improve forecast accuracy and process efficiency.* Develop a standard for forecast error measurement. The commonly used forecast accuracy measurement is MAPE, but also consider WAPE (weighted absolute percentage error across product groups). Clearly define where the data comes from, how the metrics are to be calculated, what are the lag times (one- to three-month frozen horizon), how to determine the appropriate lag times, the level of hierarchy for the measurement, and whether there are any specifics to the inclusion or exclusion of special SKUs.

Introduce FVA as soon as possible to improve not only forecast accuracy but also efficiency in the demand planning process. Eliminate or reduce the non-value-added touch points, and continue to include the value-added touch points.

Technology

■ *Before a company can consider investing in new technology, they need to formalize the demand planning process, identify and source the data requirements, and finalize technology requirements.* It is important that the technology has the capabilities, functionality, and proper workflow to support and enable the future state. The biggest mistake companies make is purchasing the technology before the process and workflow activities have been documented, assessed, and formalized. This also includes identifying the demand planning roles and responsibilities, including skill-set requirements.

In many cases, companies go ahead and purchase the technology solution before they have completed the process and workflow requirements without identifying the data requirements and how to source the data. Before the technology can be implemented, there must be a single view of all the data required to support the process. This includes not only structured and unstructured data. The data must be quality ready to assure optimal technology performance. Also, the enterprise data warehouse (or demand signal repository), including supporting data marts, need to be optimized to support both descriptive and predictive analytics. In many cases, the data are not in a high-quality state and are almost always optimized for descriptive analytics (reporting), not predictive analytics.

- *It is important to develop standard templates for data gathering and for presenting the demand planning results, which includes performance metrics.* It is recommended to allow flexibility with the tools and files used in analysis and planning, as long as there is adherence to the data source and master data. Ensure that your demand planning source data include all demand markets, channels, brands, product groups, products, and SKUs. In addition, identify and document the systems that contain the demand information for all regions and all customer types.

- *Start working with the IT organization to establish a governance model for the demand planning master data.* The demand planning process requires quality data for products, customers, and internal locations.

- *Delay making a big technology investment until you are able to clearly articulate the requirements for your technology solution.* Once the technology requirements are documented it is recommended to write a request for information (RFI) from three to five potential software vendors. This provides the opportunity to review the capabilities and functionality across several software vendors and validate your requirements.

- *Upon review of the RFIs select one to three software vendors to complete an RFP (request for proposal) to evaluate and choose the appropriate technology solution.* This will require a demo of each solution, and possibly a POV (proof-of-value) using a subset of your data (select one or two markets, brands, product groups, products, and SKUs). This will include a business case with the results of the POV along with a formal proposal from each software vendor.

SUMMARY

The journey to next generation demand management follows a logical structured flow. First, the company must be convinced that moving to next generation demand management is the only way to support short- and long-term growth and profitability. The organization will need to detail the *what:* What is the end state and what are the intermediate steps needed to reach it? With the company's buy-in and support, the next challenge is to clarify the *how*: How can the company progress from current state to future state? Past case studies of companies that have seen the benefits of becoming demand-driven have helped executives answer the *why* question.

The next generation demand management framework is a radical change from the traditional supply chain demand forecasting and planning function. This new approach takes companies beyond demand-driven to a more holistic view of the supply chain with the inclusion of the commercial organization as a key component that has accountability and ownership of the unconstrained demand forecast. It focuses not only on increasing customer service levels, reducing inventory costs, waste, and working capital, but also on demand generation, revenue, and profitability. The strategic roadmap provides a migration path from current state to future state that includes changing people skills and behavior; the integration of horizontal processes; using predictive analytics to improve forecast accuracy; and using scalable technology to facilitate and enable the process.

Index

Page references followed by *f* and *t* indicate an illustrated figure and table, respectively.